Cities and networks in Europe
A critical approach of polycentrism

Cities and networks in Europe
A critical approach
of polycentrism

Editor:
Nadine Cattan

ISBN: 978-2-7420-0677-9

Éditions John Libbey Eurotext
127, avenue de la République
92120 Montrouge, France
Tél.: 01 46 73 06 60
E-mail: contact@jle.com
Site Internet: http://www.jle.com

Editor: Maud Thévenin

John Libbey Eurotext
42-46 High Street
Esher, Surrey
KT10 9KY
United Kingdom

© 2007 John Libbey Eurotext. All rights reserved.

It is prohibited to reproduce this work or any part of it without authorisation of the publisher or of the Centre Français d'Exploitation du Droit de Copie (CFC), 20, rue des Grands-Augustins, 75006 Paris.

List of contributors

Guy Baudelle, Jean Monnet European Chair, RESO, University of Rennes 2, France

Niels Boje Groth, Danish Centre for Forest, Landscape and Planning, University of Copenhagen, Denmark

Jean-Paul Carrière, Polytechnic School, Department of Planning, University of Tours, CITERES, France

Nadine Cattan, CNRS – Géographie-cités, Paris, France

Pierre Cornut, Institute for Environmental Management and Territorial Planning, Free University Brussels (ULB), Belgium

Patrice Cosaert, University of La Rochelle, France

Michael F. Davie, University François-Rabelais of Tours, Espaces, Nature et Culture, University of Paris-Sorbonne, France

Simin Davoudi, School of Architecture, Planning and Landscape, Institute for Research on Environment and Sustainability, Newcastle University, United Kingdom

Cynthia Ghorra-Gobin, CNRS, Espaces, Nature et Culture, Institut d'études politiques de Paris, France

Erik Gløersen, Nordregio, Sweden

Francesca Governa, Dipartimento Interateneo Territorio, Politecnico e Università di Torino, Italy

Peter Hall, University College London, United Kingdom

Grégory Hamez, CEGUM, University of Metz, France

Guillaume Lesecq, UMR Géographie-cités, Paris, France

Sarah Luyten, Katholieke Universiteit Leuven, Social and Economic Geography, Belgium

Louis Marrou, University of La Rochelle, France

Kathy Pain, The Young Foundation, Globalisation and World Cities (GaWC) Study Group, Loughborough University, United Kingdom

Marcel Roelandts, Institute for Environmental Management and Territorial Planning, Department of Geography, Free University Brussels (ULB), Belgium

Carlo Salone, Dipartimento Interateneo Territorio, Politecnico e Universitá di Torino, Italy

Francesca Silvia Rota, Dipartimento Interateneo Territorio, Politecnico e Università di Torino, Italy

Søren Smidt-Jensen, Danish Centre for Forest, Landscape and Planning, KVL, Danemark

Mathieu Van Criekingen, Free University Brussels (ULB), Fonds National de la Recherche Scientifique (F.N.R.S.), Human Geography Laboratory, Belgium

Christian Vandermotten, Institute for Environmental Management and Territorial Planning, Free University Brussels (ULB), Belgium

Alberto Vanolo, Politecnico e Università di Torino, Italy

Bas Waterhout, Delft University of Technology, OTB Research Institute, The Netherlands

Wil Zonneveld, Delft University of Technology, OTB Research Institute, The Netherlands

Contents

Introduction
   N. Cattan IX

Part I. Evaluating polycentrism:
Is polycentrism effective to strengthening territorial cohesion?

Delineating urban territories. Is this a relevant issue?
   P. Hall 3

The urban typologies and the construction of polycentric spatial perspectives: The example of the Atlantic area
   J.-P. Carrière 15

Towards an improved understanding of urban profiles and polycentric development potentials: Reflections on ESPON 1.1.1
   E. Gløersen 27

Innovation and polycentrism in the Mediterranean Latin arc
   A. Vanolo 39

European polycentrism: Towards a more efficient and/or a more equitable development?
   C. Vandermotten, M. Roelandts, P. Cornut 51

Part II. Polycentrism: What is behind the concept?

Polycentricity: Panacea or pipedream?
   S. Davoudi 65

Polycentrism, equity and social cohesion in Europe
   G. Baudelle 75

The ideo-centricity of urban poly-centricity
   N. Boje Groth, S. Smidt-Jensen 81

Polycentricity, equity and competitiveness: The Dutch case
   W. Zonneveld, B. Waterhout 93

Brussels: Polycentricity as "images on the map", not in reality
   M. Van Criekingen, P. Cornut, S. Luyten 105

Networking Italy. Polycentrism and networks in Italian regional policies
   F. Governa, C. Salone 113

Part III. Networking: What potential for the polycentrism?

Cities as nodes of research networks in Europe
   F.S. Rota 125
Students mobility, gender and polycentrism in Europe
   N. Cattan 139
The network of transnational cooperation programmes in North West Europe and in the Atlantic area
   G. Hamez, G. Lesecq 149
Integrating the European space-flows and places in North West European city-region networks
   K. Pain 161
Why Hawaii or the Azores are an adequate representation of polycentrism?
   L. Marrou 173

Part IV. Polycentrism: A view point from experiences outside Europe

Territorial development and polycentrism made in USA: Between the logic of the market and a federal organization
   C. Ghorra-Gobin 183
National versus regional and international networking in the Arab world
   M.F. Davie 189
East Asia: An example of regional integration via networks and flows
   P. Cosaert 199

Introduction

The aim of the book *Cities and networks in Europe. A critical approach of polycentrism* is to look at the dominant representations that at present underpin the issues of territorial organisation and planning in Europe. Cities and networks are often envisaged, both in scientific research and in operational debate, as inevitably driving territorial development. However, because they are always positioned within logic of economic and political competition in which only processes of wealth generation are taken into account, the conceptualisation of European territorial integration has often been reduced to two conventional models: the centre-periphery model and the hierarchical model of urban networks. The European space is thereby depicted in one of these two ways: either in terms of strong centres to which peripheral territories manage to tie themselves to a greater or lesser degree, or of major metropolises in whose shadow secondary cities lie hidden. Limiting European organization territorial to these two schema means that integration is limited.

Today, in academic debates and public policies reference to polycentric territorial development has to some extent, at least in debate, changed the picture. Rather than being viewed in a polarised, pyramidal manner, spatial dynamics are being read in terms of interconnection and articulation. In addition, reflection undertaken in collaboration with European Spatial Development Perspective (ESDP) on the subject of polycentric territorial strategies has encouraged politicians and spatial planners to include the principle of "territorial cohesion" in the priorities of European public policies, in the same way as economic and social cohesion are included.

From considerations which associate conceptual approaches and analytical studies, this book makes it possible to understand in what manner polycentrism, viewed as an alternative to metropolisation could sow the seeds for new readings, at various scales, of the organisation of European territory. Even if interpretation to date is still incomplete and biased, polycentrism is perceived as if it is in accordance with the principles of equity, cohesion and sustainable development.

The main challenge of this book is to explain why it is worthwhile revisiting some rather too static representations of territorial systems in Europe. The aim is to promote the emergence and the consolidation of new, critical ways of looking at the issues of territorial dynamics: how they are to be managed, how they should be viewed, putting emphasis both on theoretical and conceptual viewpoints, and on empirical and implementational approaches.

The book is organized around four parts. Each questions the very notion of polycentrism starting from a specific point of view. Part one tends to evaluate the relations between a polycentric territorial organization and a more balanced and sustainable development according to the principle of cohesion. Part two questions the very definition of the polycentrism both from a theoretical and conceptual point of view and from its use in the public policies.

The aim of part three is to contribute to the reflections on polycentrism that put emphasis on its relational aspects taking into account networks of exchanges and of cooperation. By way of comparison, part four questions the representation of polycentrism and territorial integration entertained in other cultural areas.

PART I: EVALUATING POLYCENTRISM: IS POLYCENTRISM EFFECTIVE TO STRENGTHENING TERRITORIAL COHESION?

In most work on urban systems in Europe, typological projects dominate widely. From indicators said to be "structuring", work of this sort has always led to characterising cities one against the other, independently from their geographical position and especially from their interdependence one on the other. This has enabled the development of a certain number of functional urban and territorial models, which have their use. However approaches of this type, because they partition our perception of territories, define limits and mask the very concept of the urban network. Indeed, a general criticism could be drawn from all of the studies on typologies: usually only extreme cases are analysed. Everything that takes place at the top or bottom end of any hierarchy interests researchers and spatial planners. Nobody pays any attention to what happens in between, that is, to the more common facts which represent, however, the major part of the reality.

From concrete examples based on various geographical levels, part one examines how far different systems of measuring and classifying towns and cities actually contribute to better understanding territorial dynamics, and to support greater efficiency in the elaboration of development strategies.

In Europe today any consideration of cities and urban networks comes up against the issue of urban boundaries. Because the definitions of the city and of the statistical systems that underpin this notion vary from one country to another harmonisation is a challenge. The main obstacle is however elsewhere. In a context of general spread, the way in which to define the boundaries of urban areas now comes up against the conceptualisation *per se* of the city. After having drawn the history of the successive attempts to define urban territories, Peter Hall's paper confirms that defining a city-region can be considered as a solved problem, although delineation should be requestioned after each census round, and adapted to each EU countries figures. His paper also highlights that measuring the polycentricity[1] of several European city-regions may be easy in morphological terms. The empirical experiment of collection of indicators in seven city-regions leads him however to conclude that further researches are required to evaluate the functional aspects of polycentric figures.

Mainly based on a morphological approach of the urban networks, the two following papers bring concrete answers to the contributions that can be made by urban typologies and clas-

---

1. We use either polycentrism or polycentricity in this book.

Introduction

sifications to understand the potential development of certain categories of cities with regards a polycentric perspective. From the example of Atlantic Arc, Jean-Paul Carrière shows that urban classifications highlight the fact that attention must be related to the meso-scale and not to the macro-level as that is often proposed in the theoretical as well as in the more empirical studies. Erik Gloersen arrives at a quite similar conclusion. While profiling the Metropolitan Economic Growth Areas (MEGA) he noticed that more emphasis should be put on the secondary nodes. His methodological approach underlines also the relevance of profiling cities rather than ranking them. This means that attention must be paid to the relative importance of the various functions of a city rather than on their size. This is the only way to provide a different image of the European cities that challenges the core-periphery representation.

The last two papers of this part question explicitly the link between the polycentric spatial structures and the socioeconomic performances of these territories. From the example of fifteen regions in the Latin Mediterranean Arc, Alberto Vanolo shows that it is not possible to determine a relation between a regional polycentric index and the innovative potential of these regions. However, his study shows that the hypothesis of a "facilitation" of knowledge diffusion in polycentric contexts seems to be conceivable. The debates continue in the paper of Christian Vandermotten et al. underlying the fact that the scientific uncertainties remain large as for the advantages and disadvantages of the levels of polarization or polycentricity. Having computed two complementary measures of polycentricity for all the European macro-regions and countries this study shows that there is no relation between polycentrism and economic efficiency. Evaluating the link between polycentrism and spatial equity, the authors conclude however that because polycentrism is vague and multiform, their study are not enough for putting into question a policy that promote a more balanced and sustainable development.

PART II: POLYCENTRISM: WHAT IS BEHIND THE CONCEPT?

The concept of polycentrism made it possible to place the reflection on the territories in the centre of the strategies of development in Europe. It has, indeed, introduced the principle of territorial cohesion in the priorities of the European public policies as well as economic and social cohesion. Experts agree to think that the polycentrism is the most promising guiding principle in the search for a balanced and sustainable territorial development. As a process, polycentrism became a major challenge of the policy of regional and spatial planning of the European Union.

However, nowadays, in the academic as well as in the political debates, the polycentrism refers sometimes only to the spatial forms of distribution of the cities on a given territory, whereas the concept at other times refers to the processes which underlie them. Also, polycentrism can refer to strategies of territorial planning and development or refer to a spontaneous process. In all the cases, it seems to return to differentiated mechanisms and specific strategies of development. The "polysemia" of a concept is necessary in particular within a framework as varied as the European Union. However a better identification of the processes and challenges which underlie polycentric territorialities is vital to some extends.

Far from a normative image of the polycentrism, the papers presented in part two demonstrate how important is the construction of a critical understanding and approach to the concept of polycentrism/polycentricity. The first two contributions lighten the origin, the use and the definition of polycentrism while denouncing ambiguity of the concept and its normative character. Simin Davoudi thinks that this ambiguity is both a weakness and a strength. She stresses the importance to always build an appropriate governance arrangement to support the effort of cooperating between the cities set up in a polycentric development perspective. Guy Baudelle underlines in his conclusion that despite the vague definition of the concept, its ideological characteristic makes it an equitable project for achieving the European objectives.

Four following papers analyze the interpretation of the polycentrism in the regional and national policies of different European countries. A thorough study of these policies makes it possible to renew certain dominant meanings related to spatial and institutional logics that support a polycentric territorial development. Based on the analysis of the development strategies of three medium sized-cities in Denmark and Sweden, the work of Niels Boje Groth and Soren Smidt-Jensen moderates certain generally accepted ideas. They indeed show that proximity, although relevant, is not the guiding principle for choosing partners in the territorial cooperation projects. They indeed underline that spatial proximity is not a condition of polycentrism: cities go for the best and most relevant partners independently of their geographical position. By unravelling the policy changes in the Netherlands, Wil Zonneveld and Bas Waterhout question another dominant idea. Their analysis underscores that whatever the goals of policy are, *i.e.* competitiveness or cohesion, there is a great level of territorial selectivity in the Dutch regional-economic policy. Consequently, the focus is always on the strongest regions of the country.

The last two papers of this section deal with polycentrism in Belgium and Italian regional policies. By taking into account the case of Brussels, Mathieu Van Criekingen, Pierre Cornut and Sarah Luyten explain that the economic specialisation which obeys basically a logic of market, is ongoing in Brussels metropolitan areas but that the political structures which could make it possible to develop the co-operations between actors and territories are today absent. Consequently, these authors underline that any attempt to support polycentric structures by specialisation of the economic urban functions must be assisted by mechanisms of networking, co-operation and governance. As in response to that, Francesca Governa and Carlo Salone demonstrated that the Italian version of polycentrism in regional policies is nowadays focused on the role of actors aiming for common goals through networking activities. They show that the increasing competitiveness of the territories resulting from the processes of devolution goes hand in hand with the development of territorial and institutional partnerships and cooperation. This paper moderates the idea of conflicting strategies when speaking about competitiveness and cohesion.

By and large, the papers presented in this part underline the need for preserving a relatively broad palette of the models of territorial development in Europe. They propose a polycentric reading which holds account of the diversity of the local contexts, the differences in urban structures and the multiplicity of the forms of administration and governance at regional as well as at urban levels. One should be aware that any reference to a single model of territorial development is perilous.

Introduction

PART III: NETWORKING: WHAT POTENTIAL FOR THE POLYCENTRISM?

The concept of a worldwide economy based on networks of relationships is not new. However the functionality of a network of relationships is rarely taken into account into theories on space and its dynamics. The reasons given by many scientists to explain that it is difficult to take the realities of exchanges into account consistently relate to material or technical contingencies, ranging from lack of access to relational data to the methodological complexity of using such data. It is true that these limitations are considerable. Yet the debate is incomplete, while at the same time it seems that any attempt to give meaning to space, and to the populations, in terms of linkage and interdependence, rather than in terms of zone and distribution, meets resistance in various forms: symbolic, ideological, and institutional.

By viewing territories and cities in terms of the way they articulate one with another *i.e.* in terms of relational functionality the ambition of part three is to understand how mobility and exchange recombine the European space and modify consequently our perception of several spatial concepts and theories. Most of the work on spatial integration and globalisation focuses on what is perceived as structuring flows, such as financial flows, commercial exchanges, freight or commodity flows. Thus these works focus on the functional integration of economic activities across the globe. The mobilization, in this section of a rather broad range of networks of exchanges and co-operations, such as cultural, scientific, knowledge, information and immaterial that are considered in the dominant literature as less structuring makes it possible to propose an alternative reflection on the role played by flows as a factor in producing and organising territory. The papers presented in this section show also how today a reference to polycentric territorial systems with regard exchanges and co-operations provides a necessary counterweight to the dominant visions and perceptions of the European networks and cities dynamics.

The first two papers underline the need for a more critical approach to classic understanding of the European spatial integration that give too much importance to the concepts of hierarchy, areas of influence, borders and blocs. Analysing the research partnerships between the cities, Francesca Sylvia Rota shows that network hierarchies are not fixed and that the networks formed by non-capital cities are more dynamic than the capitals cities network. As in echo with that, Nadine Cattan shows that the student mobility between the cities is polycentric and balanced *i.e.* that no city or pair of cities dominates the network of exchanges. In a European context where 61% of migrating students are female, her work highlights moreover the fact that migratory behaviour of female students go further to questioning the neo-classic models of spatial mobility than do those of male students.

Based on the study of the transnational cooperation programmes in North-West Europe and in the Atlantic Arc, Gregory Hamez and Guillaume Lesecq observe the existence of two different spatial integration processes: a rather megalopolitan and hierarchical organisation in North West Europe and a more polycentric and balanced networking in the Atlantic Arc. Focusing on the integration processes in North West Europe, Kathy Pain's paper addresses a key debate about the impact of inter-urban flows associated with advanced business services. Analysed at the level of Mega-City-Regions the network connections prove the need for face-to-face contact in knowledge business services. Studying the network connectivities at multiple territorial scales leads the author to conclude that polycentricity is a much more complex than is acknowledged in spatial policies.

In the last paper of this section, Louis Marrou develops an original hypothesis: maritime archipelagos are relevant examples to observe polycentrism at work. This paper shows that the very notion of an archipelago is concerned with linkages and connections and that several archipelagos are territory without a centre. Consequently, the author supports the interesting idea that maritime archipelagos are perfect polycentric objects because they are mainly the pioneers of networking.

Part three underlines that today new forms of territorial organisation and integration are emerging as a result of spectacular growth in networking both in terms of exchanges and cooperation. Political decision-makers must understand that if a balanced and sustainable integration of the European territory is to be achieved, it will be through spatial planning that takes more and more account of networks themselves and less and less of urban poles. This networking process nevertheless does not produce the same effects in the different areas of the European territory. Part three shows that various types of polycentricity are occurring across Europe. Consequently one cannot understand the dynamics of territorial integration in Europe without taking into account this diversity.

PART IV: POLYCENTRISM: A VIEWPOINT FROM EXPERIENCES OUTSIDE EUROPE

By way of comparison, the aim of part four is to set European views of territorial organisation and planning, and in particular polycentric development and territorial cohesion enjoying fairly wide consensus today in Europe, against representations entertained in other "cultural areas". Working on the United States, Cynthia Ghorra-Gobin shows that the US urban system is characterized by polycentrism that is rooted in the institutional, political and historical culture of the country. She also highlights the fact that polycentrism is not necessarily associated with a coherent spatial pattern. Europe has much to learn from the polycentrism made in USA. The author concludes that precautions must however be taken for well determining the challenges: it is worthwhile analyzing the US specificity in the light of the relation between the logic of market and the political regulation.

Another example is given by Michael Davie starting from the Arab world and the Middle East experience. After a historic insight, the author explains that the geopolitical situation prevents any reflection on the constitution of regional networks and consequently of polycentric organisation. His work however shows that invisible forms of networking compensate the weakness of state planning systems and support networking between the North and the South of the Mediterranean instead of networking inside the Arab area. Patrice Cosaert with the example of regional integration in East Asia shows that in the context of economic growth the national borders are not a problem for networking. His paper shows how East Asia experiments polycentric development and how by becoming a "regional bloc" this region takes part in globalisation. Regionalization and globalisation are two complementary processes.

Part I
Evaluating polycentrism:
Is polycentrism effective
to strengthening territorial cohesion?

Delineating urban territories. Is this a relevant issue?

Peter Hall
University College London, United Kingdom

Perhaps the attempt to find a meaningful urban territory is a little like James Thurber's Unicorn in the Garden: a mythical beast. Even if not, it proves a little difficult to capture.

DEFINING URBAN TERRITORIES: THE BASIC CHALLENGE

The basic challenge is multiple:

– such units are not physical (morphological) units, like the UK's conurbations, or the French agglomerations;
– neither are they administrative units – though administrative units must usually be used to define them;
– they need to be based on Castells' "Space of Flows"; flows of people, information, goods, on a regular basis: daily (commuting), weekly (shopping, local paper);
– therefore, they must be Functional Urban Regions (FURs).

To overcome these problems, American urban analysts have long employed the concept of the Metropolitan Statistical Area (MSA): a functionally-defined urban region that goes out beyond the physically-built-up area to encompass all the areas that have regular daily relationships with a core city. The concept of the FUR lies 50 years or more ago, in the Metropolitan Areas used by the United Census and other American agencies, and widely accepted there as a statistical base. The concept has undergone many detailed changes in these five decades:

– in 1949, the Bureau of the Budget (predecessor of OMB) first defined a Standard Metropolitan Area (SMA);
– in 1959, this became the Standard Metropolitan Statistical Area (SMSA);
– in 1983, it was renamed the Metropolitan Statistical Area (MSA);
– in 1990, a new concept was developed: the Metropolitan Area (MA) including Metropolitan Statistical Areas (MSAs), Consolidated Metropolitan Statistical Areas (CMSAs), and Primary Metropolitan Statistical Areas (PMSAs);
– in 2000 yet another complication was introduced: the Core Based Statistical Area (CBSA), including Metropolitan and (a new concept) Micropolitan Statistical Areas.

The Metropolitan Area concept has thus been regularly updated and revised at each successive census – but, importantly, the basic concept has stayed the same for over half a century. It has never provided a basis for local government (which in the United Sates is strictly state-based) but it plays a major role in policy uses – especially, the allocation of Federal funds. To be precise: in its latest (2000) manifestation, a Core Based Metropolitan (or Micropolitan) Statistical Area is defined as consisting of:

– a core area containing a substantial population nucleus;
– plus adjacent communities having a high degree of social and economic integration with that core;
– and comprising one or more entire counties.

Further:

– Each CBSA must contain at least one urban area of 10,000 or more population;
– Each Metropolitan Statistical Area must have at least one urbanized area of 50,000 or more inhabitants;
– While each Micropolitan Statistical Area must have at least one urban cluster of at least 10,000 but less than 50,000 population;
– The County (or counties) in which at least 50 percent of the population resides within urban areas of 10,000 or more population, or that contain at least 5,000 people residing within a single urban area of 10,000 or more population, is Central County (counties);
– Additional outlying counties are included in the CBSA if they meet specified requirements of commuting to or from the central counties.

New England has no counties, so here, a similar set of areas is developed, using cities and towns: New England City and Town Areas (NECTAs). This produces a total (at the last redefinition) of 362 Metropolitan Statistical Areas and 560 Micropolitan Statistical Areas.

"EXPORTING" THE METRO AREA CONCEPT

United Kingdom

As long ago as 1968, work at the London School of Economics for the Royal Commission on Local Government in England (the Redcliffe-Maud Commission) adopted the American Metropolitan Area concept and applied it to South East England [8]. But, applied to the actual task of reorganising local government, it proved somewhat of a Procrustean Bed: fitting reasonably well in the shire counties of midland England, it was less satisfactory in less densely populated areas like East Anglia, where the FUR does not produce a sufficiently large unit in terms of population to be efficient in providing local government services [13]. However, the concept was then applied nationally in studies that led in 1973 to publication in the book *The Containment of Urban England* [17]. There, too, it gave good results across much of the country but less satisfactory results in sparely-populated rural areas like Devon and Cornwall or the Lake District.

Europe

In 1980, Hall and Hay extended the concept to Europe. They defined and analysed data for a set of 539 uniform Functional Urban Regions (FURs) in western Europe, and a decade later a larger follow-up study by Cheshire and Hay, funded by the European Commission, updated and deepened the work for a set of 229 larger FURS in the then 12-member EC area, and conducted a further detailed analysis of a subset of 53 FURS [15 6].

This and subsequent work [3-5, 20], though updating the data base from the 1990 census round, had to rely on the original FUR definitions based on data from the 1970 census round or nearest equivalent. In consequence the definitions have become in many cases out-of-date and misleading. This was demonstrated in the work of the GEMACA group [18] which showed for example that while the boundaries of the Paris urban region had remained relatively stable to 1991, those of London had expanded substantially. In the USA, the equivalent MSAs are regularly redefined on the basis of the latest Census and other data.

The GEMACA criteria are particularly interesting because this was an EU-wide project and the rules it employed, though derived from the American ones, were subtly different:

– An Economic Core, consisting either of a number of neighbouring municipalities where jobs $> = 20,000$ and employment density > 7 jobs/ha; or: a municipality $> 20,000$ jobs plus neighbouring municipalities where employment density > 7 jobs/ha.
– A Morphological Agglomeration, consisting either of a number of neighbouring municipalities where population density $> = 7$ inhabitants/ha, and totalling at least 60 000 inhabitants, or a municipality $> 60 000$ inhabitants plus neighbouring municipalities where population density > 7 inhabitants/ha.
– A FUR (or labour market area): neighbouring municipalities in which more than 10% of the working population works in the main economic centres on a daily basis.

THE MEGA-CITY REGION: A NEW SPATIAL CONCEPT

This concept was taken up and further adapted in the POLYNET study, funded by a 2.4 million Euro grant from the European Commission under the Interreg IIIB (North West Europe). POLYNET however develops a new urban phenomenon, in course of formation in the most highly-urbanised parts of the world: the Mega-City Region. The term comes from Eastern Asia, where it was originally applied to areas like the Pearl River Delta and Yangtze River Delta regions of China, the Tokaido (Tokyo-Osaka) corridor in Japan, and Greater Jakarta [14]. It is a new form: a series of anything between twenty and fifty cities and towns, physically separate but functionally networked, clustered around one or more larger central cities, and drawing economic strength from a new functional division of labour. These places exist both as separate entities, in which most residents work locally and most workers are local residents, and as parts of a wider functional urban region connected by dense flows of people and information along motorways, high-speed rail lines and telecommunications cables It is no exaggeration to say that this was the emerging urban form at the start of the twentieth-first century.

The expression "megacity" may recall the earlier term coined by Jean Gottmann in his 1961 book, Megalopolis. But there is a subtle distinction. As defined by Gottmann in his celebrated 1961 study of the Boston-to-Washington corridor, Megalopolis was *"an almost continuous stretch of urban and suburban areas from southern New Hampshire to northern Virginia and from the Atlantic shore to the Appalachian foothills"* [9]. That suggested a physical definition: a continuously urbanized area. Later, in response to criticism, Gottmann made it clear that he meant something different: Megalopolis was *"the cradle of a new order in the organization of inhabited space"* [9], defined in terms of Standard Metropolitan Statistical Areas; in other words a functional definition.

The extreme physical expression is the Mega-City Region: a pattern of extremely long-distance deconcentration stretching up to 150 kilometres from the centre, with local concentrations of employment surrounded by overlapping commuter fields, and served mainly by the private car. The precise spatial details vary from country to country according to culture and planning regime: in the United States, lower-density and less regulated with "Edge Cities" or "New Downtowns" on greenfield sites, exclusively accessed by the private car; in Europe, medium-density, regulated through green belts and other constraints, and centred on medium-sized country market towns or planned new towns [7, 21].

Megacity Regions are certainly developing, or have already developed, in Europe. POLYNET has analysed and compared the functioning of eight such regions:

a. South East England, where London is now the centre of a system of some 30-40 centres within a 150-km. radius.
b. Belgian Central Cities comprising Brussels and a surrounding ring of large– and medium-sized cities, with a high degree of interdependence and a total population of ca 7 million.
c. The Randstad in the Netherlands, encompassing the cities of Amsterdam, The Hague, Rotterdam and Utrecht, but now extending outwards to include the cities of Almere, Amersfoort and Breda.
d. RhineRuhr is one of the world's largest polycentric Mega-City Regions, embracing 30-40 towns and cities with a total population of some 10 million people, in this case with no obvious "core city".
e. The Rhine-Main region of Germany, encompassing core cities of Frankfurt am Main, Wiesbaden, Mainz and Offenbach, but extending widely outwards as far as Limburg in the north, Aschaffenburg in the east, Darmstadt in the south and Bad Kreuznach in the west.
f. The European Metropolitan Region (EMR) Northern Switzerland, an incipient "Mega-City Region" extending in discontinuous linear pattern from Zürich and its region westwards towards Basel.
g. Greater Dublin, within a 50-60 km. radius, but particularly northward along the Dublin-Belfast corridor.
h. The Paris Region represents a special case: through the 1965 *Schéma Directeur*, outward decentralisation pressures have been accommodated in new city concentrations within the agglomeration, with little impact on surrounding rural areas. But recent research shows that the region's economic core is not the historic Ville de Paris, but a "Golden Triangle" bounded by the city's western arrondissements; La Défense; and the suburbs of Boulogne-Billancourt and Issy-les-Moulineaux [1, 11, 12].

The underlying hypothesis is that falling costs of transportation and (more particularly) communication, combined with new informational agglomeration economies, lead to the emergence of a highly complex "space of flows" [2] within the "Mega-City Region": lower-level service functions may be dispersed out from higher-order central cities to lower-order cities [19] while highest-order services remain clustered in core "First Cities". The entire complex however achieves major agglomeration economies through clustering of activities, not in any one centre, but in a complex of centres with some degree of functional differentiation between them.

The distinguishing features of the POLYNET research are:

- Its focus on the Mega-City Region:
- Its analysis of relationship at different spatial scales, from the mega to the micro;
- Its use of information flows in the knowledge economy – specifically, in the Advanced Producer Services (APS) – both through telecommunications and face-to-face, and both internal (node to node) and external;
- Its central hypothesis that Mega-City Regions are becoming more polycentric: specifically, that MCRs are subject to "concentrated deconcentration" through a progressive redistribution of functions: in the core city or cities, continuing concentration of higher-order service functions (financial and business services, design services, media, higher education, health...); in secondary cities, growth of more routine functions (R&D, high-tech manufacturing; niche roles, such as university cities). However, all the cities and their functions are highly symbiotic and highly interconnected.

POLYNET consequently addresses new and interrelated research questions How are virtual and material flows of information and people reconfiguring intraregional relationships? Are functional relationships between top-level and other centres in these regions changing? To what extent are other urban centres dependent on, or independent of, service industry concentration in core cities? (Here the focus of inquiry is largely intraregional). In what ways are changes in regional functional relations affecting the cross-border connectivities of these regions within Europe and globally? To what extent will changes contribute to, or damage, transnational service business connectivity? (Here the focus is on cross-border relations). In what ways are these flows different as between polycentric Mega-City Regions (like the Randstad or RhineRuhr) and the much more "monocentric" Paris region? Can it be said that one or the other pattern is more sustainable, and if so in what ways and to what degree?

It was therefore essential, as a starting point for POLYNET, to review and update the basic European data base, updating the basic definitions of functionally defined city-regions, using where possible the 1999/2000/2001 Census round, extending it to smaller regions than in the GEMACA data base, and providing an extended analysis of basic data, including population, employment, income, unemployment and other key socioeconomic variables. After examination of various possible models, we have adopted a variant of the GEMACA criteria for defining Functional Urban Regions (FURs) in our eight study areas:

FURs: comprise a core defined in terms of employment size and density, and a ring defined in terms of regular daily journeys (commuting) to the core:

Cores: Using NUTS 5 units (the smallest units for which published data are generally available), define cores on the basis of: 7 or more workers per hectare, and minimum 20 000 workers in either single NUTS 5 unit or in contiguous NUTS 5 units.

Rings: Using NUTS 5 units, where possible, define rings on the basis of 10% or more of the residentially-based workforce commuting daily to the core[1]. Where they commute to more than one core, allocate to the core to which most commuters go.

---

1. The threshold levels depend on the size of national building blocks – *i.e.* the size of NUTS 5 units. They required modification on the basis of local knowledge and experience.

The Mega-City Region (MCR): Having defined FURs that were uniform, as far as possible, within and also between our eight study areas, we then needed to aggregate them into the basic units for comparative study: the eight Mega-City Regions (MCRs), of which South East England is one[2]. In a sense, there is a significant element of circularity here: since our objective was to study functional polycentricity, we could only seek to define MCRs when we had completed the research; but we had to start with a working definition. Bearing in mind that this could only be rough and approximate, we decided that the basic criteria should be one of contiguity:

Megacity Region: Defined in terms of contiguous FURs, and thus similar to the so-called Consolidated Metropolitan Statistical Areas, CMSAs, used in the United States. Contiguity is the sole criterion. There may be functional relations (cross-commuting) between the constituent FURs, or there may not; this will emerge only in the course of the analysis.

POLYNET: Key results

For both individual FURs (and, by definition, for aggregate MCRs), the eight study area teams assembled basic data on population, employment, and commuting (including cross-commuting between FURs in MCRs).

The resulting MCRs display a huge size range *(Figure 1)*:

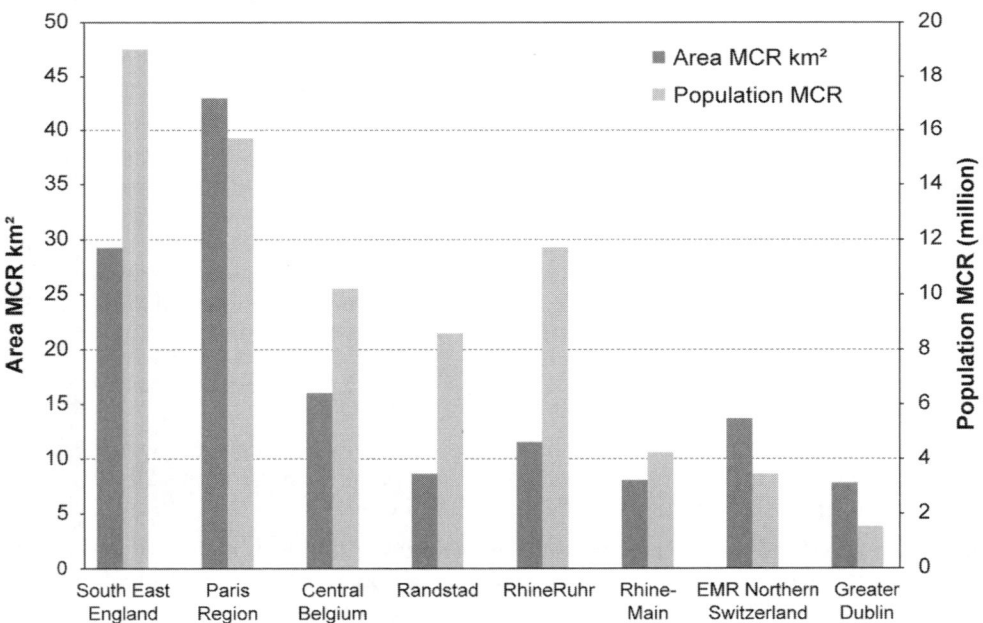

Figure 1. *Megacity regions: areas and populations 2000.*

---

2. The others are the Dutch Randstad, Central Belgium, RhineRuhr, Rhine-Main, Northern Switzerland, the Paris Region and Greater Dublin.

– Area: minimum, 7,800 km² (Dublin); maxima, 27,332 km² (SEE), 43,000 km² (Paris Region).
– Population: minimum, 1,600,000 (Dublin); maxima, 15,600,000 (Paris Region), 18,560,000 (SEE).
– But 5 out of 8 MCRs are between 8,000 km² and 16,000 km² in area, and between 8 million and 11 million in population.

In terms of internal structure:

– Six MCRs are dominated by one central FUR: London (9.5 m), Brussels (3.1 m), Frankfurt (2.4 m), Northern Switzerland (1.1 m), Paris (10.7 m), Dublin (1.0 m);
– Two FURs are strictly polycentric, with no dominant city: Randstad and RhineRuhr;
– But a majority have between 5 and 25 constituent FURs;
– The MCRs vary in polycentricity, but are predominantly "semi-polycentric" with one (or two) dominant FUR/s: Amsterdam-Rotterdam, Brussels, Frankfurt, Northern Switzerland, Paris *(Figures 2 and 3)*.

The internal dynamics of the eight FURs show a general trend to decentralisation:

– South East England: the London FUR is growing, the others even faster;
– The Randstad: the four big city FURs are declining, others are growing;
– Central Belgium: here, growth is found in Brussels and Flanders, decline in the Walloon industrial belt;
– RhineRuhr: core cities are losing to suburbs; smaller city FURs are growing;

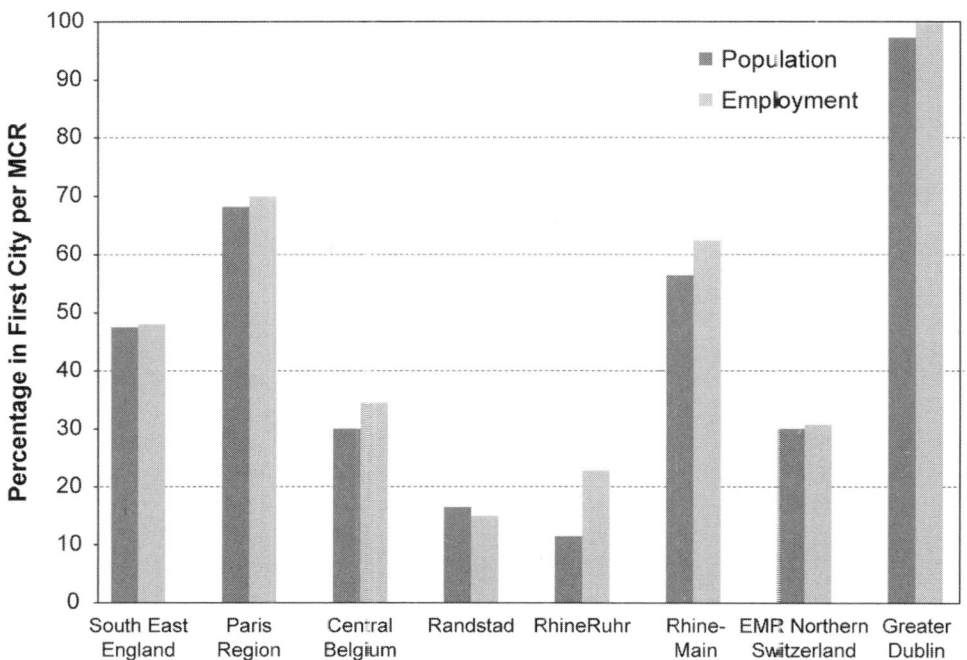

Figure 2. *Megacity regions: first city dominance, 2000.*

– Rhine-Main: this presents a complex picture: Frankfurt is growing (through migration from the five Neue Länder), while smaller FURs are growing faster, but Wiesbaden is losing;
– Paris Region: Paris and some distant FURs are growing, others declining; there is a split between a dynamic west and a less dynamic east;
– Dublin: the Dublin FUR is growing (but its growth is slowing); smaller places are growing faster.

For employment, the same trend to decentralisation is evident *(Figures 4 and 5)*:

– Randstad: there is growth in (some) city FURs, but faster growth outside;
– Central Belgium: the Walloon industrial towns are losing;
– RhineRuhr: Ruhr FURs are losing, Rhine FURs gaining;
– Rhine-Main: Frankfurt and Mainz FURs are growing, but the rest are stagnating/losing;
– Northern Switzerland: there is overall growth, but FURs of industrial towns have lost;
– Paris Region: Paris shows weak growth, some outer city FURs strong growth, FURs around eastern towns weak growth.

Employment structure shows a general shift from manufacturing and goods-handling to services, especially Advanced Producer Services, but with considerable variations. Services are strong generally, especially in core city FURs, but are also growing at periphery; the major exception is RhineRuhr.

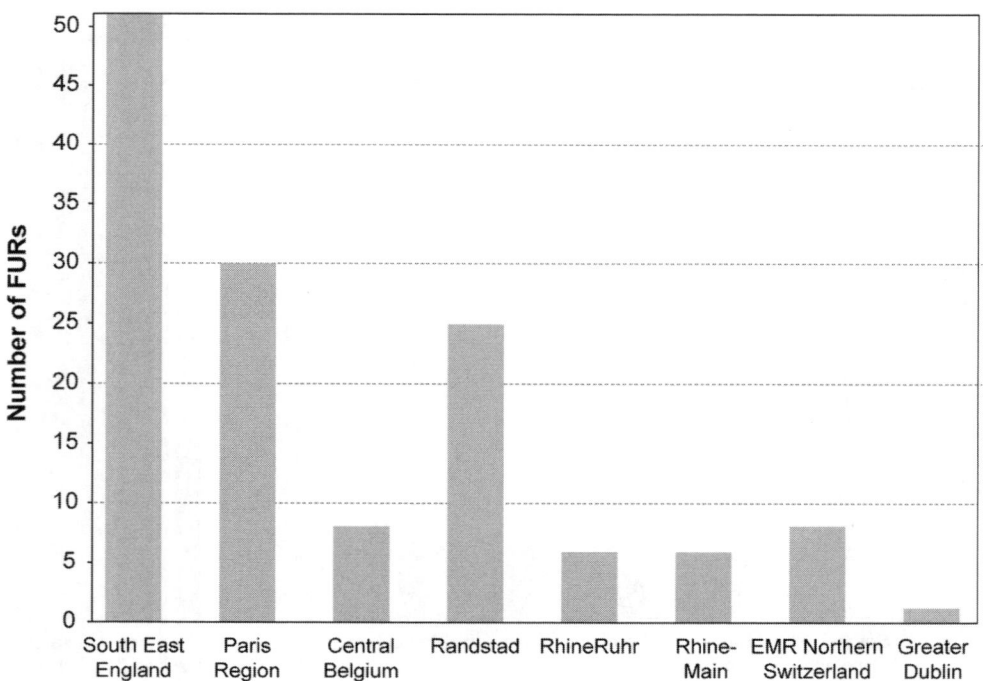

Figure 3. *Megacity regions: number of functional urban regions, 2000.*

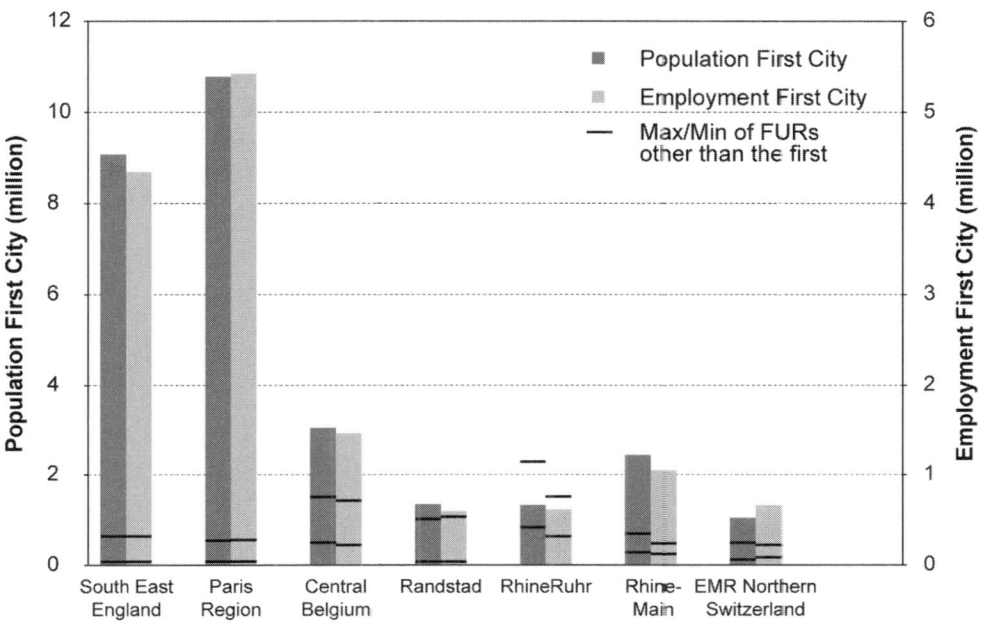

Greater Dublin is omitted since it has only one FUR.

Figure 4. *Megacity regions: comparative functional urban regions population and employment 2000.*

Commuting shows a general trend to increasing number and average length of commuter trips, with more trips "peripheral", i.e. not to the central "First City" FUR. But there are also some surprises. In the supposedly polycentric Randstad there are no big flows from the south into the Amsterdam core, nor between Randstad cities generally. In Central Belgium Brussels is dominant, but there are strong cross flows and reverse flows between rings in the so-called Flemish Diamond north of Brussels. In RhineRuhr Düsseldorf dominates the picture, but there are strong two-way-pair flows. In Rhine-Main Frankfurt is dominant; here, peripheral cross-flows are negligible. In Northern Switzerland, likewise, Zürich dominates; here there are some long-distance flows, as well as cross-flows between neighbouring FURs. The Paris Region is highly monocentric, but there are some local commuter fields farther out. Dublin displays extreme monocentricity.

MEASURING POLYCENTRICITY

The study went on to a key objective: to measure the degree of polycentricity in each FUR. It employed three well-known and well-tested methods. The first, the rank-size rule, produces two distinct groups: a larger group strongly primate (South East England, Central Belgium, Rhine-Main, Northern Switzerland, Paris Region, Dublin), with a smaller group non-primate

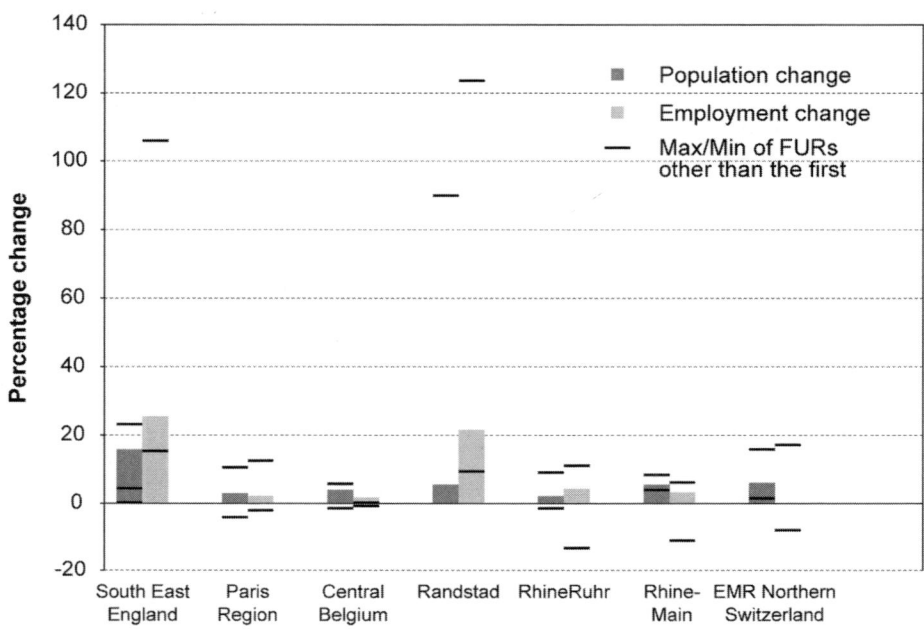

Figure 5. *Megacity regions: functional urban regions population and employment change 1990-2000.*

(Randstad, RhineRuhr). However, in the first group it appeared that primacy was "superimposed" on a lognormal (rank-size) distribution, as in South East England.

The second, self-containment, used an index developed by Ray Thomas (1969). It shows an interesting set of distinctions. In the Randstad the larger FURs are quite self-contained; in Central Belgium, all were self-contained; in RhineRuhr they were quite self-contained, but declining; in Rhine-Main, the largest FURs were self-contained, the others not so; in Northern Switzerland all were self-contained; but Zürich especially so; in the Paris Region Paris was almost completely self-contained; elsewhere there were outflows.

Finally the study developed general measures of polycentricity [10]. The index of Special Functional Polycentricity generated separate indices for in– and out-commuting; General Functional Polycentricity combined them. The conclusion, at first surprising, is that in all eight MCRs there were low degrees of polycentricity, ranging from only 0.02 in the Paris Region to a maximum of 0.15-0.20 in Randstad and RhineRuhr *(Table I)*. But, as the Dutch team commented, this apparent paradox was only to be expected:

"A value of 1.0 would mean that all FURs in the greater Randstad area are equally well connected to each other in terms of commuter flows and that the entire working population works in a place different from their place of residence. Next to being a polycentric utopia, it would also be a clear recipe for traffic chaos and environmental degradation "[23].

Table I. Special and general polycentricity indices 2000

Metropolitan City Region	Special functional polycentricity index (in-commuting)	Special functional polycentricity index (out-commuting)	General functional polycentricity index
South East England	0.14[a]	0.16[a]	0.15[a]
The Randstad	0.16	0.15	0.16
Central Belgium	0.04	0.04	0.04
RhineRuhr	0.20[b]	0.17[b]	0.19[b]
Rhine-Main	0.07	0.09	0.08
EMR Northern Switzerland	0.03	0.03	0.03
Paris Region	0.02	0.02	0.02
Greater Dublin	0.06	0.06	0.06

[a]Calculation based on 2001 data with rings at NUTS 4.
[b]Calculation based on 151 NUTS 5 units, not on FURs.

Conclusion

What conclusion, therefore, can we draw? Maybe the beast is not after all mythical, but is difficult to define – and there is more than one species of the genus. A city region may be easy to define, a Mega-City Region much harder: what exactly is its defining essence? Polycentricity, the other concept, appears equally elusive, since there are at least two meanings: physical or geographical, considered in this paper, and functional in terms of flows of information, requiring further research. This is the essence of the POLYNET study, which is fully reported in the book The Polycentric Metropolis [16].

REFERENCES

1. Beckouche P. (Ed). *Pour une métropolisation raisonnée : diagnostic social et économique de l'Île-de-France et du Bassin parisien*. Préfecture d'Île-de-France, Datar, Paris, La Documentation Française, 1999.

2. Castells M. *The Informational City: Information Technology, Economic Restructuring and the Urban-Regional Process*. Oxford: Basil Blackwell, 1989.

3. Cheshire PC. A New Phase of Urban Development in Western Europe? The Evidence for the 1980s. *Urban Studies* 1995; 32: 1045-63.

4. Cheshire P.C. Cities in Competition: Articulating the Gains from Integration. *Urban Studies* 1999; 36, 5-6: 843-64.

5. Cheshire PC, Carbonaro G. Urban Economic Growth in Europe: Testing Theory and Policy Prescriptions. *Urban Studies* 1996; 33: 1111-28.

6. Cheshire PC, Hay DG. *Urban Problems in Western Europe: An Economic Analysis*. London: Unwin Hyman, 1989.

7. Garreau J. *Edge City: Life on the New Frontier*. New York: Doubleday, 1991.

8. G.B. Royal Commission on Local Government in England, 1968. *Research Studies 1: Local Government in South East England*, by the Greater London Group, the London School of Economics and Political Science, London, HMSO.

9. Gottmann J. *Megalopolis: The Urbanized Northeastern Seaboard of the United States*. New York: Twentieth Century Fund, 1961.

10. Green N. *General Functional Polycentricity: A Definition. POLYNET Working Papers*. London: Institute of Community Studies/The Young Foundation & Polynet Partners, 2004.

11. Halbert L. (2002a). Services aux entreprises: vers une nouvelle géographie économique métropolitaine. *Note Rapide de l'IAURIF* 2002; n° 8, Bilan Stratégique du SDRIF, Paris, IAURIF.

12. Halbert L. (2002b). Les emplois supérieurs en Île-de-France. Vers de nouvelles polarités ? *Note Rapide de l'IAURIF* 2002 ; n° 12, Bilan Stratégique du SDRIF, Paris, IAURIF.

13. Hall P. Geography: Illogical? (The Maud Report Examined). *New Society* 1969; June 19: 954-55.

14. Hall P. Planning for the Mega-City: A New Eastern Asian Urban Form? In *East West Perspectives on 21st century Urban Development: Sustainable Eastern and Western Cities in the New Millennium*, Brotchie J, Newton P, Hall P, Dickey J (Eds). Aldershot: Ashgate, 1999: 3-36.

15. Hall P, Hay D. *Growth Centres in the European Urban System*. London: Heinemann, 1980.

16. Hall P, Pain K. *The Polycentric Metropolis: Learning from Mega-City Regions in Europe*. London: Earthscan, 2006.

17. Hall P, Thomas R, Gracey H, Drewett R. *The Containment of Urban England*, 2 vol. London: George Allen and Unwin, 1973.

18. IAURIF. *North-West European Metropolitan Regions: Geographical Boundaries and Economic Structures*. Paris: IAURIF, 1996.

19. Llewelyn Davies. *Four World Cities*. London: Comedia, 1997.

20. Magrini S. The Evolution of Income Disparities among the Regions of the European Union. *Regional Science and Urban Economics* 1999; 29: 257-81.

21. Scott AJ. (Ed) *Global City-Regions: Trends, Theory, Policy*. Oxford: Oxford U.P, 2001.

22. Thomas R. *London's New Towns: A Study of Self-contained and Balanced Communities*. London: PEP, 1969.

23. Werff M. van der, Lambregts B, Kapoen L, Kloosterman R. *POLYNET Action 1.1: Commuting & the Definition of Functional Urban Regions: The Randstad*. London: Institute of Community Studies/The Young Foundation & Polynet Partners, 2005. http://www.polynet.org.uk/

The urban typologies and the construction of polycentric spatial perspectives: The example of the Atlantic area

Jean-Paul Carrière[1]

Polytechnic School, Department of Planning, University of Tours, CITERES, France

The European Spatial Development Perspective (ESDP) published in 1999 proposed the goal of a polycentric model for the development of Europe, with the aim of achieving social as well as territorial cohesion following the Treaties of Maastricht and Amsterdam. Member states agreed to implement planning policies which would promote this goal. The polycentric model is considered to be the strategy best able to minimise regional disparities in development whilst at the same time creating a more competitive European economy as suggested by the Lisbon summit (2000). The main challenge for this strategy is to reconcile the aim of reducing spatial imbalances with the aim of competitiveness, aims that are often regarded as conflicting.

The ESDP itself reflects concern about current development trends which have led to a core-periphery model of development in Europe, a monocentric model which is regarded as a threat to the European project. In response, the ESDP suggests a spatial scenario for the future of Europe based on a balanced development of "world economic integration zones". These correspond to the 13 transnational macro-regions of the INTERREG III program[2]. Among them is the Atlantic Area where there is a widely shared interest in avoiding a peripheral role in Europe.

Polycentrism in this chapter is used in the same sense as that defined by the ESPON[3] 1.1.1 report: "potentials for polycentric development in Europe" [5, 2]. In particular, this means that polycentrism is clearly a multi-scalar spatial organisation model. For this reason, we focus on the urban system and the part played by the different levels of the urban hierarchy in the spatial organisation of a macro-region such as the Atlantic Area. Secondly, we include

---

1. We would like to thank Pr. Stuart Farthing (University of the West of England), member of the scientific committee of the Atlantic Spatial Development Perspective (ASDP), for having contributed to the challenging task of translation of this chapter.
2. The INTERREG Programme is an European communal initiative programme financed by the structural funds.
3. European Spatial Planning Observation Network.

both aspects of polycentrism: the "morphological" and the "relational" aspects. This means that the presence of several big cities (morphological polycentrism) inside a macro-region of this type does not on its own constitute a sufficient condition for promoting the development of a world economic integration zone, able to be a counterweight to the "Pentagon" (the set of the richest European regions). In order to bring about balanced development in Europe, there must also be strong interactions between the centres within a region, and some determination to cooperate between cities and between cities and regions, on all scales.

This chapter draws on the findings of the research we have done with the members of the scientific committee for the Atlantic Spatial Development Perspective (ASDP). Briefly, the aims of the ASDP were:

– to translate the proposals of the ESDP to the Atlantic scale, and in particular the proposal of a polycentric spatial structure, in which cities and urban networks play a key role,
– to evaluate the whole macro-region, and to establish whether it can be regarded as a "World Economic Integration Zone",
– to make policy recommendations concerning inter-regional/transnational co-operation, in order to implement the project of a European multi-scalar polycentrism more effectively.

Based on the hypotheses and concepts briefly mentioned above, the ASDP proposes a territorial vision for the development of the Atlantic European façade, regarded in its entirety as a macro-region, including some strategic proposals for sectorial policies as well as territorial policies (particularly for new polycentric urban spatial organisation and interregional areas of cooperation)[4]. Given the strong link between the structure of the urban system and trends in spatial development, our main aim here is to focus more attention on the classification of urban areas and on how this classification can assist in the process of strategic analysis and evaluation, a process which is needed as a preliminary step in the creation of a polycentric territorial perspective on the European scale.

URBAN TYPOLOGY AND VARIOUS SCALES OF POLYCENTRISM

The role played by urban areas is an essential element in any policy for turning the Atlantic Area, a heterogeneous set of regions[5], into a future component of a polycentric European space. But how can we analyse the urban system of this macro-region in a way that helps us to understand the potential that exists for developing the polycentric model in Europe?

---

4. The ASDP was conceived by a team of experts from the 5 countries involved: Ireland, the UK, France, Spain and Portugal. The work was done in collaboration with the forward studies unit for the maritime peripheries, which depends on the Conference of Peripheral Maritime Regions of Europe (CPMR), and is under the control of the monitoring committee formed by the 20 Atlantic Regions co-financing the study, in complement to the European INTERREG III B Atlantic Area Programme. The final report is available now on the CPMR website and a shorter version was recently published by the CPMR [4].
5. The Atlantic Area *(Figure 1)*, defined in order to implement the INTERREG III B programme, involves 44 Regions NUTS II, where 73 million inhabitants live (a number very similar to that of the population of the 10 new members of the EU!)

In order to carry out a strategic evaluation of the Atlantic urban system and, at the same time, of the spatial structure of the whole area, four levels of spatial analysis were identified, corresponding to four levels of urban and regional systems. They do not necessarily coincide with any administrative divisions. We distinguish *(Figure 1)*:

– Metropolitan areas: these have an administrative, economic, and political power of influence over a supra-regional scale area, and a fairly strong power of attraction internationally. They show considerable territorial influence, a high degree of connectivity, a large range of highly internationalised and diversified activities, as well a wide range of rare and high-tech services.
– Intermediate cities: these can be defined as single cities or sometimes as poly-nuclear ensembles of separate urban areas. They are important nodes in transport networks. The scale of their areas of influence is supra-regional or at least regional. Whereas the top level in the urban structure is relatively weak, the network of Atlantic intermediate cities constitutes a real asset, even if they do not all have the same potential.
– Medium-sized towns: these correspond to lower levels of the urban hierarchy and provide commonly available functions. They are the centre of a sub-regional labour market. In this category are all the towns that, although they have a significant population, either do not have the full potential to be considered as intermediate cities, or are too remote and isolated to be part of a metropolitan or polynucleated intermediate system.
– Rural areas: by definition, these encompass all the areas that are predominantly rural, and covered only by a network of local centres, small towns or villages. A distinction needs to be made between those rural areas that have real potential thanks to high levels of diversification in activities (crafts, industries, tourism...), and those areas that are already suffering from the effects of a significant decline.

The link between these four levels of analysis can be illustrated by the following graph *(Figure 2)*, which in particular shows the strategic role of the intermediate cities in the Atlantic area. Polycentricity is made up of "bunches of grapes of cities" [6], structured in more or less permanent networks, and capable collectively of offering a sufficiently attractive level of higher services.

Figure 2 reveals that intermediate cities play a key role on the regional-national scale, *i.e.* the so-called meso-scale of polycentricity [5], whereas, the metropolises can be regarded as European nodes, able to become counterweights to the European core, the "Pentagon of capitals" and to further a polycentric spatial organisation on the macro-scale. Given the large number of intermediate cities in the Atlantic Area, in comparison with the relative weakness of the much smaller set of metropolitan regions, it appears that this network can hinge two different levels in the urban hierarchy, having on the one hand strong links with the European metropolitan areas, generally outside the Atlantic area itself (London, Paris, Madrid...) and on the other hand with more rural areas, and with cities of the same ranking. *Figure 2* also shows the essential role of the small and medium sized cities in terms of functional polycentricity on the micro-scale, *i.e.* the intraregional level.

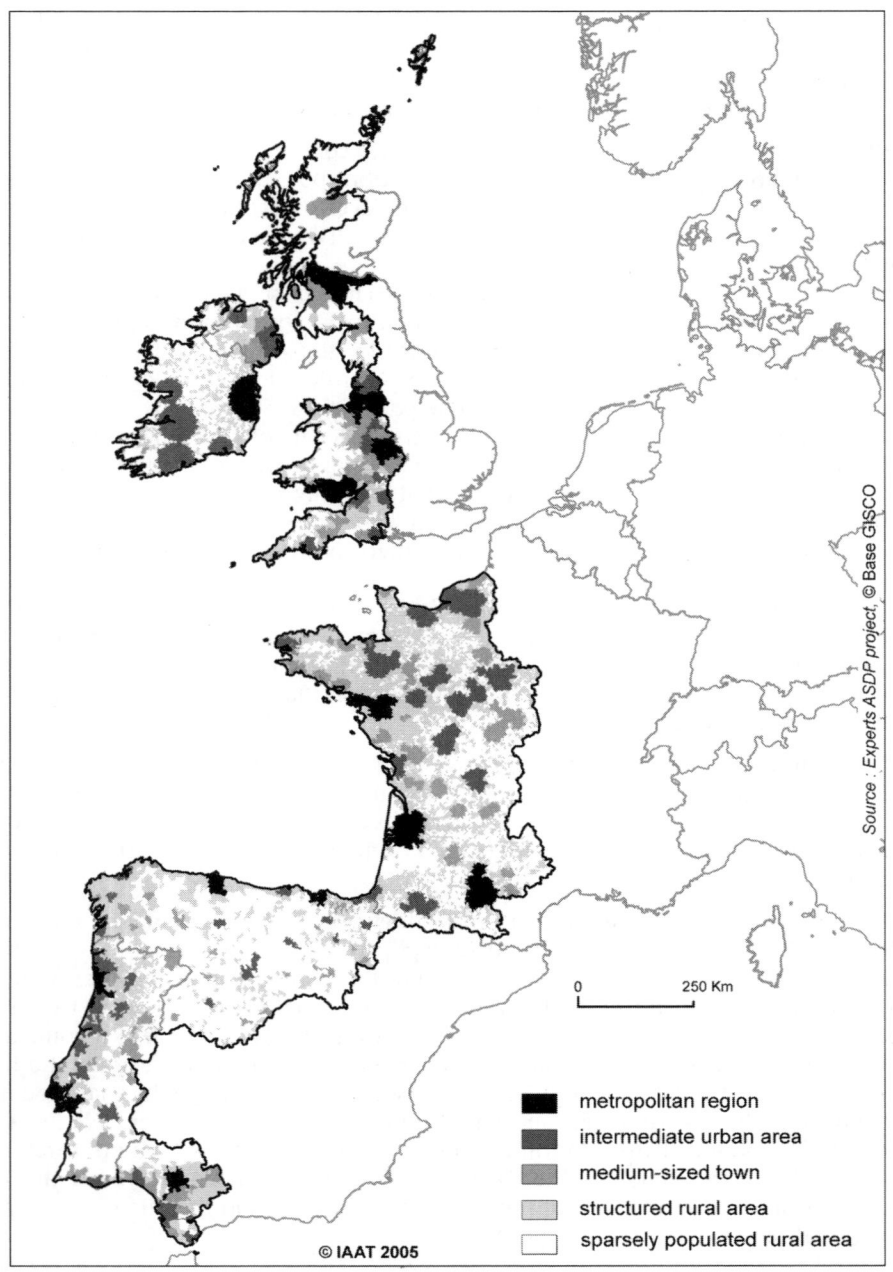

Figure 1. *Location of the different territorial and urban systems in the Atlantic area. With the permission of CPMR.*

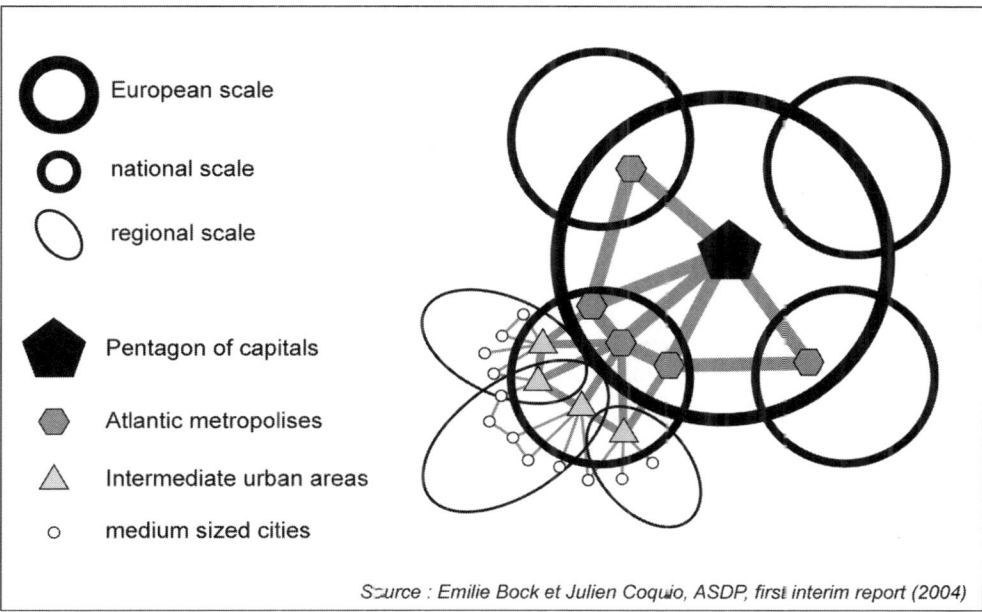

Figure 2. *The links between the four levels of analysis: the scales of polycentrism. With the permission of CPMR.*

URBAN CLASSIFICATION AS A BASIS FOR GENERATING SPATIAL PERSPECTIVES

The Atlantic area is not a World Economic Integration Zone

Having solved the methodological problems and having selected the cities in each of the four spatial analysis categories *(Box 1)*, the research consisted in an evaluation of the performance of each city (metropolis, intermediate or medium-sized) in order to assess how far the Atlantic city network could further both a polycentric Europe and a polycentric internal spatial organisation, within the Atlantic area.

Their performances and levels of influence were measured by means of a multi-criteria analysis, utilising several indicators and covering four main fields: demography (population, demographic growth, proportion of young people, migrations..), economic performance and competitiveness (GDP, GDP *per capita*, indicators of sectorial specialisation, employment, Research, Innovative and development activities, business headquarters...), connectivity (performances of the air, sea, road and railway transport systems...), urban functions and facilities (administrative functions, universities, fairs, hotels...).

The evaluation of the performances of the cities underlines the weakness of the top level of the urban hierarchy in the Atlantic area. But, beyond this relatively obvious result, the analysis shows that there are variations in the performances of the Atlantic cities. On the first

> **Box 1. Atlantic urban typology: some methodological problems**
>
> Classifying cities and urban areas that spread across different national territories in an area such as the Atlantic area, poses some methodological and practical problems which had to be solved in a pragmatic manner.
> – Because of the lack of a pan-European statistical data system, it was first necessary to select the set of data and indicators that were the most readily available for the whole area? However, the most recent indicators in each country were not available: generally speaking, nearly all data used were those for 2002 and calculated at the NUTS 4 or 3 level.
> – The hardest problem for our research was secondly linked to the lack of correlation between the level of the functions provided by cities and their population size when comparisons are made across national boundaries. Hence we chose to give priority not to the size criterion, but to the level of the functions provided and the visibility of the cities, assessed by national experts. For example, English, French or Spanish cities with a population of several hundred thousands are included in the intermediate category, whereas Irish or Portuguese cities of the same category only have populations of some tens of thousands. In Portugal, Ireland or Scotland, small towns with populations below 30,000 deliver a range of services equivalent to that provided by much larger towns in the other countries.
> – Because of large differences in urban spread and average densities, the third problem was that the definition of urban boundaries differs between countries (for example Spain and France). Urban morphology is strongly shaped by national contexts. Considering the need to take account of the national or regional realities, national definitions of functional urban areas were used in order to collect the data and to conduct analyses.

level of our spatial analysis system as defined in the first part (corresponding to the metropolitan area level), our research makes it possible to identify three different types. A first type concerns those metropolitan areas with a strong influence and visibility on the international scale, such as Dublin, the Manchester – Liverpool system, Birmingham and Lisbon. A second type corresponds to metropolitan areas with minor influence and lower levels of accessibility. Glasgow, the Welsh Cardiff-Swansea system, Nantes, Bordeaux, Toulouse and Bilbao are the best examples. A third type gathers metropolitan areas with limited competitiveness and weaknesses concerning several indicators. Porto, Sevilla, Ciudad Astur (the Asturian system with Oviedo – Gijon – Aviles) fit this type. In comparison with the most powerful and influential intermediate city systems, such as Le Havre – Rouen or Rennes – Saint-Malo, the position of these metropolitan areas often does not appear better in relation to some indicators of demographic or economic mass and dynamics.

On the second level of our spatial analysis that corresponds to the intermediate cities, our research provides evidence of a wider diversity of situations. Three main types can however be easily identified. The first corresponds to intermediate cities with supra-regional influence and strong socioeconomic performances: for example, Bristol, Cork, the polynucleated system of Rennes – Saint-Malo, Le Havre – Rouen or Vallalolid – Palencia. The second type concerns the intermediate cities with regional or infra-regional influence, poor international connections and weak performances. This type covers a great number of intermediate cities. But the largest type includes intermediate cities that are in an intermediate situation i.e. their performances vary a lot according to the indicators taken in account.

The situations of the third spatial analysis level, corresponding to the medium sized towns' category, also vary a lot according to the indicators taken into account.

A synthesis of the above analysis, at this stage of our study makes it possible to draw three intermediate remarks:

– The Atlantic area is characterized by a relative weakness in the first level of the urban system. None of the large cities appear to be in a position to compete seriously with the major European cities. Most of them could be described as "incomplete metropolises" in that they do not have the full range of higher functions, and they also do not always have a strong international influence enabling them to compete on the territorial market with the other major urban areas of the Pentagon. No Atlantic metropolis can claim to be among the top international metropolises, otherwise known as global cities, to use the term coined by Sassen (1991).
– The Atlantic area offers a high density of intermediate city networking. Since they are widespread throughout the area, this can be viewed as a real asset if they manage to develop strong relationships among themselves, using informal and formal co-operation links.
– The Atlantic area comprises a strong set of medium-sized towns. Rural areas are also predominant and constitute one of the major characteristics of the Atlantic area as a whole, if we do not focus exclusively on the more built-up coastal zones.

If, to these observations, we add the deficiency of connections between the cities and the regions themselves, as well as the weaknesses of the urban system in several domains (such as in high-tech activities and research development, for example...) this research leads us to conclude that there is marked spatial heterogeneity within the Atlantic area, and this cautions us against being too optimistic. The Atlantic area cannot be regarded currently as a "World Economic Integration Zone", in the ESDP sense of the word, even if the spectacular development of Atlantic interregional co-operation shows that it should be viewed as an appropriate area for new development projects.

The meso-scale: Potential areas of development

However, these results do not mean that there should be no development strategy and no way forward for the polycentric project. They lead us to believe that priority should be given to developing polycentrism on meso– (groups of Regions) or micro– (Cities and Regions) scales, rather than on macro scale (the whole area). The objective is not to replace one scale (the Atlantic area) with another (sub-areas), but rather to reflect in concrete terms on the need to consider action and co-operation on two distinct and complementary levels. That is why ASDP strategic guidelines for the development of the Atlantic area call for a meso-scale strategy.

Using the urban typology mentioned above, as well as other quantitative and qualitative findings concerning the competitiveness and connectivity of the Atlantic regions, we identified several types of very specific sub-areas. The polycentric project needs to take this diversity into account. The meso-scale approach is not in conflict with the idea that the Atlantic Area as a whole can also be considered as a transnational area within Europe, where its regions share a certain number of interests and common problems which require joint cooperation. It introduces a complementary geographical level that should be taken into account in any polycentric development strategy.

In this perspective, our study subdivides the Atlantic area macro-region into the following two sub-areas: the "motor" sub-areas and the "integration" sub-areas. Motor sub-areas concern regions (NUTS 3) which have the best performance on all indicators and are at the top level in regional economic development within the Atlantic area. They are also the areas where the cities have the greatest influence. This confirms the evidence of a correlation between the level of regional development and the performance of the cities. Integration sub-areas correspond to regions which present more weaknesses and are often undergoing processes of urban and regional decline. However, looking to the future, they need to reduce the gaps with the motor sub-areas and to be integrated into them (as it has been the case with some Irish or Spanish regions).

Motor sub-areas have comparative advantages: in particular, they are organised around metropolises and intermediate cities with considerable international influence and visibility; they are endowed with good connections, high-tech sectors, a good level of diversification of their regional economy, and they score high on the composite index of regional development... As shown on *Figure 3* five "motor sub-areas" have been identified as follows:

– Greater Dublin and the South-East of the Republic of Ireland;
– The Cardiff-Bristol-West Midlands-Liverpool– Manchester axis;
– The North Western part of the French Atlantic area;
– The cross-border area between the North-East of the Spanish Atlantic area and the South-West of France;
– The West Iberian Atlantic area (the coastal areas of Galicia and Portugal).

Integration sub-areas do not have cities with great influence and have many handicaps. In between the five "motor sub-areas" there are large intervening spaces where the population density and relative level of development are lower, the time-distance relationship between cities is much greater, there are fewer international connections, cities have less influence and the economy is much less diversified. These are regions that need to be included in a more balanced development in the Atlantic area because they are lagging very far behind other areas. Within this category some have greater inherent weaknesses than others, caused particularly by the more serious phenomena of depopulation and geographical isolation. It is therefore necessary to make a second sub-division between "high-potential integration sub-areas" and "weak integration sub-areas". However, the boundaries separating them are blurred, they remain highly interwoven and overlap *(Figure 3)*.

To organise the "motor sub-areas" and their links with the "integration sub-areas" is a vital objective that has to be achieved in a polycentric perspective. The task is to define development areas inside the Atlantic area on the basis of "motor sub-areas" with an examination of how high-potential or weak "integration sub-areas" can be integrated into them. It requires more inter-regional, cross-border and transnational co-operation in order to achieve this integration, and to create new projects and development areas. We can identify five major projects and development areas, each one organised around a more or less coherent urban system, which includes metropolises and networks of well-connected and cooperating intermediate cities. This perspective is founded on the hypothesis that cities are the drivers of regional development. The five major projects and development areas *(Figures 3 and 4)* are:

Urban typologies and polycentric spatial perspectives

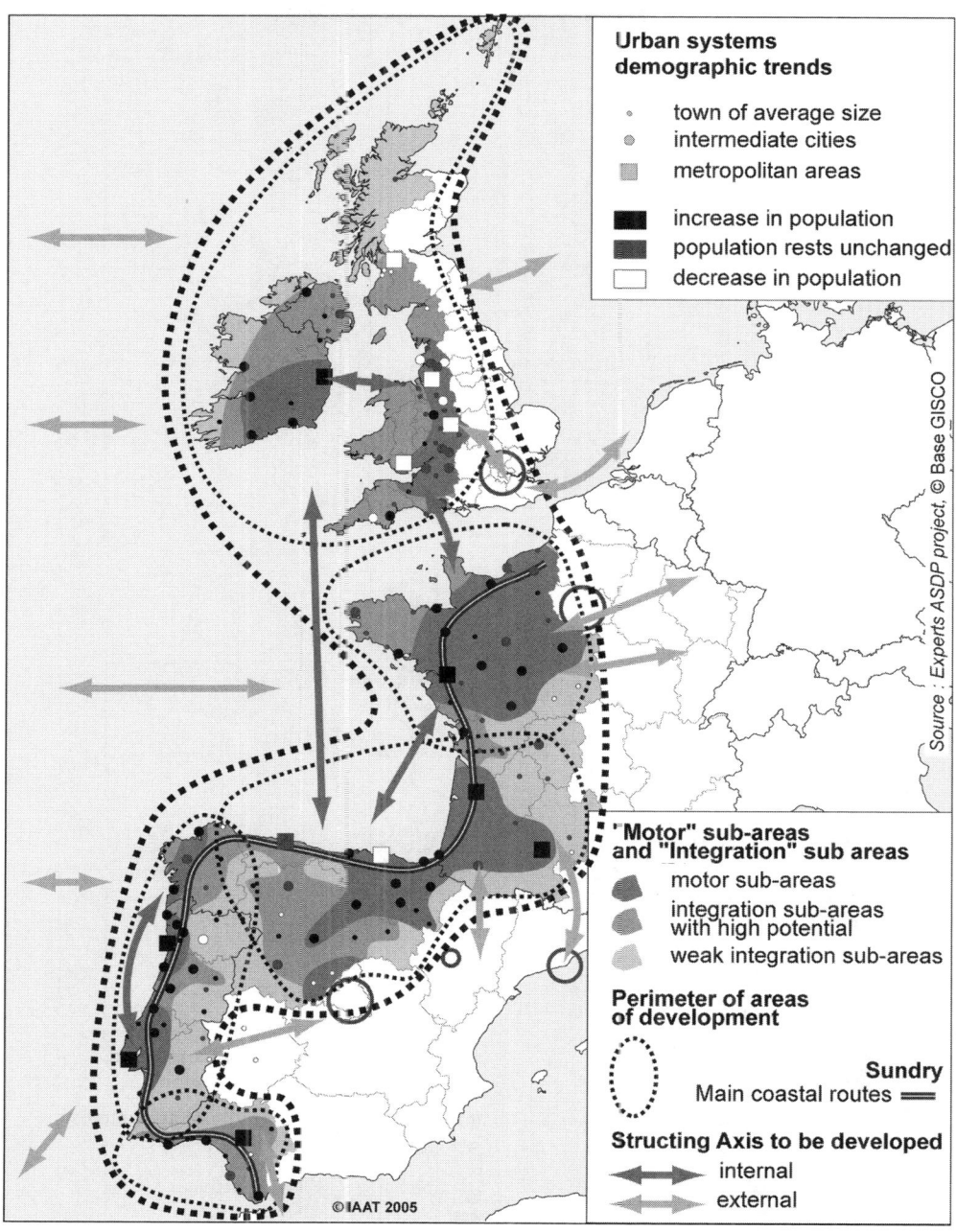

Figure 3. *Spatial vision for the Atlantic area. With the permission of CPMR.*

Cities and networks in Europe – Evaluating polycentrism

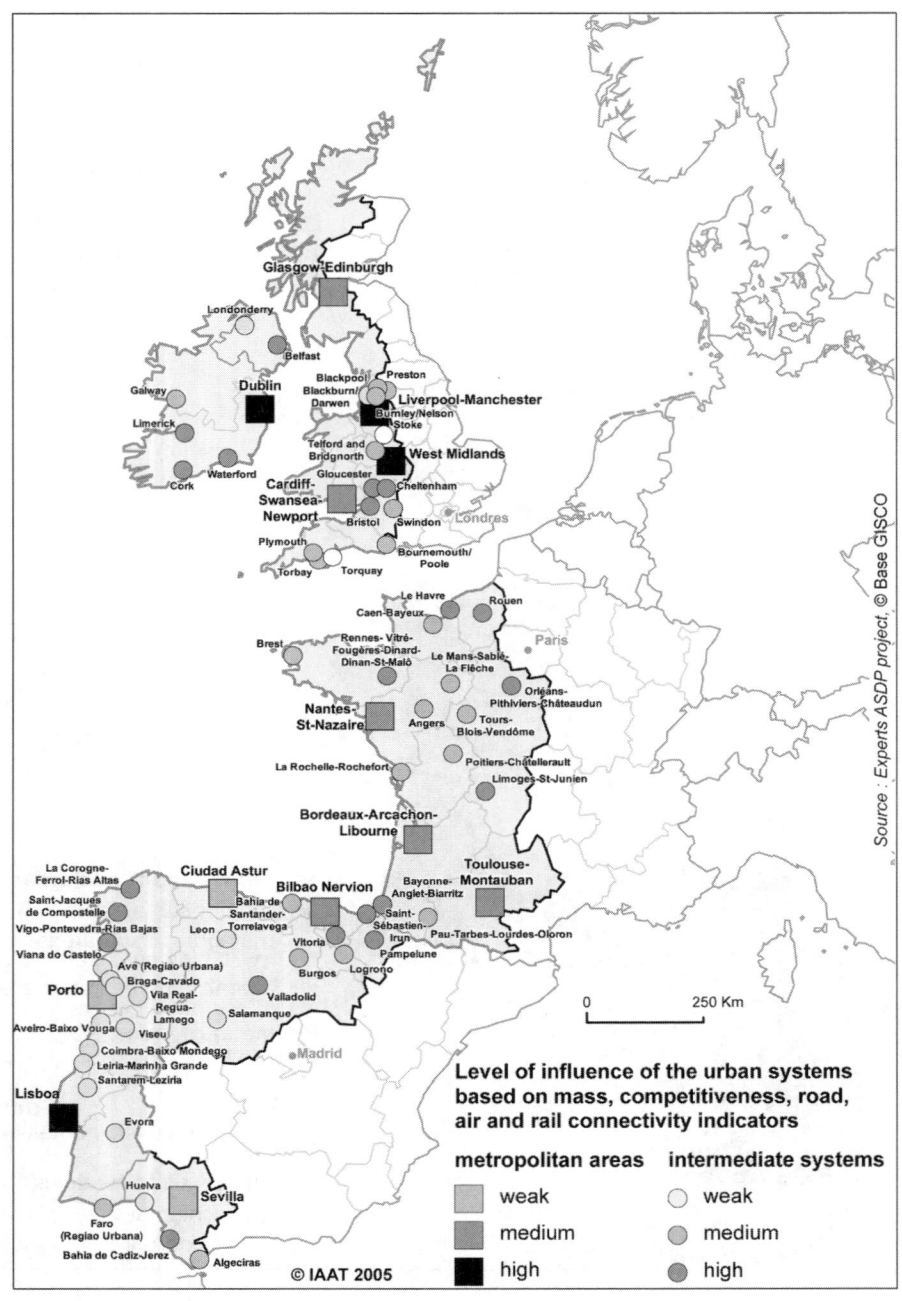

Figure 4. *Scales of influence of the Atlantic metropolises and intermediate cities. With the permission of CPMR.*

– The British Atlantic area: the main issue is the need for the Irish Sea and its coasts to be jointly managed.
– The French North-West area: the area is strongly connected to Paris and also includes the adjacent sub-areas.
– The French-Spanish area: the major challenge is to create appropriate links between the two national components by strengthening cross-border co-operation and finding suitable solutions, taking into account the environmental constraints specific to the mountain environment.
– The Western Iberian area: this zone is characterised by its role as a transition point between three worlds, Latin America, Africa and Europe (in fact all Atlantic regions are likely to play an increasing role as an interface between Europe and the overseas continents of America or Africa in the context of ever-expanding globalisation).
– The Southern Iberian area: This area is a particular case because it has a dual Atlantic and Mediterranean identity.

It should be emphasised that these five development areas within the Atlantic area as a whole were agreed by the General Assembly of the Regions, and members of the Atlantic Arc Commission of the CPMR when the ASDP final report was presented.

These areas should be considered as components in their own right of the overall unit formed by the Atlantic area. Sectorial and territorial policy recommendations, to be implemented through inter-regional co-operation, have been put forward for each of these projects and development areas.

Promoting intraregional cooperation within the sub-areas in order to implement territorial and sectorial recommendations does not exclude inter-regional cooperation on the Atlantic scale, through stronger proactive inter-regional co-operation based on a set of themes and key projects that bring together the common interests of the Atlantic regions, and incorporate the qualities that define and create the identity of the Atlantic area within Europe as a whole.

Conclusion

According to the principles set out at the summits of Lisbon and Göteborg, and the polycentric model suggested by the ESDP, the meso-scale strategy suggested in this chapter aims to enable the territories and the cities of the Atlantic area to become more attractive, to overcome their peripheral status within Europe, and to achieve more sustainable growth. In this perspective, cities play a key role in regional development on the sub-area scale, as well as on the Atlantic area scale. That is why the typology used has such an important place in the ASDP approach, both in spatial analysis, and also in relation to the polycentric perspective proposed. Achieving better territorial and socioeconomic integration within the sub-areas, as well as within the area as a whole, requires polycentricity to be strengthened. One precondition for doing this is some understanding of the strengths and weaknesses of the urban system, and an assessment of how far cities are able to participate in the process of building polycentric World Economic Integration Zones in Europe. In this sense, the Atlantic urban typology is a key element in elaborating the spatial perspective suggested.

Quoting the ASDP, it seems clear that: "Promoting a policy for more attractive and more accessible Atlantic cities may lead to improved territorial cohesion and help to make the

Atlantic area more competitive. This is a vital element for the development of polycentrism at the Atlantic area level." But, this recommendation can be itself regarded as the result of the analysis of the "Atlantic urban system" that we have introduced in this chapter.

REFERENCES

1. Carrière JP. L'aménagement du territoire en Europe : vers une approche polycentrique multiscalaire ; analyse à partir de l'Espace Atlantique. In *Le développement territorial : regards croisés sur la diversification et les stratégies*. Guesnier B, Joyal A. Poitiers: ADICUEER, 2004: 63-80.

2. Carrière JP. Une réflexion sur la construction du polycentrisme en Europe : apports et limites du rapport Potentials for polycentric development in Europe. *Revue Territoires* 2005 ; 2030, n° 1 : 47-63.

3. Carrière JP, Bock E. Le développement des villes intermédiaires au Portugal : un enjeu stratégique dans la perspective du polycentrisme. *Revue de géographie des Pyrénées et du Sud-Ouest* 2005 : 71-85.

4. Atlantic Spatial Development Perspective. CPMR, 2006.

5. Potentials for polycentric development in Europe. ESPON 1.1.1, 2004.

6. Kunzmann KR. Planning for spatial equity in Europe. *International Planning studies* 1998; 3 (1): 101-20.

7. Sassen S. *The global city*. Princeton University Press, 1991.

Towards an improved understanding of urban profiles and polycentric development potentials: Reflections on ESPON 1.1.1

Erik Gløersen
Nordregio, Sweden

Polycentricity is acknowledged as a central objective for spatial planning in Europe. However, as shown by Davoudi (2003), this does not imply that a consensus has been reached when it comes to the meaning of the concept. Analyses related to the polycentric development of the European territory first need to identify their understanding of the concept. When Nordregio was awarded the role of lead partner for the study on "The Role, Specific Situation and Potentials of Urban Areas as Nodes in Polycentric Development", also known as "ESPON[1] project 1.1.1", the main reference was the European Spatial Development Perspective (ESDP) approach of polycentricity. This resulted in a focus on the European macro scale, at which the ESDP encourages the identification of "several larger zones of global economic integration in the EU" which can be promoted as potential strongholds for a continental polycentric territorial organization.

The general objective of the present article is to describe how the analyses undertaken within the ESPON 1.1.1 research project have led us to question this "ESDP understanding of polycentricity". The first section argues that ESPON 1.1.1 results based on an ESDP-inspired focus on rank (rather than on functional specialisations) lead polycentric thinking down a dead end road. The second section presents some alternative methods, susceptible of providing a more nuanced view of the roles and functions of cities at different levels in the urban hierarchy.

A TYPOLOGY OF CITIES BASED ON MASS CRITERIA

Positioning the ESDP hypothesis on polycentricity in the academic debate

The ESPON 1.1.1 project produced a typology of cities as a test of ESDP hypotheses on polycentricity. It attempts to identify empirically potential "larger zones of global economic in-

---

1. European Spatial Planning Observation Network.

tegration" which could counterbalance the Pentagon. These zones are meant to be composed of multiple large metropolitan regions. The methodological setup of ESPON 1.1.1 therefore focuses on identifying urban masses, *i.e.* localised demographic and functional accumulations that could develop into a stronghold for global economic integration.

The focus on large cities as the main context for global integration is not specific to the ESDP. In the works of Saskia Sassen (1991) globalisation has been equated to the rise of a few major metropolises. Their strength is only indirectly connected to demographic size, as it derives from the production of financial and producer services. She however explains that these sectors only can thrive in vast labour markets, where a wide range of specialised competences can be pooled. John Friedmann's (1995) account of world city research also focuses exclusively on major metropolises, even if he maintains that this scientific framework is also a "way of asking questions about cities in general", and not only of establishing "world cities" as a separate category of urban nodes. In their typology of the world's most prominent urban nodes, Beaverstock *et al.* (1999) admittedly point out that "megacities" and "world cities" are not equivalent categories, quoting Zurich as an example of a "world city" that is not a "megacity". But this is rather to be considered as an exception to the general rule: global integration is, according to all these authors, best understood through the prism of major metropolitan regions that have asserted themselves as global cities. The ESDP has in this respect complied with a dominant, but contested research trend [16, 9].

The idea of multiple metropolitan regions forming a "geographical zone of global economic integration", which is developed in the ESDP, is on the other hand not grounded in the literature on global cities. As a geographical form, it is admittedly reminiscent of Jean Gottmann's "Megalopolis" [7]. Gottmann used this term to designate the "urbanised northeastern seaboard of the United States", but did not claim that the concept should have any explanatory dimension. As noted by Baigent (2004) the concept of Megalopolis was consequently "doomed [...] to obscurity" in geography. She however notes that the concept paradoxically thrives in other contexts. The success of the'Global integration zone' concept in European planning communities can be considered as a manifestation of this maintained fascination for the "Megalopolis" idea.

The rationales behind the two concepts are however different. While Gottmann used the Megalopolis as a framing concept for a regional monograph, Mehlbye (2000) describes how the "Global integration zone" concept underpins a shift away from spatial planner's proclivity to envisage only one possible core area in Europe. Polycentricity based on identifying "several larger zones of global economic integration in the EU" derives from the opinion that the challenges of European peripheries cannot be met by connecting them to this single core. As an alternative to infrastructure investments developing monocentric core-periphery connections, Mehlbye suggests to focus on connections between metropolitan regions outside of the European core area. Based on this analysis, ESPON 1.1.1 set out to identify which the metropolitan regions to be connected in such a way could be.

The MEGAs level: A focus on rank

In ESPON 1.1.1, cities were approached in terms of Functional Urban Areas (FUAs), corresponding to travel-to-work areas around each urban node. This first implies that the city was conceptualised as a daily-life living environment rather than as an administrative territory or a continuous built-up area. An underlying hypothesis of the FUA approach is furthermore that the boundaries of the travel-to-work areas correspond to a possible delimitation of each urban economic region, *i.e.* that certain types of interaction between economic actors are directly or indirectly connected to daily commuting patterns. This is not obvious. One can for example hypothesise the existence of wider commercial functional interaction areas, *e.g.* for industrial clusters and sub-contracting relationships. Further empirical evidence needs to be gathered on this issue.

Irrespective of these limitations, 1595 FUAs were selected as relevant European nodes, based on quantitative criteria[2]. These FUAs were characterised according to seven sets of statistic criteria, as described in *Table I*. Because of data availability problems, the measures were not compiled in a database. Instead, grades (from 0 to 4 or 5) were attributed to each city according to certain threshold values. In this way, some of the FUAs for which quantitative data were not available could be included in the analysis, with the help of experts assessing the category to which they were most likely to belong for each function.

Table I. *Functions considered for the characterisation of FUAs*

Feature/Functions	Measured variable
Population (mass function)	Population
Transport function	Airports (passengers), ports (container traffic)
Tourism function	Number of beds in hotels (and similar)
Industrial function	Gross "value added" in industry
Knowledge functions	Location of university, number of students
Decision-making centre	Location of top 500 companies
Administrative functions	Administrative status of FUA

Five of these seven functions were used for the classification of FUAs. This classification was produced by calculating the average score for the five functions. The grades were in other words added up; arbitrary threshold were then applied to distinguish FUAs of local/regional importance, national/transnational importance and Metropolitan European Growth Areas (MEGAs). By applying this method, 76 MEGAs were identified, including all national capital cities except Nicosia, and a selection of major regional capital cities. It should be noted that no dynamic indicators such as population trends were included in this analysis. This has created a certain discrepancy with national perceptions of where dynamic regional metropolitan areas are to be found. The classification may indeed rank a major, but lethargic regional capital city higher than a smaller active one with high growth over the last decades.

The classification method also reinforces the focus on mass and rank, rather than on profile. Some implicit hypotheses are indeed made when adding together different scores. First, the

---

2. Cities were considered as relevant nodes if their urban core exceeded 15,000 and the total FUA population either exceeded 50,000 inhabitants or amounted to 0,5% of the national population. Some smaller cities of particular functional importance were also considered [1].

numerical value of the score is presupposed to reflect the distance between each category: When a city with over 100,000 hotels beds is given the score "5", and a city with 50,000-100,000 beds is given the score "4", and when these values are added up in combination with scores for other types of urban functions, then a city scoring "5" is implicitly considered 25% "better" than a city scoring "4". The information that is lost when constructing these categories and when applying such a strong hypothesis can be problematic.

The second and most important hypothesis is that a city becomes a relevant major node in European polycentricity only insofar as it cumulates demographic mass with a high-level concentration of most of the five functions considered in the analysis. The analysis will for example not identify small cities with an exceptionally high number of students, as the "knowledge function" cannot compensate for low values in the four other functions when scores are added up.

This raises fundamental questions concerning our understanding of polycentricity. As described in the introduction to the present section, the ESPON 1.1.1 classification of FUAs was inspired by the quest for potential alternative "zones of global integration" outside the European core. This core is equated to the area delimited by London, Paris, Milan, Munich and Hamburg, known as the Pentagon. The underlying hypothesis is that the Pentagon has attracted a concentration of globally relevant functions because of its demographic and economic mass. In other words, the ESDP conceptualisation of global integration zones interprets the correlation between mass and global functions as a causal linkage. Following this logic, the relevant nodes for European polycentricity must be carried out through the identification or constitution of metropolitan entities with sufficient mass outside of the Pentagon. We term this search for alternative Global Integration Zones the "ESDP hypothesis" on European scale polycentricity.

The FUA classification methodology follows this ESDP rationale by identifying cities that accumulate functions, rather than to focus on centres of excellence within certain sectors only. This results in a MEGA classification that gives the impression that there is a strong potential for polycentric development across Europe *(Figure 1)*.

Going further with regards to the logic of mass, the ESPON 1.1.1 project tests the hypothesis that neighbouring peripheral nodes would join forces in order to constitute entities with greater mass, susceptible of counter-balancing the Pentagon. Consequently, ESPON project 1.1.1 modelled the effect of an increased integration between neighbouring cities on the European urban hierarchy. The resulting changes in the urban hierarchy *(Figure 2)* show that the promotion of metropolitan integration across Europe actually leads to stronger hierarchical contrasts between the core and the periphery.

More generally, a territorial strategy with the objective of changing the European urban hierarchy as such has little chances of succeeding, given the high degree of inertia of these systems. The growth model of the Pentagon cannot be reproduced in other parts of Europe, insofar as this model is based on unique concentration of people and economic actors. Polycentric development strategies can however promote a more multipolar Europe by facilitating the emergence of alternative development strategies throughout its territories, and at all levels of the urban hierarchy. The next sections describe methodologies susceptible of identifying specialisations in the urban system susceptible of upholding such a polycentric territorial strategy. The objective of this alternative method is to identify the main vectors of polycentric development potential, namely secondary centres with a dynamic, endogenous development model.

Urban profiles and polycentric development potentials

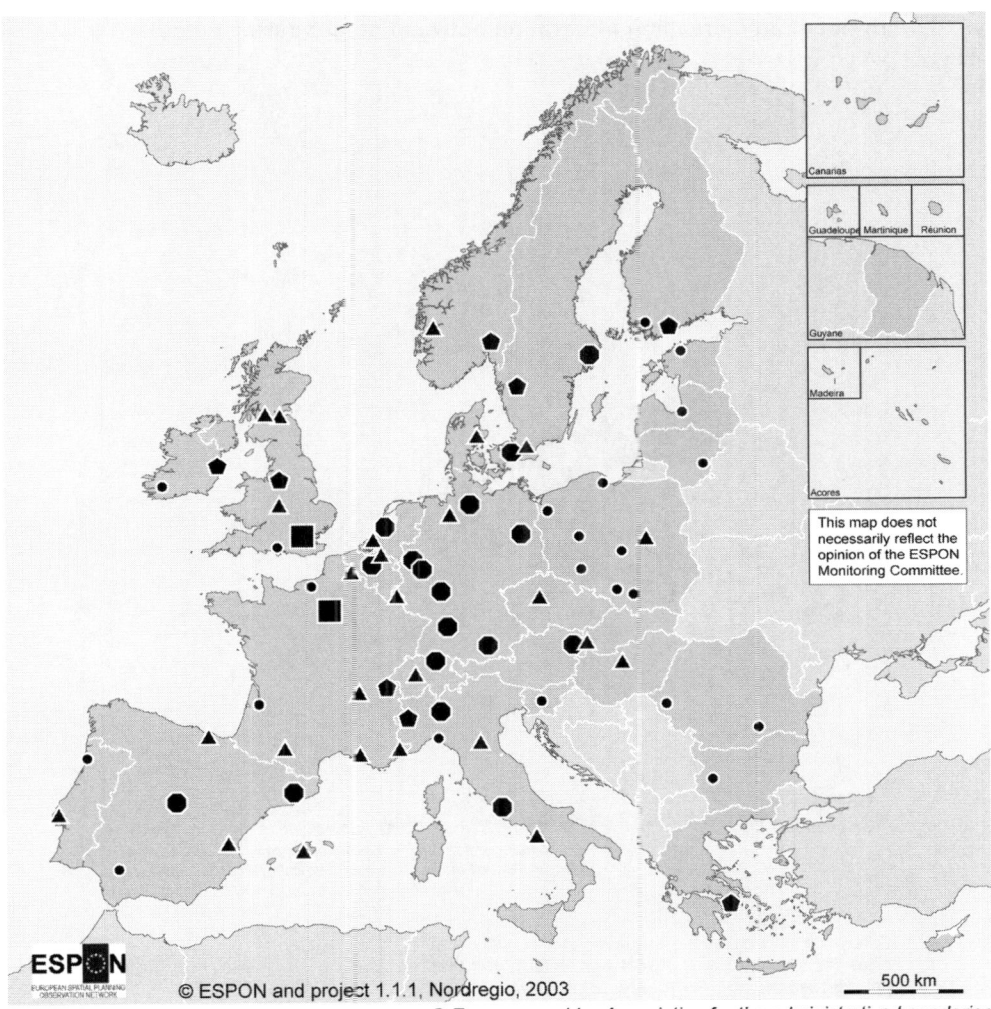

- ■ Global nodes
- ● European engine
- ⬟ Strong MEGA
- ▲ Potential MEGA
- • Weak MEGA

Figure 1. *Metropolitan European Growth Areas classification and EU polycentricity perspective.*

Effect of an increasing integration between neighbouring cities

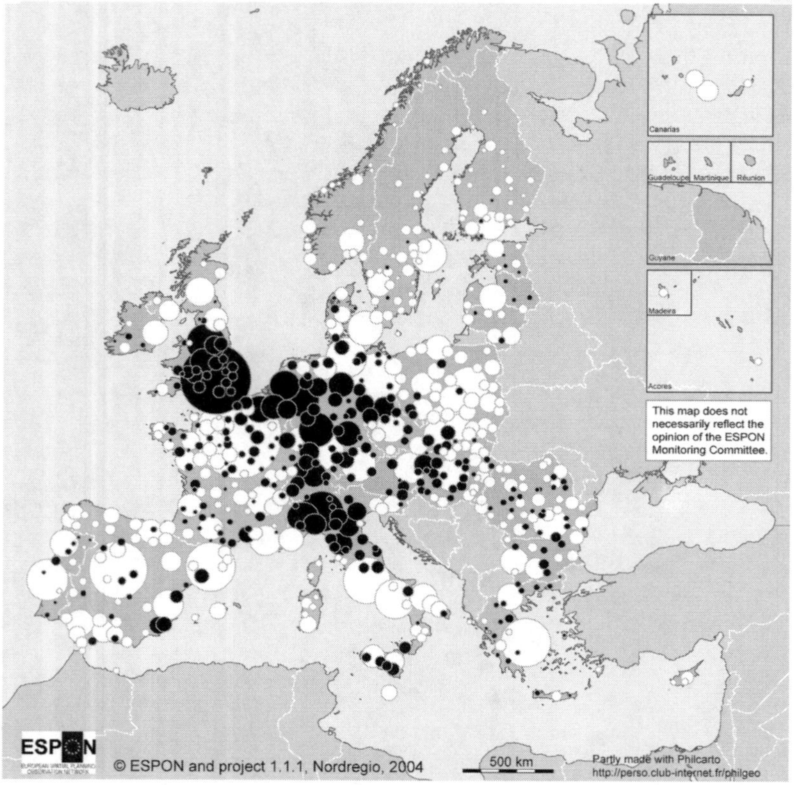

© Eurogeographics Association for the administrative boundaries
Origin of data: Eurostat, National Statistical Offices, National Experts
Data sources: Nordregio, ESPON NUTS 5 database
PUSH delimitation: RRG
PIA identification: Nordregio

Difference between the European rank of individual cities (according to their PUSH population), and that of corresponding Polycentric Integration Area (considering the main node of each PIA only):

■ Cities gaining relative importance through polycentric integration (PIA rank > PUSH rank)

☐ Cities losing relative importance through polycentric integration (PIA rank < PUSH rank)

For this calculation, areas accessible in 45 minutes around all European FUA centres were first delimited. If two such neighbouring areas overlapped by over one third, the smaller city was then integrated into the larger one. These new integrated entities were labelled Polycentric Integration Areas, or PIA.

FUA population according to national FUA definition
- 11 175 000
- 7 650 000
- 2 900 000
- 850 000
- 13 000

Figure 2. *Regional polycentricity across Europe increases the contrasts between core and periphery.*

PROFILING CITIES RATHER THAN RANKING THEM

In the previous section, we described how the ESPON 1.1.1 project developed an approach of polycentricity on the basis of the ESDP vision of the concept at the European scale, by focusing on mass and rank rather than on urban profiles. This implies that the combination of social and economic characteristics that describes each city's specific function and potentials is not regarded as the prime focus of polycentricity. Instead, the focus is on the territorial imbalances in the spread of large metropolitan areas across Europe. The methodology used reflected this perspective. The ESPON 1.1.1 report however concluded that polycentricity based on mass and rank will not contribute to improve the territorial balance in Europe. The initial methodological choices were consequently partly invalidated by the findings. The study consequently concluded that the focus of polycentric policies should be on functional specialisation in secondary cities.

In the present section, we present a methodology in line with this kind of perspective on the urban system. The focus is shifted away from ranking lists, as these reproduce the current hierarchical structure in the urban system. They furthermore fail to reveal nodes that could potentially challenge the core-periphery contrasts and promote an improved territorial balance. The objective is to show that cities can be classified not only according to their size, but also according to the relative importance of different functions. A secondary city can host a major university, research facility or industrial plant. From a European polycentric policy point of view, it is important to gather knowledge about where such phenomena occur, in view of understanding how hierarchical patterns can be challenged.

Ascendant classification is useful when one wishes to produce typologies without any *a priori* hypothesis on the classes to be produced. In the present case, we have used a classification method based on k-means. This implies that categories are built in such a way that as little of the variation between cities as possible occurs within the categories and, inversely, as much variation as possible is concentrated between categories. The classes are in other words designed so that each group of cities is as different as possible from the other ones. A categorisation in five classes, based on the five parameters demographic mass, transport, knowledge function, decision-making and administration, was chosen.

The results are interpreted by comparing the average score for each variable within the categories with the average overall score. The difference between the two average scores is illustrated in *Figure 3*. These results confirm the importance of hierarchy as a factor of differentiation within the European urban system. Indeed, three of the five categories gather cities for which all functions are, on average, either over– or underrepresented.

Cluster 1 comprises cities where all functions are generally heavily overrepresented. The 37 cities in this category are generally national capitals or metropolitan regions of high economic importance, or so called nodal regions (Hamburg, Amsterdam, Antwerpen, Rotterdam, Frankfurt, Zurich, Frankfurt, Düsseldorf, Barcelona and Porto). The inclusion of Valletta in this cluster however shows that a high grade with regards to administrative functions is an important structuring element. The name of this cluster, "First tier nodal regions and capital cities", indicates this ambivalence. The category should ideally be subdivided in order to isolate the European nodal regions.

Cities and networks in Europe – Evaluating polycentrism

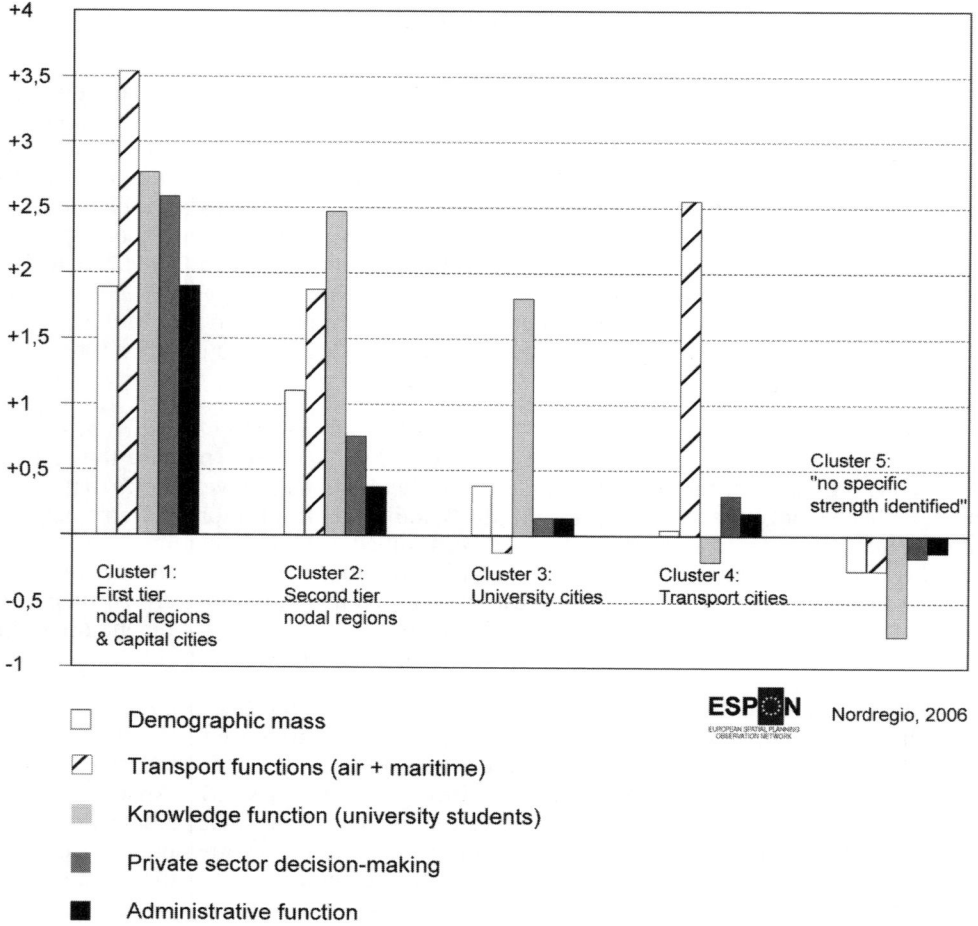

Figure 3. *Characterisation of the five clusters of cities (identified by applying a k-means ascendant classification method to the FUA grades).*

Cluster 2 comprises 74 cities where all categories are as previously overrepresented, but to a more reduced extent. The overrepresentation of administrative, decision-making and transport functions is less significant than in Cluster 1, while Universities are on average as well represented. We have named this category "second tier nodal regions".

The vast majority of the urban areas (1,126 cities and towns) belong to Cluster 5, and have scores that are generally weak or average, and no specific strength covered by any of the 5 indicators used. These are the urban areas whose development could most contribute to increase polycentricity at the meso– and micro-scales. FUAs in this cluster are referred to as "Cities with no specific strength identified", in order to underline that a wide range of additional profiles, potentially involving a prosperous economic situation or a high development potential, would have been identified if a wider range of indicators had been used.

The two remaining clusters however show elements of functional differentiation. Cluster 3 confirms the presence of knowledge functions in lower tiers of the urban hierarchy. This cluster comprises the 327 cities that have higher education facilities, but only weak or average scores in other respects. It is important to note that cities in clusters 1 and 2 can also have major higher education facilities. We have not termed this group of cities the "university cluster" in exclusive sense. The name of the cluster instead refers to the fact that the presence of a University is the main distinguishing trait of these cities identified through the indicators used. In the same way, one would more easily refer to Cambridge or Heidelberg as "university cities", than London or Berlin, even if a higher number of students may be found in the two latter cities.

Cluster 4 represents the same kind of situation for transport functions. The 32 cities in this cluster generally have weak or average scores in all respect, except for transport. These are generally harbour cities (*e.g.* Helsingborg and Le Havre), or cities with major air traffic due to tourism (*e.g.* Ibiza and Larnaca) or due to the presence of air freight hubs (*e.g.* Luxembourg). In the same way as for the "university cluster", major transport functions can also be found in cities belonging to clusters 1 and 2.

Figure 4 maps the FUAs belonging to each of the 5 clusters. The main added value of the method lies in clusters 3 and 4, which identify secondary urban nodes that have developed a significant strength within a given activity. A similar analysis with a wider range of indicators (*e.g.* proportion of employees high-technology, leisure or cultural activities) would be likely to reveal additional cities with a parallel type of profile. In other words, this methodology can reveal motors of economic development situated outside of the traditional centres of power and wealth. A better knowledge about these dynamic secondary nodes would provide useful insights for the design of a European polycentric development strategy.

Conclusion

The FUA analysis of ESPON 1.1.1 broke new grounds through its geographical scope, and the number of urban areas that were taken into account. Compiling FUA delimitation for 29 countries, and corresponding statistical data was a major challenge, which was overall successfully overcome. The study was designed as a test of certain hypotheses on polycentricity deriving from the ESDP. This test was in some regards inconclusive, especially as empirical evidence shows that creating *"several larger zones of global economic integration in the EU"* having characteristics similar to those of the Pentagon is not a realistic way forward. The study however neither had the time nor resources to draw all the consequences from these conclusions, by designing and implementing alternative analytical approaches.

The results of the study however remind us that the primary objective of a polycentric development strategy cannot be to change the urban hierarchy. Polycentricity must instead seek to avoid a reproduction of hierarchical relations leading to constant concentration, with metropolisation in some parts and depopulation in others. The main focus of research undertaken with a polycentric perspective should therefore be the assertion of secondary nodes within the urban system. We have argued that functional specialisation is a major aspect of

Cities and networks in Europe – Evaluating polycentrism

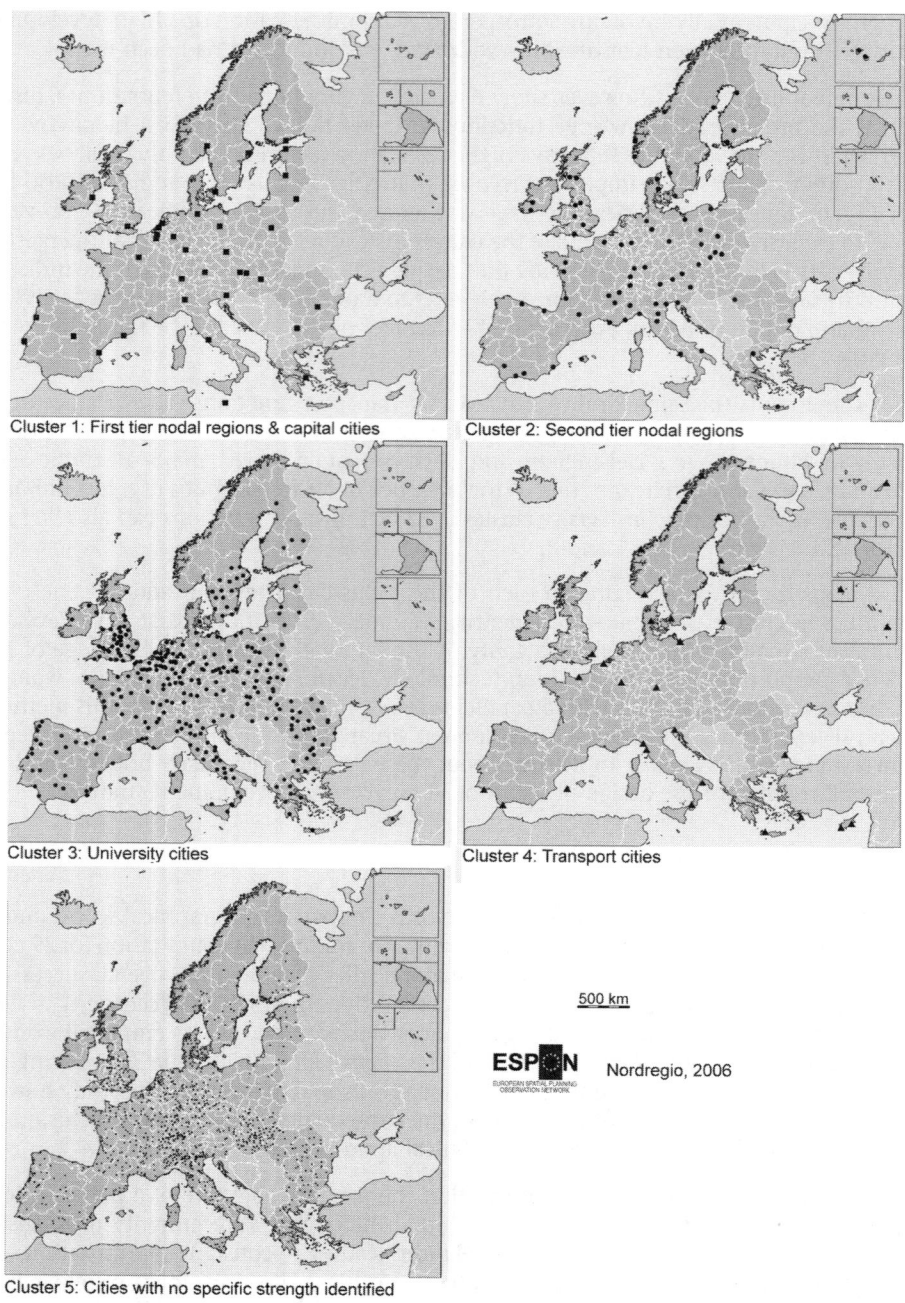

Figure 4. *Typology of Functional Urban Areas.*

this assertion. This however does not imply that one should underestimate the importance of institutional arrangements, either as vectors of local empowerment or as inhibitors of local growth dynamics.

The present article has described a method that could be applied for this purpose. The results should be understood as a contribution to the current dialogue on how the European urban network should be approached, offering an alternative to the MEGA and FUA classification of the ESPON 1.1.1 report. They do however not provide a satisfactory account of the European urban network, insofar as there is fundamental need to rethink the conceptualisation of the city and urban region as such. An analysis of the European urban system with a polycentric perspective should therefore take into account the complexity of multi-scalar urban interaction, and would need to combine different typologies for each of these scales.

REFERENCES

1. Antikainen J. The concept of Functional Urban Area. Findings of the ESPON project 1.1.1. *Informationen zur Raumentwicklung*, Heft 7, Bonn: Bundesamt für Bauwesen und Raumordnung, 2005.

2. Beaverstock J, Smith RG, Taylor PJ. A roster of world cities. *Cities* 1999; 16: 445-58.

3. Baigent E. Patrick Geddes, Lewis Mumford and Jean Gottmann: divisions over "megalopolis". *Progress in Human Geography* 2004; 28, 6: 687-700.

4. Commission of the European Communities. ESDP–European Spatial Development Perspective – Towards Balanced and Sustainable Development of the Territory of the European Union. Brussels: European Commission, 1999.

5. Davoudi S. Polycentricity in European Spatial Planning: from analytical tool to normative agenda. *European Planning Studies* 2003; vol. 11, n° 8: 979-99.

6. Friedmann J. Where we stand: a decade of world city research. In *World Cities in a World System*. Knox PL, Taylor PJ (Eds). Cambridge: Cambridge University Press, 1995: 21-47.

7. Gottmann J. Megalopolis the urbanized north-eastern seaboard of the United States. New York: Twentieth Century Fund, 1961.

8. IAURIF. *Growth sectors – clusters in Dublin, London, Paris and Rhineruhr – Synthesis and recommendations*. Final report of INTERREG IIC project n° 051, GEMACA II, ISBN: 2-7371-1430-6. Paris : Institut d'Aménagement et d'Urbanisme de la Région Île-de-France, 2002.

9. McCann E. Urban Political Economy Beyond the "Global City". *Urban Studies* 2004; vol. 41, n° 12: 2315-33.

10. Mehlbye P. "Global Integration Zones – Neighbouring Metropolitan Regions". *Informationen zur Raumentwicklung*, Heft 11/12. Bonn: Bundesamt für Bauwesen und Raumordnung, 2000.

11. Nordregio, 2000. *Study Programme on European Spatial Planning*. Nordregio Report 2000, 4, Stockholm, Nordregio.

12. Nordregio, 2004. *ESPON 1.1.1 – Study on urban areas as nodes in polycentric development*, final report of a study commissioned by the European Spatial Planning Observatory Network (ESPON), available for download at www.espon.eu.

13. Moriconi-Ebrard F. *Geopolis: pour comparer les villes du monde*. Paris: Anthropos/Economica, 1994, 246 p

14. Rozenblat C, Cicille P. *Les villes européennes – analyse comparative*. Paris: DATAR/Documentation française, 2003.

15. Sassen S. *Global city: London, New York, Tokyo* Princeton: Princeton University Press, 1991.

16. Smith RG. World city actor networks. *Progress in Human Geography* 2003; vol. 27, n° 1: 25-44.

Innovation and polycentrism in the Mediterranean Latin arc

Alberto Vanolo
Politecnico e Università di Torino, Italy

The Mediterranean Latin Arc is an area that includes the coastal regions stretching from Andalusia to Campania. The idea of this geographical entity is closely related to certain summary representations of the European territory proposed by geographers and urban scholars, pointing to a "centre-periphery" model, with a strong (in terms of socioeconomic indicators) Western European core and weaker "peripheral" regions [7]. In particular, this centre-periphery model refers to the existence of a central backbone, an urban structure already identified by Brunet (1989), which includes the London region, Randstad Holland and the Ruhr area, continuing along the Rhine axis down to Lombardy. This area has a better economic and urban performance than the more peripheral regions, and in recent years, several scholars have emphasised the need to strengthen other geographical development axes to encourage a more balanced structure; suggestions include an "Atlantic Arc" (proposed by Crpm: www.arcatlantique.org) or a "Mediterranean Latin Arc" [6]. The latter area has unclear geographical boundaries, and in this sense has been defined by Boulifard (1994) as a "variable geometry area". A general picture, based on a series of theoretical contributions and empirical analyses [14], is presented in *Figure 1*. This area constitutes the geographical context for the analysis, which looks at the dynamics and potential of the region from two specific perspectives: polycentric territorial development and technological innovation.

From an analytical point of view, the study is based on observation of industrial clusters. These geographical elements play a major role as innovation spillovers. In particular, as indicated by Malmberg and Maskell (2002), innovation is created and spread in two ways: first through horizontal relations between businesses, *i.e.* companies carrying out the same functions in the value chain, and hence acting as potential competitors, able to directly observe and imitate each other. The second dimension is vertical and concerns suppliers and customers, attracted by the opportunities offered by geographical location within the cluster, such as the possibility of establishing privileged relationships (trusting, rapid, informal) with other companies. Moreover, as businesses specialise, they increase the local stock of knowledge, by concentrating on problems and inefficiencies that are otherwise neglected. And finally, severe disintegration of the production process within a polycentric structure determines the need to build stable networks to coordinate the activities of businesses, making it easier to share knowledge [11]. In this sense, industrial clusters may act as nodes in a reticular and polycentric regional structure: the aim of developing "innovative polycentrism" corresponds, on the one hand, to promoting several regional clusters of innovation, and on the other, to furthering functional interactions between clusters as a means of spreading knowledge.

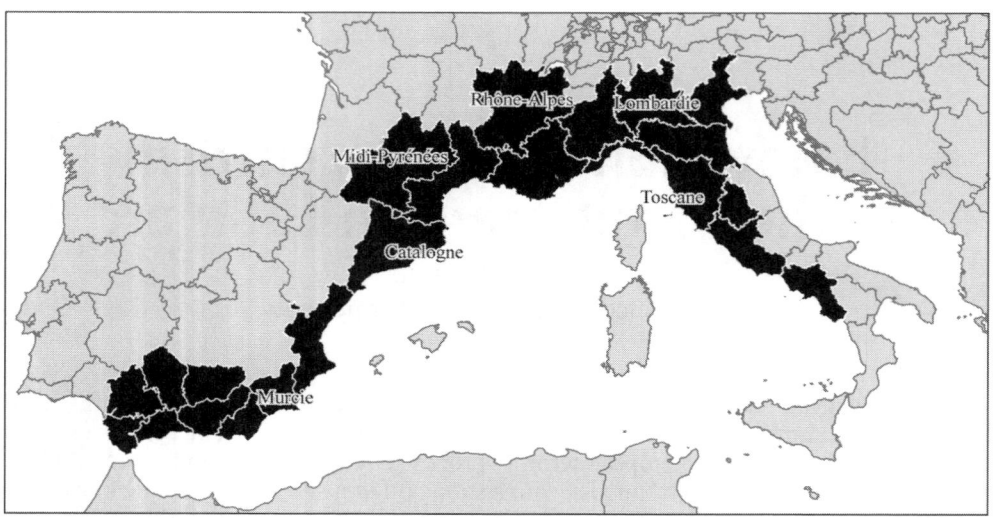

Source : ESRI Database

Figure 1. *The Mediterranean Latin Arc.*

The aim of this paper is to elaborate an analytical scheme to evaluate and compare the level of innovativeness in regions in the Arc, along with their level of polycentrism (or, conversely, polarisation), based on the assumption that polycentric structures favour the diffusion of knowledge by means of the aforementioned horizontal and vertical relations. The first paragraph introduces the general methodology; paragraph 2 focuses on the potential for innovation of a selected number (15) of clusters; paragraph 3 evaluates the level of polycentrism of the territorial structures considered. Finally, paragraph 4 combines the results obtained in the previous two paragraphs, to build a summary representation of the industrial geography of high technology in the Arc and to put forward some reflections and theoretical conclusions.

FIELDS STUDIES: DEFINITION OF INNOVATIVE CLUSTERS

Defining innovation in local systems starts with the identification of some clusters characterised by a high endowment of technological functions in terms of enterprises, universities, polytechnics, and research centres operating in high-technology fields[1], since these are the main players involved in the process of creating, spreading, and reproducing (*i.e.* training and educational activities) knowledge locally [12].

---

1. Six hi-technology sectors have been identified by means of Acs (1996): i) biotechnology and biomedical; ii) information technologies and services; iii) high technology machinery and instruments, iv) defence and aerospace; v) energy and chemicals; vi) high technology research.

Innovative clusters are identified by considering the main characteristics that are considered in literature:

- proximity of socioeconomic players and, consequently, concentration of players and resources within a limited space;
- specialisation in particular industrial sectors;
- variety of subjects and organisations operating in the territory;
- relativity of the size of the cluster: a small cluster may not be particularly significant within a strongly developed regional context, but it may act as an engine of regional development in a peripheral area.

When considering the proximity of subjects, it is necessary to choose an appropriate territorial statistical reference unit. Nuts 2 and 3 are too broad, while the municipal unit hides relationships between subjects located in wider metropolitan areas. This is the classic theory-method problem of defining self-contained territorial units. The main instrument used for this purpose is the everyday urban system. Data were initially collected at municipal level and then aggregated. In the case of Italy, local labour systems (*sistemi locali del lavoro*) [9] were used, for France the *zones d'emploi* [8], and in Spain, the urban areas defined by the Dirección General de Vivienda (2000 [5]). Next, the share of business located in each system was calculated in proportion to the total level of high-tech industry in the region (Nuts 2) for each of the six high-tech sectors considered, using the formula:

$C_{sl} = I_{sl}/I_{sr}$

where:

C share (concentration) of businesses
I number of businesses   l local system (local labour system, zone d'emploi or urban area)
s high-tech sector   r region (Nuts 2)

For the purposes of this analysis, systems with the following characteristics were considered innovative clusters:

1. A concentration of at least one third of the total regional endowment of industry within at least one of the six sectors considered; this responds to the need to consider the systems in relative terms, with an emphasis on local concentrations and industrial specialisation. The quota (one third within any of the six high-tech sectors), established as a result of numerous empirical tests, has the potential to identify more than one cluster within every region.
2. The presence of at least one university or polytechnic, and at least one research centre, all operating in a high-tech sector. This lays emphasis on the variety of players involved in innovative processes.

In this perspective, 15 innovative clusters have been identified:

- Italy: Turin, Milan, Genoa, Padua, Bologna, Florence, Rome, Naples;
- France: Lyon, Toulouse, Montpellier, Marseille-Aubagne;
- Spain: Barcelona, Valencia, Seville.

TYPOLOGY OF THE INNOVATIVE LOCAL SYSTEM

For a more precise assessment of the innovative potential of these 15 clusters, we introduced further data to the analysis. In addition to the "traditional" input and output variables[2], data concerning the existence of organisations and institutions that influence or encourage innovation in the territory are taken into account. These data concerned[3]:

– the existence of organisations involved in the production and diffusion of knowledge: companies, academic institutions and research centres, science and technology parks;
– the international reach of the local system, measured using the following criteria: number of international flights (inbound and outbound) during the year, hotels, international research projects involving local players (in 5th EU Framework Programme), headquarters or offices of international organisations (such as OECD or UN) and European Info-points;
– availability of facilities for innovative enterprise: business and financial services, fairs and exhibitions, members of the European Venture Capital Association;
– the cultural milieu, particularly important for defining social assets that encourage an innovative climate [12], measured in terms of the existence of museums and libraries with an international standing, and universities and research centres operating in humanistic and non-technological fields (seen in residual terms compared to "high technology" institutes);
– the socioeconomic and welfare conditions, measured in terms of GDP *per capita* and unemployment rates. A bad performance in this field may be the consequence of a weak capacity to innovate; however, at the same time, conditions affected by uncertainty, instability, and dissatisfaction may hinder innovative processes [13].

The 15 clusters were evaluated for innovativeness using the principal components analysis. This statistical instrument enabled us to reduce the original number of variables (more than 20 in our case) and replace them with a smaller group of components (new variables) that were nearly as informative as the original group. In our case, the calculation identified five components, accounting for 86.9% of the original variance *(Table I)*.

The first component expresses the level of internationalisation and the scientific potential of the clusters, showing elevated correlations with the variables for international reach, the existence of research centres and participation in international scientific networks. Thus, the ability to produce and use knowledge seems to be closely related to inclusion of clusters within the supra-local networks. The technological and production milieu shows high correlations with the presence of companies, business services and patents. Local reproduction of knowledge refers to academies and science parks. Socioeconomic welfare presents a direct correlation with GDP *per capita* and an inverse one with unemployment rates. These aspects are of vital importance, not only for the well-being of the population, but also for innovative

---

2. These are expenditures (share of GDP) and employment (share of active population) in R&D activities; patent applications every 1,000 inhabitants.
3. Data refer to 2001 or 2000. Statistical sources: i) enterprise: *Amadeus database* by Bureau Van Dijk. Here are enterprise satisfying at least one of the following criteria: a) at least 1 million € operating revenue; b) at least 2 million € total assets; c) at least 15 employees; ii) other sources: *The Banker*, 2001, n. 907; *The Europa World Yearbook* and *The World of Learning*, Europa, London, 2000; www.iaspworld.org; *Regio 2002*, Eurostat, Brussels; www.evca.com; *The Hotel Guide*, Meggen, 2000; www.europa.eu.int; *Guida Mondiale delle Fiere*, Pianeta, Turin, 2000.

Table I. Cluster potential in the fields of technological innovation.

Clusters	Components and factorial scores				
	Internationalisation and scientific potential	Technological and production milieu	Local reproduction of knowledge	Socioeconomic welfare	Research and development
Milan	+	+	+	+	+
Barcelona	+	+	+		+
Lyon		+	+		+
Rome	+	+	+		+
Marseille-Aubagne		+		−	+
Naples	+		+	−	−
Montpellier		−	+	−	+
Turin	−		+	+	
Florence	+		+	+	
Bologna	−			++	
Padua	−	+	−	+	−
Valencia	−			+	−
Genoa		−	−		+
Seville			+	−	
Toulouse	−	−			+

Source: Amadeus database, The Banker, The Europa World Yearbook, Eurostat, Guida Mondiale delle Fiere, The Hotel Guide.

processes, since innovation is not a phenomenon that takes form in laboratories and research centres, away from the local context, but rather is a social process. A widespread climate of well-being can therefore facilitate social relations, encouraging the spread of trust, cooperative attitudes, and personal satisfaction. Finally, the fifth component refers to expenditure and employment rates in research and development, in both the public and private sectors.

This statistical exercise allows us to classify the clusters according to how these components are combined. This classification never focuses on technological performance, but rather on the existence of factors and conditions that favour innovative processes. In this sense, it represents the potential of the clusters in the field of technological innovation. For this reason, there are different cases within the same groups:

− The first level refers to strongly innovative clusters. Here, all five factors present high scores and, at the same time, there are no significant weaknesses. Barcelona and Milan represent by far the most innovative nodes, while Lyon and Rome represent second level ones.

– The second level includes moderately innovative clusters, a large category including territories with high technological potential, but with marked problems with one of the five components. Naples, Marseille-Aubagne and Montpellier have unemployment problems, and there industrial weakness in Naples and Montpellier. Turin is included here on account of its weak international reach. The situation in Florence is particular: even though the system shows no specific weaknesses, the area's technological potential is not really high from any of the perspectives, and for this reason it was not included in the previous group.
– The third level is for traditional clusters, *i.e.* clusters characterised by good economic and industrial performance, but with low levels of innovation. Bologna, Padua and Valencia present "traditional" specialisations and the need to enhance their capacity for innovation.
– Finally, in declining clusters a low capacity for innovation is linked to unemployment and industrial decline, particularly in Seville. Toulouse is in industrial recession, and the situation is similar in Genoa, although it must be noted that the city is actually undergoing extensive transformation of the old economic base, with increasing emphasis placed on the port and the cultural sector (never included in previous data).

REGIONAL ORGANISATION AND DIFFUSION OF THE INNOVATIVE POTENTIAL OF CLUSTERS

In addition to innovation potential, it is also important to estimate the role played by the various clusters within their regions. In fact, one local system can act as an engine of innovation within its wider (regional) territorial context, while another may simply represent a hierarchically dominant area located in a weaker regional context. For this reason, the theoretical concept of polycentrism has been transposed into the analysis emphasising two different dimensions: the presence of several clusters within a region refers to a widespread territorial structure, while the existence of relations between clusters indicates the degree of interdependence within the regional structure.

This was done with the aid of the map presented in *Figure 2*. The dark circles are the 15 innovation clusters analyzed in the previous pages, and the light ones show areas that are characterised by significant concentrations of industry – *i.e.* concentrations of at least 20% of the total regional endowment of business in at least one of the high-tech sectors under examination (see part one). We will call these light circles "significant industrial concentrations", as they never satisfy all the requisites previously introduced representing the innovation cluster (for example they never have universities), and they merely represent concentrated areas of business. *Figure 2* also shows the connections between the local systems, linking those that are close to each other (within the same or adjacent region or separated by another one) and share one or more specialisations. The importance of these lines is related to the hypothesis that common industrial and technological specialisations facilitate the spread of knowledge and innovation, based on the mechanisms of horizontal and vertical relationships between businesses.

Figure 2 therefore enables us to establish two aspects of regional polycentrism. First, the number of clusters and "industrial concentrations" (*i.e.* the number of circles) refers to the spread of industry in the regional territorial structure. We will distinguish between regions with a high industrial spread (5 or more clusters or industrial concentrations), those with an inter-

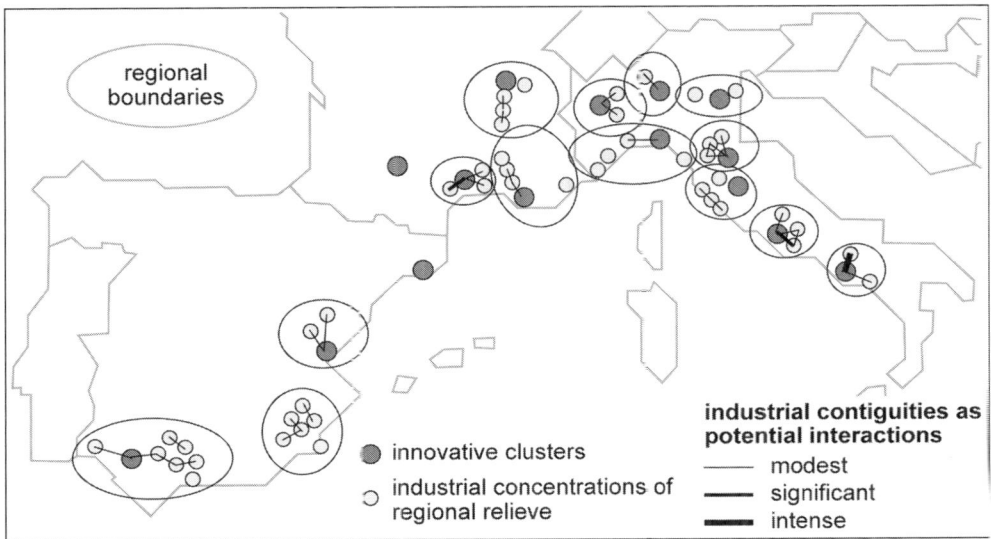

Figure 2. *Concentrations and contiguities in industrial concentrations.*

mediate spread (3 or 4), and those with a low industrial spread (1 or 2), *i.e.* strong polarisation. Secondly, the number (and the intensity, as the lines present different thicknesses according to the number of shared industrial specialisations) of linkages (lines) allows us to quantify the potential interdependence between industrial concentrations within the region[4], encouraging diffusion of knowledge through horizontal processes along the cluster.

According to these two aspects of polycentrism, there are three categories of regional organisation: the first is polarisation and combines a small number of clusters with very weak linkages between them. It includes Toulouse, Barcelona, Padua and Genoa. The second category involves an intermediate situation with Bologna, Turin and Valencia. Here the clusters are more numerous and the connections between them start to be significant. The third and final category is polycentrism, where clusters are very numerous and very interdependent. Marseille, Montpellier, Milan, Seville, Lyon, Naples, Rome and Florence possess this kind of polycentric regional organisation.

DEGREES OF POLYCENTRISM AND LEVELS OF INNOVATION POTENTIAL

All of these factors raise the question of what the link is between the innovation potential of an area and its level of polycentrism. This question is central to academic literature and among political developers and decision makers. In fact, it can be argued [2] that cities in a

---

4. The classification is as follows: low interdependence (0-1 contiguities), medium (2-3) and high (4 or more). Double intensity connections (2 common specialisations) have been considered as weight 2, and those with triple intensity as weight 3.

polycentric structure benefit from certain external economies, on the one hand, thanks to a common labour market or highly specialised services such as universities, and on the other, by taking advantage of their different complementary aspects and specialisations. Basically, according to traditional economic theory, all cities can rely on economic sectors in which they enjoy specific comparative advantages, to further technological specialisation. At the same time, it is reasonable to suppose that frequent interaction between the nodes of a polycentric structure, together with the sharing of problems and perspectives, will promote the extensive diffusion of ideas, solutions and, more generally, knowledge.

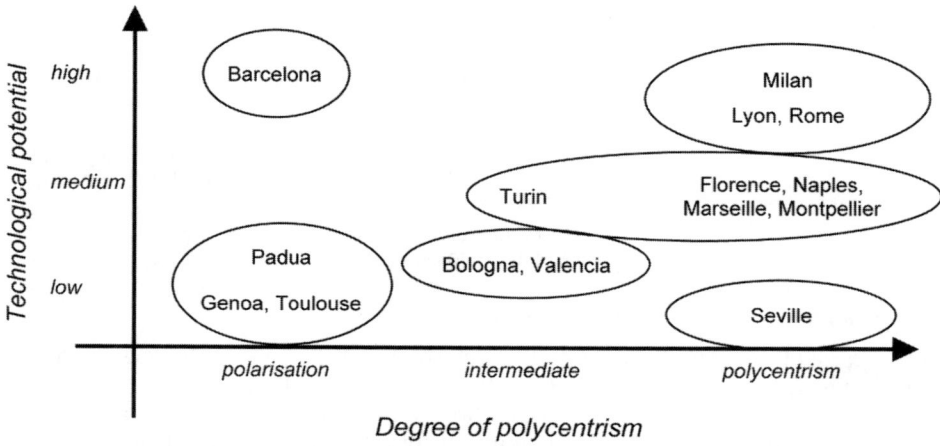

Figure 3. *Combination of technological potential and polycentrism.*

The combination of the classification by innovation potential, on one hand, and the three categories of regional polycentric organisation, on the other, shows that it is not possible to determine the existence (and the logical direction) of a causal relationship between polycentrism and technological potential *(Figure 3)*. However, with the exception of Barcelona and Seville, the hypothesis concerning the supposed "facilitation" of the diffusion of knowledge in polycentric contexts seems to be conceivable, since the cities with higher levels of polycentrism perform better in terms of technological potential, confirming that regional networking plays a crucial role in innovative phenomena [11].

Such a perspective of the relationship between polycentrism and innovation may be read on different geographical levels. In this sense, a concise vision of the previous results provides us with a map of spatial models of innovation in the Mediterranean Latin Arc *(Figure 4)*. The 15 innovation clusters are classified according to their innovation spillover potential, so are displayed as "significant industrial concentrations". This map sums up the industrial geography of high technology in the Latin Arc and allows us to formulate some general descriptive considerations:

– With the exception of the Barcelona pole, the Iberian area appears to be extremely weak in terms of innovation. Nevertheless, it is important to note the high degree of polycentrism in the Southern area, particularly in Andalusia and Murcia, while the technological potential of Catalonia appears to be almost exclusively concentrated in Barcelona.

Innovation and polycentrism in the Mediterranean Latin arc

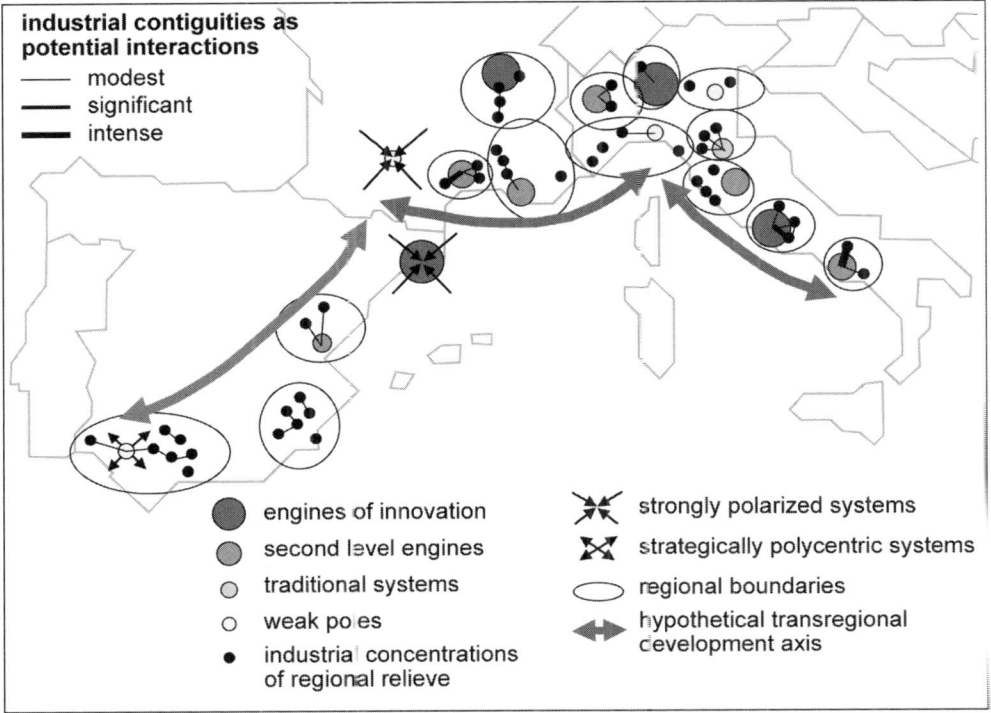

Figure 4. *Spatial models of innovation in the Mediterranean Latin Arc.*

– In Italy, the Western Po axis (Piedmont and Lombardy) and the Central regions hold high technological potential and polycentric territorial structures. The most problematic clusters are Padua and Genoa, which are technologically and industrially weak.

– The French-Italian axis constitutes one of the strongest forces in the Latin Arc, thanks to the two main engines of innovation, Milan and Lyon. It should be noted that Genoa and Toulouse present problematic socioeconomic and technological situations, and are isolated by poor polycentric structures.

These regional models of innovation allow us to formulate some reflections of a transnational nature. The French-Italian border, with the exception of Liguria, is an area with great technological potential, particularly rooted in regional polycentric structures in the two French regions. Conversely, the diffusion of innovation along the Spanish-French border is a problematic issue owing to the presence of strongly polarised structures on either side of the Pyrenees.

Conclusion

The empirical analysis can supply some theoretical cues for a deeper understanding of the concept of polycentrism. In particular, it has been identified, at regional level, as the intersection of two analytical factors:

1. The first refers to the more common and intuitive meaning of polycentrism, that is, the existence in a territory of several clusters within a basic widespread industrial fabric.
2. The second considers the possible existence of significant relations between and interdependency of the clusters.

This allows us to introduce one simple, nevertheless useful, terminological distinction: areal polycentrism, indicating those territorial configurations in which only the first analytical factor is satisfied, and reticular polycentrism, referring to both. This distinction implies huge differences in terms of policies and strategies *(Table II)*.

As for the production/reproduction of knowledge, in areal polycentrism the phenomenon of innovation is specific to the inner technological capabilities of clusters, whereas reticular polycentrism becomes a regional feature, deriving from the interaction between several clusters; the development of complementary networks is therefore worthwhile. Therefore, while in the case of areal polycentrism the strategies of territorial competition affect, above all, the single clusters, in the case of reticular polycentrism, it is also possible to formulate cooperative strategies for the development and promotion of the regional system as a whole.

In terms of innovation policies, the areal perspective is distinct from traditional diffusion-oriented policies, whereas reticular polycentrism is coherent with network-oriented policies. This is seen in the most recent orientation of EU policies, aimed at encouraging not only the diffusion of knowledge, but also the promotion of networks, in order to foster the participation of peripheral and marginal territories. The mere availability of knowledge, in fact, does not constitute an advantage for a centre if there is no demand for innovation and, furthermore, the capacity to transform knowledge into a competitive advantage for local enterprise. The formation of a regional polycentric system, on the other hand, can work towards functional specialisation and inclusion of the clusters into regional-scale economic processes.

Table II. *Areal and reticular polycentrism.*

	Areal polycentrism Isolated poles	*Reticular polycentrism* Interdependent nodes
Innovation	Specific innovation processes	Innovation systems
Competition	Specialisation	Complementary networks
Innovation policies	Diffusion-oriented	Network-oriented
Objectives	Diffusion	Local development

After all, areal polycentrism evokes the theoretical contributions of post-war regional sciences (*e.g.* Myrdal's contribution), where much of the debate regarded the promotion of the spread (transfer of capital and production factors) and backwash effects (of development) from the dominant pole towards the rest of the territory. Alternatively, reticular polycentrism responds to the wider objectives of local development of the regional system, as it must not be considered as a sum-zero distribution process, but rather as a development path based on the activation of those endogenous processes operating only on a supra-local scale. It therefore becomes clear that hierarchy and polycentrism do not conflict with each other: in a reticular system, the major clusters (and urban centres) can act as gateways for participation in the hierarchical lower urban systems of supra-local networks.

REFERENCES

1. Acs Z. American high-technology clusters. In *Evolutionary Economics and the New International Political Economy*. De la Mothe J, Paquet G. (Eds). London: Pinter, 1996: 183-219.

2. Bailey N, Turok I. Central Scotland as a polycentric urban region: useful planning concept or chimera? *Urban Studies* 2001; 38, n° 4: 697-715.

3. Boulifard C. Images et scénarios de développment de l'Arc Méditerranéen : un état des Lieux. Paris : Quaternaire, 1994.

4. Brunet R. *Les villes européennes, Datar-Reclus*. Paris : La Documentation Française, 1989.

5. Dirección General de la Vivienda, la Arquitectura y el Urbanismo. *Atlas estadístico de las áreas urbanas en España*. Madrid: Ministerio de Fomento, 2000.

6. European Commission. *Europe 2000 + Co-operation for the Spatial Development of Europe*, Luxembourg: Office for Official Publications of the European Communities, 1994.

7. European Commission. Sixth Periodic Report on the Social and Economic Situation and Development of the Regions of the European Union. Luxembourg: CEC, 1999.

8. Insee. *Atlas des zones d'emploi*. Paris : Insee, 1998

9. Istat. I sistemi locali del lavoro 1991. Roma: Istat. 1997.

10. Malmberg A, Maskell P. The elusive concept of localization economies: towards a knowledge-based theory of spatial clustering. *Environment and Planning A* 2002; 34, n° 3: 429-49

11. Rosenberg N. *Exploring the Black Box: Technology, Economics and History*. Cambridge: Cambridge University Press, 1994.

12. Saxenian A. Regional systems of innovation and the blurred firm. In: *Local and Regional Systems of Innovation*. De la Mothe J, Paquet G. (Eds). Norwell: Kluwer, 1998: 29-43.

13. Sweeney G (Ed). *Innovation, Economic Progress and the Quality of Life*. Cheltenham: Edward Elgar, 2001.

14. Vanolo A. Per uno sviluppo policentrico dello spazio europeo. Sistemi innovativi territoriali nell'Europa sud-occidentale. Milano: Franco Angeli, 2003.

European polycentrism: Towards a more efficient and/or a more equitable development?

Christian Vandermotten, Marcel Roelandts, Pierre Cornut
Institute for Environmental Management and Territorial Planning, Free University Brussels (ULB), Brussels

A more polycentric urban network, as opposed to monocentrism, is a central objective of the official European policies of planning and dominates its rhetoric [6]. The ESPON[1] report 1.1.1 [8] aims to investigate it in depth. More polycentrism – the concept being used as well at the intrametropolitan level, at the intranational level and at the European level as a whole – is supposed to help containing urban sprawl, to favour cooperative strategies and networking between the cities, and, at the upper scale, which we intend to examine here, to lead to more efficient economies and at the same time to more equitable regional developments. The polycentric project is now so present in the official documents that questioning the content and the validity of the concept could seem out of place. However, we intend to show that this concept is often unsubstantial, ambiguous, badly defined, used as well from a morphological (the urban pattern) as from a functional point of view (the flows, the effective networks)[2], confusing the geographical scales and more a normative than a scientific one [5].

Our main question is thus to examine if it is true, looking at the empiric pieces of evidence – *i.e.* morphological polycentricity as a measurable scientific object, and not as a territorial planning political goal -, that more polycentric national and European structures could lead simultaneously to more equity and effective regional development, to less inequalities between the regions and to a more effective, competitive and better integrated European economy, favouring also the sustainable development.

---

1. European Spatial Planning Observation Network.
2. PJ. Taylor and the GaWC project are tempting to investigate this badly known aspect. However, Taylor's methodology is based on the arguable assumption that a network of intrafirm flows, possibly immaterial, is associated to the presence of subsidiaries of each firm in the advanced services sector in different cities. So, it is supposed that horizontal flows between subsidiaries exist as well as vertical links between the subsidiaries and their headquarters. More, these so-called intrafirm networks are supposed to be a proxy of more global networking between the main cities around the world. If firms are surely working more and more inside networks, their pattern doesn't correspond necessarily to corresponding polycentric networks between cities, nor to logics of proximity and complementarities between neighbour cities.

MEASURING THE MORPHOLOGICAL POLYCENTRICITY OF THE EUROPEAN URBAN PATTERN

The ESPON report provides the sole more or less comparable measure of the functional urban areas (FUAs) of the European cities, even if those data are yet sometimes defective[3]. The FUAs include the urban economic cores and their labour pools. From our point of view, we will take into account in two parallel analyses the whole set of FUAs with more than 50,000 inhabitants (we are then at the level where regional cities are organizing local spaces and providing current or semi-current services for the population in a Christallerian logics) and the only FUAs with more than 200,000 inhabitants, which seems to be a very minimal level for cities aiming to play a substantial role as places of regional economic dynamisation.

The ESPON report computes a national polycentricity index based on three normative assessments:

– A linear rank-size distribution indicates a better urban pattern because of not dominated by a single big city.
– An uniform pattern of the cities disseminated through the national territory is better than a pattern of urban clusters polarised on certain parts of the national territory.
– In a polycentric pattern, accessibility should have to be identically available for small and big FUAs.

On this basis, the ESPON complex index adds indicators supposed to account for these three dimensions[4]. It characterises each country by a synthetic value interpreting its polycentricity, notwithstanding the size of the country. Beyond the normative character assigned to the rank-size law, a logical incoherence appears at first, as this index takes into account as well the distribution of the population of the FUAs as their GDP, when a scientific analysis should have precisely as objective to measure if more or less polycentricity implies more or less equity in the regional distribution of the product. Moreover, considering the Gini index of the size of the Thiessen's polygons designed around the centres of the FUAs on the basis of the mediatrices of the lines joining two neighbour cities, assuming that more equal sizes of these polygons indicates more polycentricity (and not Reilly's polygons which consider the relative size of each city on a gravitation law basis), means in a normative perspective that equality of the size of these polygons is an objective *per se*, notwithstanding the pattern of the population on the territory (or that the even distribution of the population on the national territory is an objective *per se*).

As for us, we have computed two measures of the polycentricity on the basis of a sole methodology, the one at the level of the States, the other at the level of more or less similar sized units, *i.e.* the small and medium-sized countries considered as a single unit, and the biggest countries divided into macro-regions of about 10 million inhabitants.

---

3. A revised list and estimation of the FUA's population is proposed in the ESPON 1.4.3 report, published March, 2007, after the writing of this paper. See bibliography.
4. The indicators are the gradient of the classification of the cities following the rank-size law, the index of primacy given by this distribution, the same indicators using the GDP, the Gini's index of the sizes of the Thiessen's polygons designed around the whole set of FUAs, the slope of the linear regression between population and accessibility of the FUAs and the Gini's index of this last measure.

Our index is computed on the basis of a simple and purely morphological methodology (as approached by the proxies of population data). We have used the cardinal ranking of the following indicators:

- weight of the main FUA in the total population of the country or macro-region;
- weight of the main FUA in the total population of the whole set of FUAs with more than 200,000 and more than 50,000 inhabitants;
- average of the differences of population between a FUA and the following one in a decreasing ranking from the most populated FUA to the one immediately beneath the threshold of 200,000 inhabitants and until the threshold of 50,000 inhabitants;
- standard deviation of the population of the set of FUAs with more than 200,000 and with more than 50,000 inhabitants.

The value of each of these seven indicators has been distributed on a scale bounded from 100 (the highest value for the indicator) and 0 (the lowest one). The arithmetic average of these seven indicators gives the cardinal global index *(Table I)*. We stress that we compute here (the proxy of) an exclusively morphological index of polycentricity, and not a measure of functional polycentricity, decisional functions appearing to be much more concentrated in most countries than the urban populations [10].

A surprise arises from the comparison between our index and the ESPON index, only computed at the level of the countries: there is perfectly not any correlation between the two indexes. In fact, this confirms the strong critics we formulate against the ESPON methodology[5].

The sole surprise arising from our ranking regarding a qualitative knowledge of the European urban patterns is the position of Hungary, which appears *a priori* to be very monocentric due to the weight of Budapest[6].

Our own index of polycentricity is not linked to the results of any territorial planning policy. It aims first at showing the product of national histories and territorial building, in a very long time perspective. The economic and political developments, sometimes from the Middle Ages, gave rise to different urban patterns, with a whole range of situations between monocentricity and polycentricity:

---

5. For instance, it is very surprising to see Ireland presented by ESPON 1.1.1 as a strongly polycentric country. This so-called Irish polycentricity is clearly linked to the dispersal on the territory of the Republic of some quite small cities, but located on the Western and Southern fringes of the territory: therefore, the Thyssen's polygons have quite similar sizes, as they put Dublin and Galway or Limerick on the same foot! It is the same for the case of Denmark. At the reverse, taking into account the dispersal of the cities on the national territory notwithstanding the total amount of population they could serve increases strongly the ESPON 1.1.1 level of monocentricity in the Scandinavian countries, due to the sole fact of the concentration of the urban pattern in the Southern regions, the North being simply empty: but is it well a territorial planning objective to attempt to fulfil it?

6. This discrepancy is due to the fact that the index is based on population data and not on an appraisal of the level of concentration of the political and economic decision. Moreover, the value of the index for Hungary is presumably for a part linked to the very restrictive definition used for defining Budapest FUA (small periurban cities at the fringe of the capital are abusively considered as separate FUAs) and also to the very weak gap of size between the FUAs with less than 300,000 inhabitants and the numerous FUAs between 50 and 100,000 inhabitants, which are the heritage of the numerous rural cities of the traditional Hungary.

Table I. *Level of monocentricity in the European macro-regions and countries.*

Countries/Regions	Index	Countries/Regions	Index
Parisian basin	86,2	**Norway**	**27,4**
North-Eastern Germany	85,4	Bavaria	27,3
Central Spain	78,7	**Sweden**	**25,4**
Latvia	**78,6**	North-Western Italy	25
Southern England	65	Northern England	24,7
Northern Ireland	64,8	Mediterranean France	24,1
Ireland	**63,9**	Northern Poland	23,3
Greece	**59,7**	**Belgium**	**23,1**
Estonia	**57,3**	**Spain**	**23,0**
Cyprus	**50,9**	**Lithuania**	**21,5**
Southern Poland	47,5	Central-Western Germany	21,4
Central Poland	47,2	North-Western Poland	20,8
Austria	**46,3**	South-Western France	20,1
Portugal	**43,9**	**Czech Republic**	**17,1**
Eastern Spain	43,9	Southern Italy	16,5
Denmark	**41,4**	**Switzerland**	**15,8**
France	42,1	Midlands	13,5
Central Italy	40,9	**Poland**	**13,4**
Wales	38,1	**Italy**	**13,3**
Scotland	36,1	**Slovakia**	**10,8**
United Kingdom	**35,5**	Eastern France	10,7
Slovenia	**33,4**	North Rhineland-Westphalia	10,6
Bade-Wurttemberg	32,5	Southern Spain	10,5
Finland	**32,1**	Northern Spain	9,3
South-Western Poland	32	**Germany**	**9,3**
Central-Eastern France	31,1	**Netherlands**	**9,3**
Nord-Pas-de-Calais	29,1	Western France	8,7
North-Western Germany	29	Saxony and Thüringen	7,7
Hungary	**27,6**	Eastern Poland	7,5
		North-Eastern Italy	2,5

Source: Eurostat, IGEAT/ULB, ESPON 1.1.1. data.

– A monocentric pattern combined with a relative sterilization of the rest of the country, for a long time characterised by out migration (*e.g.* Ireland, for a long time in a quasi-colonial context; Greece, with the exception of Thessalonica, located at the top of an international corridor).
– A restrained monocentricity, linked to an early national building, but without sterilization of the development outside the capital region (*e.g.* Denmark and Sweden, where the agrarian revolution played an important role in the initial phases of access to modernity).
– A strong monocentricity, yet more decisional than morphological, in countries with a very early territorial formation, where the powers are strongly concentrated in the capital, but however with other important cities, possibly also with their own strong historical weight. These cities can have been reinforced, as well as other medium-sized cities and intermediate areas, by regional and equilibrium metropolises policies during the last half-century, even if they remain under the control of the capital. France pertains to this type, which doesn't exclude macro-regional polycentricity, like in the East or the West of the country.
– A more or less similar situation, but where the decisional supremacy of the capital doesn't exclude big (former) manufacturing conurbations, born during the early phases of a very intense industrial revolution, implying locations on the coalfields or on the proto-industrial manpower basins, or even allows more recent urban-regional developments (*e.g.* Great-Britain).
– A more or less equilibrated bicephalous pattern, possibly with a more political and a more private economic head (*e.g.* Spain or Italy, with in this last country very strong inter-regional economic inequalities and more, in the South, regional more or less parasitic primacies, like Naples or to a certain extent Seville, which reflect the long-lasting survival of aristocratic and archaic structures in their rural environment).
– A mid-European strongly polycentric pattern, with a very dense urbanisation and a very open urban hierarchy, from millionaire cities to a dense network of medium-sized cities, in the context of old urban autonomy tradition. This model includes polynuclear conurbations, even if these don't recover necessarily truly lived identities or spaces of strong planning and economic cooperation (Delta Metropolis in the Netherlands; Rhine-Ruhr; Rhine-Main; the Walloon industrial axis). This polycentricity can be the result of late national unifications and federal systems. However, the German polycentricity doesn't exclude the extreme monocentricity of the North-East of the country, besides not a part of the medieval Germany of cities and merchants;
– Finally, Switzerland is characterised by a typical mid-European polycentricity, but without big millionaire cities nor conurbations born during the coal based industrialisation period.

POLYCENTRISM AND ECONOMIC EFFICIENCY

As we have already seen, European policies assign to polycentrism a normative value of efficiency: it is supposed to favour regional and, through this one, global development, either by adding more performing regional growths or by avoiding diseconomies supposed to affect the biggest agglomerations.

What is the evidence? If it is any, but not significant or slight correlation, it is between the level of development and more monocentricity! As a matter of static situation, the correlation between the level of monocentricity and the level of development, as measured by the GDP/inhab., is not significant as well at the scale of the States as a whole (r = 0.09) as at the scale of the macro-regions (r = 0.07). However, if the level of development of the macro-regions is defined not by reference to the European average, but to each national average, it is a slight positive but weakly significant correlation (r = 0.28): the most monocentric macro-regions, in fact those centred on the main metropolises, the most important nodes of the global world economy (London, Paris, Madrid), benefit from the highest relative GDP/inhab. It is evidently not the case for North-Eastern Germany, at the mid of the new Länder.

Table II. *Coefficient of correlation between monocentricity and economic growth.*

Relation	Period	Correlation coefficient r
Economic growth and monocentricity at the scale of the States	1980-2002	+ 0.52 (quasi-s.)
Economic growth and monocentricity at the scale of the macro-regions *(Figure 1)*	1980-2002	+ 0.42 (s.)
Economic growth and monocentricity at the scale of the States	1995-2002	+ 0.44 (s.)
Economic growth and monocentricity at the scale of the macro-regions *(Figure 2)*	1995-2002	+ 0.30 (s.)
Economic growth by comparison to the national levels of each country and monocentricity at the scale of the macro-regions *(Figure 3)*	1980-2002	+ 0.38 (quasi-s.)

What about the dynamics? Therefore, correlations appear to be more significant, and always with the same trend, as well on mid-long term (1980 to 2002) as on short term (1995 to 2002): economic results seem to be better when monocentricity is stronger, either at the scale of the States as a whole (at the limit of the statistical significance it is true), or for the macro-regions *(Table II)*.

Considering the two monocentric macro-regions centred on London and Paris, it appears that the performances are better in the first one, by comparison to the national performances of both countries (and *a fortiori* by comparison to the European standard): this means likely the better insertion of London in the world-wide networks.

To conclude, this statistical link between monocentricity and economic efficiency seems to be consistent with the main present trends towards more globalisation, which favour the main advanced services nodes of the world-wide economy.

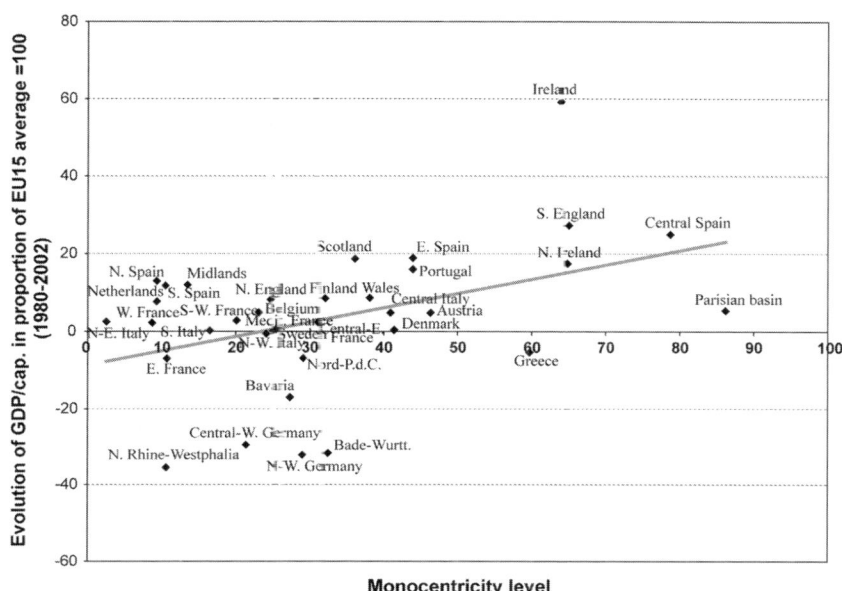

Figure 1. *Economic growth and monocentricity at the scale of the macro-regions (1980-2002).*

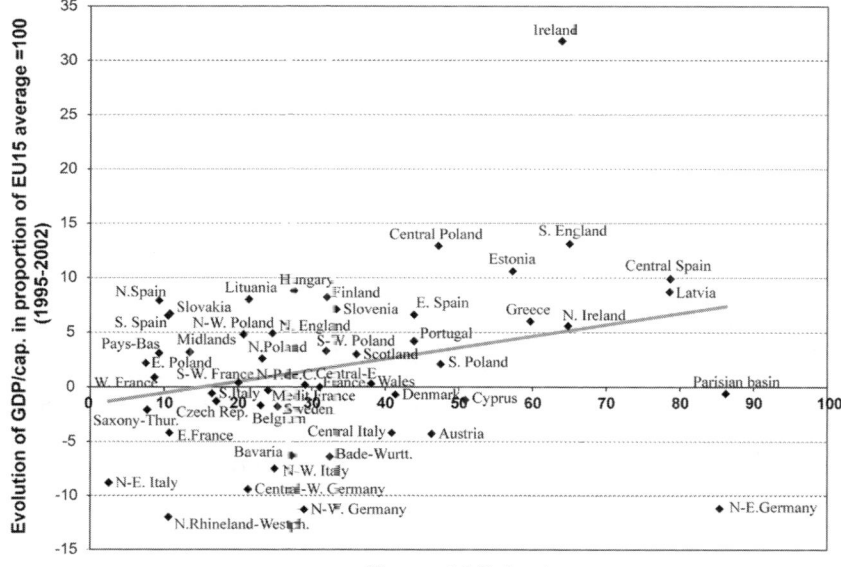

Figure 2. *Economic growth and monocentricity at the scale of the macro-regions (1995-2002).*

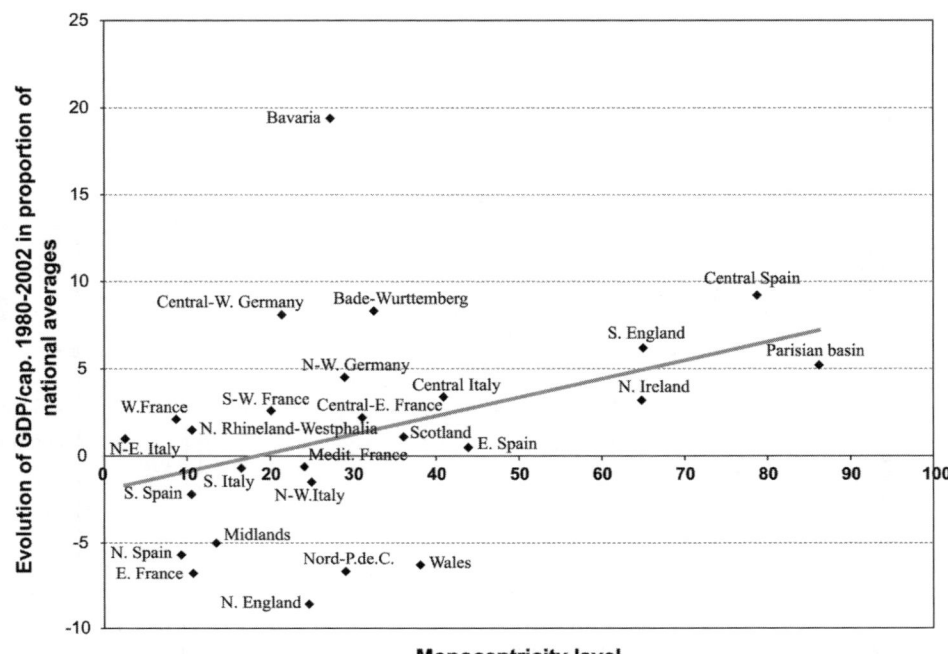

Figure 3. *Economic growth by comparison to the national performances in each country and monocentricity at the scale of the macro-regions (1980-2002).*

POLYCENTRISM AND SPATIAL EQUITY

One could object to the preceding conclusions that it reflects a neo-liberal vision, sacrificing territorial cohesion to global growth, notwithstanding its impact on the satisfaction of local people and their own right to live in their place of origin.

Indeed, at the NUTS 3 level, a slight trend can be observed to more spatial inequalities inside more monocentric countries, but statistically insignificant ($r = 0.33$) and very strongly influenced by the sole value of the small Latvia (without Latvia and Hungary, the correlation is 0). More, this conclusion ought to be corrected due to the fact that GDP/inhab. values computed at the NUTS 3 level are not weighted by an internal parity of purchase power correction, which should imply reducing the real GDP in the most central regions, where real estate and other goods and services prices are much higher[7].

---

7. In each State or macro-region, we have ranked the NUTS 3 units by decreasing level of GDP/inhab. and computed the ratio between the average GDP/inhab. of the first and the fourth quartile of the whole population.

As measured at the level of the macro-regions, internal spatial inequalities become surely more significant when monocentricity is stronger *(Figure 4)*. But, another bias has to be taken into consideration, inherent to the GDP statistics. NUTS 3 units, mainly where they are small, like in Germany, Belgium or the Netherlands, and yet more around the biggest cities (London, Paris), are an inadequate framework: many people working in the central areas, where GDP is accounted at the place of work, are indeed residing in suburban areas located outside the central NUTS 3 unit. The measure completely masks the social difficulties of the central cities, as opposed to the prosperity of the suburban areas. The position of Inner London at the first place in the ranking of the richest NUTS 3 units in Europe and of Brussels-Capital in the next position is only a pure statistical mystification.

This is very well proved by the recent computation of a regional households available income, which can usefully replace the traditional GDP/inhab., but is unfortunately only computed for the moment at the NUTS 2 level [3]. This new indicator reduces strongly the disparities inside the countries. Regional inequalities appear to become weak enough with this new index to exclude any statistical link between polycentricity and regional equity. At any way, considering the statistical relation between monocentricity and economic efficiency, the question can be put if the residual differences in available income are not weak enough for being advantageously balanced through increased inter-regional transfers. This position should perhaps be nuanced in the case of the big States with strong internal economic gaps, like Italy, between North and South, Germany, between the old and the new Länder, or Spain, but this question is in any way not reducible to the one of more or less polycentricity, as the two first countries are globally very polycentric, including in their most disadvantaged macro-regions.

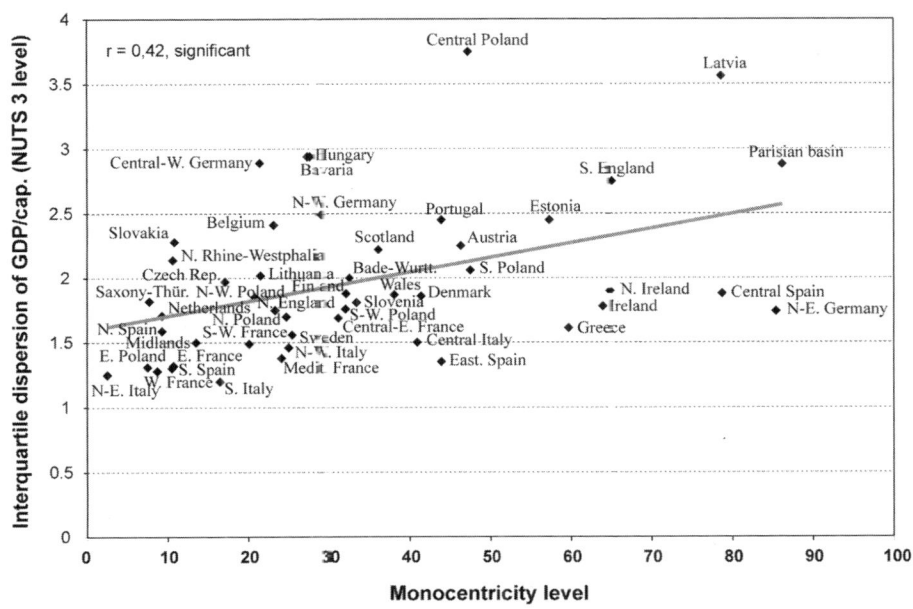

Figure 4. *Monocentricity and spatial inequalities at the level of the macro-regions.*

Conclusion

This study has only examined the question of the morphological polycentricity, at the upper geographical scales. It is not at all a plea for monocentrism. We don't want to replace one religion by another. It doesn't imply any neo-liberal and laissez-faire perspective, which should abandon the development of the regions to the rules of the market and to the concurrence between cities, regions and States, in a global economy leaving the weakest one in their problems. On the contrary, reinforcing social transfers and regional development policies seem to be very necessary where needed. These regional policies, at least in the Western European context, should perhaps target more the human capital than the infrastructural development.

Moreover, we don't deny the utility to specialize some second level cities on specific niches, if possible in coordination with more powerful near metropolises. At the reverse, we think that one of the traps of polycentrism seen as a normative doctrine is to lead to dispersing the same kinds of resources in an unreal search of space homogeneity. Such a policy of dispersal has shown its counter-productivity in the Walloon Region, characterised by a polycentricity inherited from the industrial revolution, with a strong weakness of its conurbations in advanced services and local entrepreneurship. This political willingness once stated by this Region of a strongly self-centred development, independent from Brussels and coupled with sprinkling equally the resources on the different cities of the former industrial axis, has nowhere led to efficient multiplying effects. This is often the situation in the polycentric urban patterns of the early industrialised regions, but can also be observed at the highest levels of the urban hierarchy: the international position of London or Paris is well above the one of the polycentric Rhine-Ruhr metropolitan region, even with a similar total population.

At the level of the structuration of the main metropolitan regions, which were studied in the POLYNET study, one has also to be wary on the cult of polycentrism. First, it appears that if the metropolitan region is dominated by one sole major international node, the developments in the satellite nodes are mainly linked to specialised niche activities, for instance logistics around the ports and airports or some kinds of services to the enterprises, or to back offices. The highest level directional functions prefer, even more than ever, the concentration in the central business districts, and are ready to pay very high real estate prices therefore. However, the growth of the satellite centres can led to more criss-crossed flows inside the metropolitan region, which doesn't necessarily favour more sustainable transport policies. It appears also that these deconcentrations are often not the result of a global policy at the scale of the metropolitan region as a whole, but more of slashed competitions between the centre and its peripheries, which only add bargain effects to decisions already taken by the firms and increase the social problems in the inner cities. Brussels' case is caricature of such a situation, as the inner part of the metropolitan region and its suburban parts are located in different federated Regions in the federal Belgian State. These Regions act as independent quasi-States from the point of view of economy, planning, environmental policies, without any fiscal or budgetary transfer between the peripheries and the centre.

When metropolitan areas are characterised by a more equilibrated morphological polycentricity, like in the Delta Metropolis in the Netherlands, it appears also that any concerted management between similar sized cities, like Amsterdam and Rotterdam, is non-existent.

This is opposite to the assumption that cities with interpenetrating labour pools beneficiate from the best opportunities for developing synergies.

One can argue that this attempt of demonstration was related to efficiency and spatial equity and that the question of sustainable development was not examined at all. Surely, this study remains to be done. However, it doesn't appear *a priori* evident that the management of the flows should be easier and environmentally friendlier in a polycentric pattern than in a more monocentric one. Radial concentrated flows could be more efficiently managed through corridors, using intensively public transports, than more Brownian movements in a polycentric pattern. It remains also to demonstrate if one very dense region opposed to low density regions should have a stronger environmental impact than a more equilibrated density pattern.

We stressed that the more or less polycentric urban pattern is in each country the product of a long-term history. Therefore it is likely illusory to try to "correct" radically such patterns, searching for an idealised spatial ubiquity against the most heavy trends of the contemporary economy. Planning policies have to get as a priority target reducing social inequalities, including the intrametropolitan ones, even if that implies to correct the major spatial inequalities through the transfer of resources or specific grants.

The empirical evidence of the contemporary economy is much more characterised by a metropolitan concentration and more homogeneous urban structures than by a trend towards the postulates of the normative polycentrism, *i.e.* a polycentric dispersal coupled with a specialisation of neighbouring cities inserted in global voluntarist cooperative networks. Moreover, the integrative flows between so-called networking cities and their importance and true meaning appear simply not to be measurable. The potential for polycentric development is nearly never mentioned as a key factor in partnership establishment by neighbouring cities: they are often much more competitive than cooperative. Cooperation processes are very often more effective between specialised far away cities. Finally, the intrafirm networks appear not to be similar at all to the proposed cooperative networks between cities promoted by the planners of polycentrism.

Surely, these considerations are not enough for putting into question a policy promoting more polycentrism. One could justifiably argue that public policies have to counteract some present disastrous dominant trends. Yet should it be necessary to prove that such a vague, inclusive and multiform concept as polycentrism could be the basis for alternative more valuable economic, social and ecologic policies, or that it could led to a better achievement of the Lisbon objectives.

REFERENCES

1. Allain R, Baudelle G, Guy C (Eds). *Le polycentrisme, un projet pour l'Europe*. Presses Universitaires de Rennes, 2003.

2. Beaverstock JV, Smith RG, Taylor PJ, Walker DRF, Lorimer H. Globalization and World Cities: Some Measurement Methodologies. *Applied geography* 2000; 20, 1: 43-63 (for further publications of this team see www.lboro.ac.uk/gawc).

3. Behrens A. (2003a). How rich are Europe's regions? Experimental calculations. *Statistics in focus. General statistics. Theme 1, Eurostat* 2003; 6: 1-7.

4. Behrens A. (2003b). Income of private households and gross domestic product in Europe's regions. *Statistics in focus. General statistics. Theme 1, Eurostat* 2003.

5. Davoudi S. Polycentricity in European Spatial Planning: From an Analytical Tool to a Normative Agenda. *European Planning Studies*, 2003; 11, 8: 979-99.

6. ESDP. European Spatial Development Perspective. Towards Balanced and sustainable Development of the Territory of the EU. Luxemburg: CEC, 1999.

7. Hall P, Pain K (Eds). *The Polycentric Metropolis*. London: Earthscan, 2006.

8. IGEAT *et al.*, 2007. Study on Urban Functions, ESPON report 1.4.3. To be dowloaded at www.espon.eu.

9. NORDREGIO *et al.*, 2005. The role, specific situation and potentials of urban areas as nodes in a polycentric development, ESPON report 1.1.1. To be downloaded at www.espon.eu.

10. Vandermotten C. Le polycentrisme dans une perspective historique. In : Allain R, Baudelle G, Guy C (Eds). *Le polycentrisme, un projet pour l'Europe*. Presses Universitaires de Rennes, 2003 : 17-28.

11. Vandermotten C, Vermoesen F, De Corte S, *et al.* Villes d'Europe. Atlas comparatif. *Bulletin trimestriel du Crédit Communal de Belgique* 1999 : 207-8.

Part II
Polycentrism:
What is behind the concept?

Polycentricity: Panacea or pipedream?

Simin Davoudi

School of Architecture, Planning and Landscape, Institute for Research
on Environment and Sustainability, Newcastle University, United Kingdom

The notion of polycentricity is not new and can be traced back to the urban literature of the early 20th century. What is new is its growing popularity after publication of a pan-European spatial framework called the European Spatial Development Perspective (ESDP) [3]. Yet, despite its long history and widespread usage, its precise meaning has remained elusive. It means different things to different people: planners use the concept as a strategic spatial planning tool; geographers use it as an analytical tool to explain the dynamics of urban growth; ESDP promotes it as a normative agenda; and, for some it simply represents a symbolic image. Polycentricity also means different things when it is applied at different spatial scales. This chapter aims to trace the origin of polycentricity, unpack its multiple interpretations, and provide examples of how the concept has been employed across Europe to enhance economic competitiveness and social cohesion.

POLYCENTRIC AND MULTIPLE APPLICATIONS

Traditionally the concept of polycentricity has been applied at the intraurban scale to challenge the monocentric models which were used in the pioneering work of Ernest Burgess in his famous depiction of the city as a series of concentric circles [2]. In contrast to this definition, a polycentric city is defined as a city which consists of a centre and an organised system of concentrated sub-centres [9]. This of course is different from a dispersed city which represents a disorganised urban sprawl *(Figure 1)*.

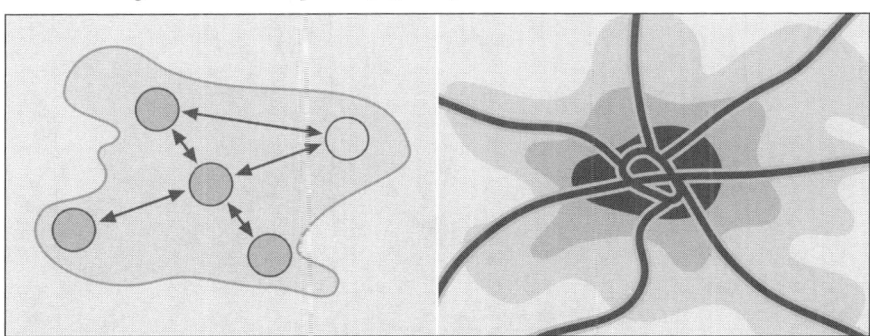

Source : adapted from Federal Office for Building and Regional Planning 2001

Figure 1. *Polycentric versus dispersed city.*

At the inter-urban scale, the focus is on the polycentric urban region (PUR), defined as a region with three or more cities that are historically and politically separate, have no hierarchical ranking, are in reasonable proximity from each other, and demonstrate a high degree of functional interconnections and complementarities. Several examples of PUR can be found in Europe such as, the Rhine-Ruhr region in Germany, which shows a sharp contrast with the Brandenburg region where Berlin is clearly dominant *(Figure 2)*. Other examples include the Flemish Diamond in Belgium (consisting of Brussels, Leuven, Antwerp and Ghent) and Padua-Treviso-Venice area in the Northern Italy.

However, the classic example of a PUR is Randstad in Holland. This consists of a ring of four large cities around an area of farmland and water, called the Green Heart. Each city thrives on a different, yet complementary, economic basis: Amsterdam benefits from proximity to Schipol Airport, tourism and finance; Utrecht has the service sector and nice surroundings; The Hague is the seat of government; and Rotterdam lives off its port *(Figure 3)*. Randstat is not an administrative or political unit, but given the proximity, connectivity and interactions between its constituent cities, it has been treated and promoted by Dutch planners as a single coherent region; as the next European Delta Metropolis capable of competing with London and Paris.

However, the conceptualisation of polycentricity at the regional level is still at developmental stage. Its definition, for example, is problematic at least on two accounts: what is a reasonable proximity? And, how do we measure functional interconnection? As regards reasonable proximity, back in 1915 for Patrick Gedess, the rule of thumb was one hour. In the ESPON research, 45 minutes drive time was used as a measure of reasonable distance which people are prepared to commute daily. As regards functional interconnection, the common criterion is travel-to-work journey but this ignores other trip-generating activities such as shopping and leisure. It also ignores flows of goods and information between firms. Nevertheless, the concept has evoked a lot of enthusiasm amongst neighbouring cities, which are keen to expand their competitive advantage by pooling their resources together.

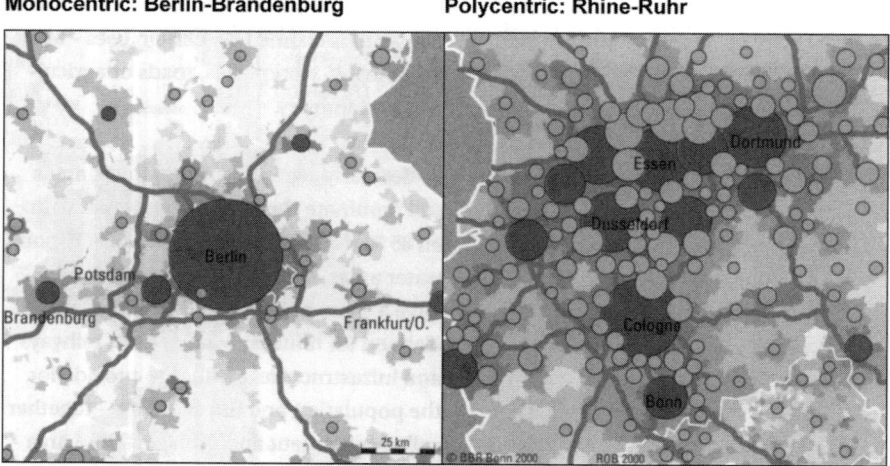

Source : Federal Office for Building and Regional Planning, 2001

Figure 2. *Monocentric versus polycentric urban region.*

Polycentricity: Panacea or pipedream?

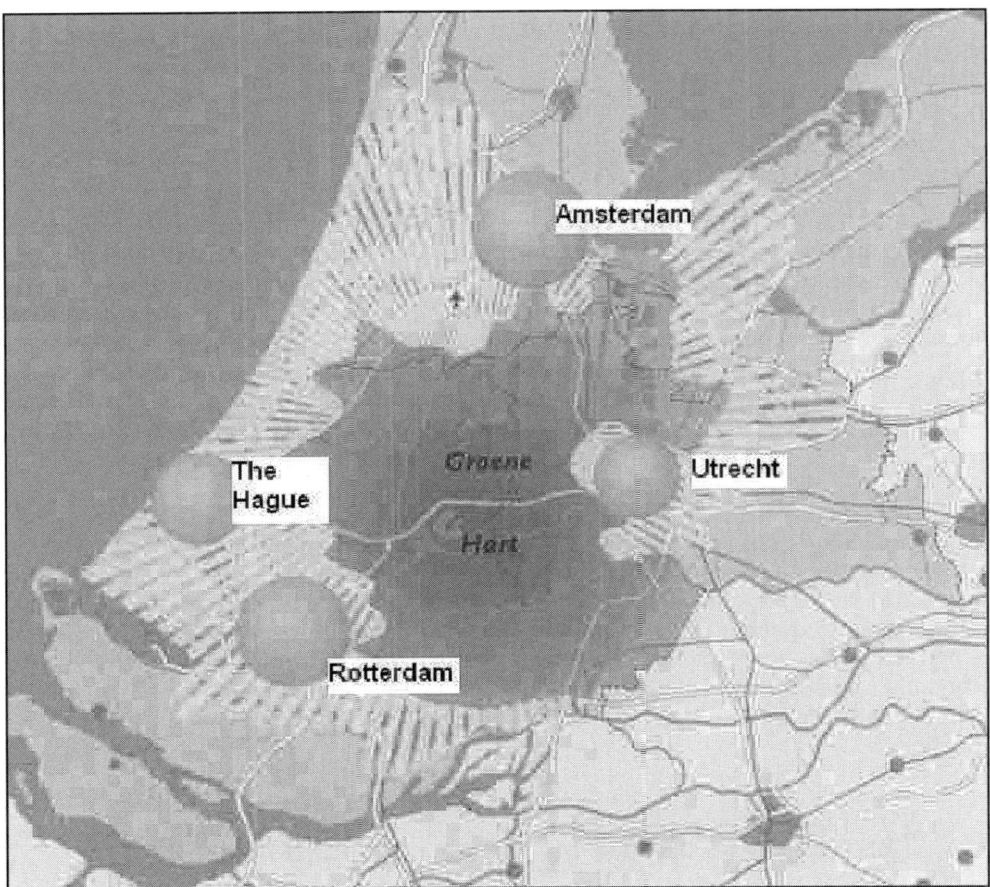

Source : adapted from Hoppenbrouwer et al, 2003

Figure 3. *The Randstadt.*

At the inter-regional scale, the concept has been used to explain the expanding scale of urban growth and the coalescence of metropolitan areas. Gottmann (1957), for example, famously coined the notion of "megalopolis" to define 600 miles of contiguous areas in the east coast of America, running from Boston in the north to Washington in the South. Another related concept is that of "urban field" invented by Friedmann and Miller (1965) to depict a new scale of urban living that extends far beyond metropolitan core and into the periphery. Doxiadis (1968) went even further and suggested that we would soon live in "ecumenopolis" or world city. His poetic vision does not seem to be too far from the contemporary trends that are taking place in, for example, the Beijing, Seoul, Tokyo urban corridor which transcends national boundaries, stretching almost contiguously along a 1,500 kilometre strip of densely populated land (98 million population) with a maximum air travelling time of one and a half hour.

At the level of Europe, the agglomeration forces have led to the uneven development of the EU territory, where a prosperous core stands against an underdeveloped periphery. This core-periphery conception of European space has been captured in a number of metaphors such as: "European Megalopolis", "Golden Triangle", the "Blue Banana", and more recently the "pentagon". The latter, which is an area bounded by the metropolises of London, Paris, Hamburg, Munich and Milan, was coined by the ESDP to describe an area which although covers only 20% of the EU15 territory, it generates 50% of its GDP and is home to 40% of its population. It is seen as the only economic zone in Europe that can compete effectively in the world market. Hence, a key aim of the ESDP is to promote new economic growth zones of global significance in order to make Europe not only more competitive but also more cohesive. For the ESDP, polycentricity is not an analytical tool but a normative agenda. This however raises a number of questions, such as:

– Is a win-win situation achievable?
– What kind of policy intervention can help position of cities/regions in the "winning camp"?
– Is PUR a panacea for economic competitiveness?
– Can a PUR be planned for?

In the paper published in the journal of European Planning Studies [4], I have tried to address each of these questions in detail. Here, I will focus on the key theme of this contribution: is PUR a panacea for economic competitiveness? The simple answer is that there is, so far, no conclusive evidence to show that a polycentric spatial structure is economically more competitive than for example a monocentric or a bipolar urban structure. However, the notion of polycentric development has provided a powerful political discourse for promoting both economic competitiveness and spatial equity through balanced development. This means that, at the EU level it has become the spatial manifestation of the concept of territorial cohesion [5].

THE CHALLENGE OF COMPETITIVENESS AND COHESION

Recent trends have shown that the drive towards polycentricity at the European level has been coupled with further monocentricity at the national level, often at the expense of the peripheral and economically fragile regions. Ireland is a potent example. The economic boom of the last decade, which has turned the country into one of Europe's star performers, has mainly gravitated in the Greater Dublin Area (GDA), making Ireland a highly monocentric country [6]. Research under the European Spatial Planning Observation Network (ESPON) has identified Dublin as one of the top categories of metropolitan European growth areas (MEGAs) which are considered as having the potential to counterbalance the "pentagon" [16].

However, while the economic growth of Dublin as the driver behind the "Celtic Tiger" has been widely celebrated, it has also raised the alarm because: firstly, its over heated economy has created a number of social and environmental problems, and secondly, its excessive growth has led to the widening and deepening of regional disparities. This is partly because in Ireland, as in most other Cohesion Countries, when the EU resources began to flow in only the major urban centres, and particularly the capital cities, had the critical mass, the infrastructure and the institutional capacity to absorb and deploy them effectively. It is therefore not surprising to see that similar trends are taking place in the new member states which will be the main recipients of the EU funds in near future. In these countries, growth has already begun to gravitate towards capital cities such as Budapest, Prague, Riga, Tallinn and Ljubljana. Even Poland, which entered the post-socialist transformation with a well-balanced urban system, has since experienced a degree of regional polarisation.

In combating such trends, many national spatial strategies have drawn, explicitly or implicitly, on the concept of polycentric development to promote functional inter-connection between second tier cities that, on their own, do not have the critical mass to be globally or nationally competitive. Again, Ireland is a potent example, where a number of neighbouring cities in the south west (Cork, Galway, Limerick and Waterford), branded as "Atlantic Gateways", are encouraged to pool their resources together and develop a Polycentric Urban Region, and hence increase their chance of becoming a new zone of economic growth and a counter balance to Dublin. Hence, the concept of polycentricity has been taken up by the National Spatial Strategy to address the problems of core-periphery by putting the emphasis on maximising the potentials of the smaller cities, rather than on redirecting resources from elsewhere to them, or seeking to halt growth in Dublin.

Similarly, in the UK, the concept of polycentric development has underpinned what is called the "Northern Way" initiative. This is a coast-to-coast megalopolis, with the 130-mile M62 corridor at its core, and encompassing three regions which include eight core City regions of Manchester, Liverpool, Leeds, Hull, Sheffield, Central Lancashire, Tyne and Wear and Tees Valley. The idea is that by developing a coherent functional space, the area will become more competitive and can act as a counterbalance to the south east. The three northern Regional Development Agencies (RDA) along with other regional partners have committed themselves to deliver on the Northern Way Growth Strategy, which sets out how the North will build upon its current and new assets to deliver its vision by 2025. The Growth Strategy:

– Looks at the North as a whole to identify pan-northern investments, which will add value to that which is being undertaken in each of the individual regions;
– Is based on how best to build on the North's strengths, defining what partners can do in the North and what Government must do to realise benefits from these assets;
– Complements the three regional economic strategies, as these define the key proposals to take forward economic development in the three regions of the North; and
– Focuses on the North of England's eight city-regions which are crucial to accelerating the economic growth of the North.

The main indicators of success of the Growth Strategy is set to be whether implementation increases private investment across the North, increases employment and increases Gross Value Added (GVA). Key successes of the Northern Way include:

– the development of a high-quality evidence-base and analytical framework for understanding the economic challenges and opportunities of the North of England;
– a commitment of the three northern RDAs to promote the science cities of Manchester, Newcastle and York, as part of their £100 million investment in university-business collaboration by 2010;
– collaboration between the eight research-intensive northern universities to increase research excellence in the North, building on existing strengths.

– agreement of a Northern Transport Compact as the focal point for setting pan-northern transport investment priorities;
– pilots to enhance the training programmes in the North of England with an entitlement to qualification in priority sectors and areas; and,
– an extension of the existing initiatives to accelerate the number of people moving from Incapacity Benefit into employment [17, 18].

FORGING SYNERGIES BETWEEN NEIGHBOURING CITIES

When it comes to the implementation of polycentric strategy, the most critical elements are the development of: economic links, functional specialisation, and complementarities; because, without these, a PUR will simply represent a morphological concept rather than an integrated functional space. In Scotland, for example, despite the fact that development has spread along an east-west corridor, dominated by well-connected cities of Glasgow and Edinburgh, research has shown that the evidence for treating the area as a fully integrated single region is weak [1]. Hence, the critical question for policy makers is how to forge functional synergies between neighbouring cities of a potential PUR. There are two key areas where policy intervention can be usefully deployed. One is often obvious and relates to development of hard infrastructure, such as efficient transport and telecommunication networks between the nodes. The other, which attracts less policy attention, relates to development of soft infrastructure, notably governing capacity and regional identity. If cities and towns are to pool together and share labour market and infrastructure facilities, they need to develop flexible and multi-agency forms of governance at the pan-PUR level, which in turn will enable them to enhance their functional synergies.

Although in many European countries, there are no formal structures of government at city-region or PUR level, the survey that we conducted for ESPON research showed that a growing number of informal partnerships and networks have been formed at the inter-municipal and inter-regional levels. However, many of these partnerships suffer from limited resources, political will and commitment, and experienced partners. It showed that building governance relations is not easy and needs sufficient time, long-term external assistance and investment and devolved powers and responsibilities [16] (Workpackage 5: Governance). If cities are to pool together their resources and create synergies and strengthen their linkages, they need appropriate forms of governance, which is capable of coordinating their activities and providing a degree of leadership and strategic directions. However, there is currently a considerable mismatch between the strategies that are promoting polycentricity and the operation of the formal government structure. In order to elaborate on this point, I will draw on the current debate about city-regions in the UK, because although it represents a smaller than PUR scale, the governance principles are similar.

It is widely acknowledged that while government operates on the basis of administratively defined boundaries, such as communes, municipalities, boroughs, local authorities and Kreise; the activities of industries, businesses, and households straddle such boundaries and take place in functionally defined areas. For example, forty per cent of the UK working population cross at least one local authority boundary during their journey to work. This figure rises for higher skilled and professional workers [14]. Furthermore, journey to work is not the only trip generating activity. People may live in one administrative area; work in another; send their children to school in a third; spend their leisure time in a fourth; use the services of a hospital in the fifth; and so on. Thus, making strategies on the basis of administrative boundaries does not make sense and will not be effective. What, then, is the alternative? How can the administrative boundaries and the wider functional areas be co-aligned? In the UK, this is currently the subject of a heated debate, which is mainly focused on the city-regions and particularly on the large metropolitan cities, which although have an extensive catchment areas, their authority is often limited to a much smaller administrative boundaries. Birmingham in the West Midland Region of England is a classic example of a metropolitan area which has evolved from coalescence of smaller independent settlements into a large contiguous built up area, but where no one local authority has administrative control over the whole area.

To overcome this fragmentation, it is crucial that a city-region approach to strategic planning is adopted. This means that governance and functional activities need to be better aligned. However, this does not necessarily mean that a single all powerful city-region authority should take over the jurisdiction of the whole area. It is even more perverse, to argue for such an authority at the level of polycentric urban regions. There are a number of reasons why such a governance structure is not desirable or effective. Firstly, it is politically sensitive, and creates unnecessary rivalries and anxieties especially amongst the smaller cities which might fear of loosing their autonomy and identity. Secondly, the geography of functional areas varies depending not only on the methodology applied to define them, but also on different functions and markets. For example, travel to work patterns may be different from patterns of travel to shopping and entertainment centres. Often, for the less frequently used services, the catchment area of metropolitan cities are much more extensive than for the daily travel to work. For example, a recent study led by Manchester University has shown the wide spread of the cultural draw of Manchester's theatres. This shows that although the majority of customers are drawn from the North West Region, there is hardly a single local authority in England and Wales which does not have at least one person attending a performance at one of the theatres [19].

Thirdly, even within one type of market, such as labour market, catchment area is markedly different for different occupations. For example, the catchment area is substantially larger for professional and managerial workers than for semi-skilled and routine workers (ibid). Fourthly, much of the debate and research on functional regions, including the one mentioned above, is dominated by an economic imperative, with little attentions to the environmental footprints of the metropolitan cities. For example, the movement of waste from metropolitan cities, such as Greater Manchester, to the rest of the region has a catchment area of its own whose boundaries do not necessarily coincide with other functional boundaries. Furthermore, the flows are always in opposite direction to the dominant economic flows. Over half of municipal waste generated in Greater Manchester travel to the nearby cities and districts such as Warrington, while about a quarter moves outside the region to Yorkshire, turning areas such as Warrington to what is locally known as the dustbin of the North West [7].

In summary, there is no single overarching city-region boundary which can catch all functions and services. Hence, there is little justification for creating a single, city-region authority. It is even less justifiable to have such a formal government structure for PUR. The "fuzziness" of the functional areas means that any tightly-drawn administrative boundaries, no matter how big or small, will become inadequate for one type of function or another; and also irrelevant sooner or later. It thus follows that, imposing a fixed structure of government over such fuzzy boundaries will do little for effective governing of the complex and dynamic functional interconnections between cities and their hinterland. Similarly, it will do little for forging synergies and cooperation and developing polycentric urban regions. In Britain, any formal restructuring of local government which demarcates a single city-region will inevitably be along the same lines as the metropolitan counties which were established by one Conservative government in the 1960s, and abolished by another in the 1980s.

Instead, what is needed is a variable geometry of more informal and flexible inter-municipal collaborations, for different functions and services. Indeed, such collaborative arrangements based on multi-agency partnerships and flexible forms of networking at various spatial scales are already happening across Europe, and have become the hallmark of the transition from government to governance. They represent alternative models of managing collective affairs, which are based on *"horizontal self-organisation among mutually interdependent actors"* [15] from both governmental and nongovernmental stakeholders.

It, therefore, seems that whilst the evidence about the degree of functional polycentrism across European regions is not yet conclusive, the move towards political polycentrism is already evident from the proliferation of institutional networks, and multilevel forms of governance. Most of these initiatives have been bottom-up. In Birmingham, the case which was mentioned earlier, there is now a concerted effort to set up partnership between existing local authorities. However, these informal polycentric governance arrangements are likely to be more effective, and command more credibility, if government provides appropriate incentives and clear mandate to encourage their establishment and to increase their chance of being sustained over time.

Conclusion

As regards the concept of polycentricity in general, two concluding remarks are worth mentioning. The first point is about the ambiguity of the concept particularly when it is applied to inter-urban scale. This is both a weakness and a strength. It is a weakness because it exposes the concept to multiple interpretations, making it possible to be used for different purposes by different people. At the same time, it is a strength because its "woolliness" facilitates its universal political acceptance, especially because it provokes a "positive" image. The present popularity of the term can be seen as the need for a conceptual basis which promotes network-based strategies for urban development in a world dominated by pressures of competitiveness. The second point, which is partly related to the above, is that polycentricity seems to be following a destiny similar to that of many other concepts that have come before it. *"They often start as a tentative notion, a provisional working model. But, all too swiftly, they become hardened into an idée fixe. Instead of using the concept as an aid to describe an emerging reality, it is coming to determine that reality"* [4]. This transformation from a descriptive and analytical tool to a prescriptive and normative agenda may not be problematic in itself, provided that polycentricity is promoted and perceived as one model of spatial development amongst many. This, however, is increasingly not the case. Hence, polycentricity now appears to be cropping up everywhere as an "ideal type" regional spatial structure, despite a lack of common definition and empirical evidence about its desirability, effectiveness, or the potential for its alleged success being replicated elsewhere by policy intervention.

However, despite these shortcomings the notion of polycentricity has provided a powerful political discourse for forging cooperation among neighbouring cities. This paper has argued that building institutional capacity and appropriate governance arrangements is crucial for the success of such cooperation. Within this context, an effective governmental policy intervention is one which focuses on incentivizing inclusive, inter-municipal coalitions across the PUR geometries which are fit-for-purpose.

REFERENCES

1. Baily N, Turok I. Central Scotland as a polycentric urban region: useful planning concept or chimera? *Urban Studies* 2001; 38 (4): 697-715.

2. Burgess E. The growth of city, an introduction to a research project. In *The City*. Park R, *et al*, (Eds). Chicago: University of Chicago Press, 1925.

3. Davoudi S. Making sense of the ESDP. *Town and Country Planning* 2000; 68 (12): 367-69.

4. Davoudi S. Polycentricity in European spatial planning: from an analytical tool to a normative agenda. *European Planning Studies* 2003; 11 (8): 979-99.

5. Davoudi S. Understanding Territorial Cohesion. *Planning Practice and Research* 2005; vol. 20 (4): 433-41.

6. Davoudi S, Wishardt M. Polycentric Turn in the Irish Spatial Strategy. *Built Environment* 2005 vol. 31 (2): 122-32.

7. Davoudi S, Evans N, Smith A. *Regional Waste Strategy Making: A National Overview*. Leeds: Leeds Metropolitan University, 2005.

8. Doxiadis C. *Ekistics*. London: Hutchinson, 1968.

9. EC. Sixth Periodic Report on Social and Economic Situation and Development of Regions in the EU. Brussels: European Commission, 1999.

10. Federal Office for Building and Regional Planning. *Spatial Development and Spatial Planning in Germany*. Berlin: BBR, 2001.

11. Friedman J, Miller J. The urban field. *Journal of the Institute of American Planners* 1965; November: 312-20.

12. Gottmann J. Megalopolis – or the urbanisation of the North-eastern Seaboard. *Economic Geography* 1957; 33 (3): 189.

13. Hoppenbrouwer E, Meijers E, Romein A. Randstad. In *Planning polycentric urban regions in North West Europe*. Meijers E Romein A, Hoppenbrouwer EC (Eds). Delft: Delft University Press, 2003: 33-80.

14. HM Treasury. Devolving decision-making: 3– Meeting the regional economic challenge. London: HMSO, 2006.

15. Jessop B. Governance failure. In *The New Politics of British Local Governance*. Stoker G (Ed). London: Macmillan, 2000: 11-32.

16. Nordregio. ESPON 1.1.1: Potentials for Polycentric development in Europe. Stockholm: Nordregio, 2004, rev. 2005.

17. NWSG. Moving Forward: The Northern Way – First Growth Strategy Report. Northern Way Steering Group, NWSG, 2004.

18. NWSG. Moving Forward: The Northern Way – Business Plan 2005-2008. Northern Way Steering Group, NWSG, 2005.

19. Office of the Deputy Prime Minister (ODPM). *A Framework for City Region: Working Paper 1: Mapping City Region*. London: ODPM, 2006.

20. Robson B. Towards a Randstad of the North. *Town and Country Planning* 2005; 74 (1): 18-19.

Polycentrism, equity and social cohesion in Europe

Guy Baudelle

Jean Monnet European Chair, RESO, University of Rennes 2, France

Introduced in the Amsterdam Treaty (1997), social cohesion is fostered in the Constitution Treaty Project and in the Third Cohesion report as an objective for the European Union. Since polycentrism as a concept is defined in the ESDP[1] as "a balanced territorial development resulting from an even spatial distribution of economic activity centres", our intention here is to evaluate to what extent polycentrism can achieve the objective of social cohesion. The gap is striking between the official success of the idea of polycentrism and the scepticism it encounters among the scientific community. This is why we intend to assess the added value of this concept as well as its practical capacity for promoting the balanced spatial planning of the European territory. We will firstly examine the diffusion of the concept in the spatial planning community despite its vague definition. Secondly, we will highlight the debate that has occurred between various disciplines. And finally, we will argue that the ideological characteristics of the concept make it an equitable project, and one which is of genuine strategic importance for achieving European objectives.

A VAGUE BUT INCREASINGLY NORMATIVE CONCEPT

The concept of polycentrism rose quickly to prominence before being officially adopted. It emerged in the early 1990s in Germany, and rapidly gained currency until it was formally acknowledged in 1995 in the first ESDP version, which outlined a path "Towards a more balanced and polycentric urban system" [9]. Here, polycentrism was explicitly defined as one of the three "principles for a European spatial development policy".

Paradoxically, this meteoric success contrasted with a very low level of scientific endorsement. Although it is to be expected that such a newly coined concept could not yet appear in urban geography and spatial planning academic manuals in the mid 1990s, or even in more specialized papers on planning published in Europe, it is astonishing that it should still be ignored in those academic works that came much later, such as in the *Dictionnaire de la géographie et de l'espace des sociétés* [18].

---

1. European Spatial Development Perspective.

The reason why acceptance by the scientific community has been so slow might lie in the fact that polycentricity has been elaborated in spatial planning circles. It is, indeed, the German regional planning Minister who promoted polycentrism as a concept, the word "concept" being an approximate English translation of the German term "Konzept" (which in fact means "project" or "plan"). Polycentrism is now assumed to be a genuine model appearing in high-profile documents (besides ESDP) coming from various instances like the DATAR/DIACT[2] [14] or the Conference of Peripheral Maritime Regions in Europe. The appeal of who seem to wear this concept in the bare. polycentrism is all the more general as it seems to be both polysemic and to correspond to the requirements of sustainable development, which makes it very "politically correct" [21].

In return, this vagueness makes it complex, flexible and thus opened to slight shifts in definition. As a consequence, the word appears to be typical of "Euro-language", of the "code words" of the new Europe [3]: being a coded term but not rigidly codified, ambiguous, with changeable outlines. Thus polycentrism seems to be more convenient as a tool in the debating arena than for reaching final conclusions. This uncertainty encourages reflection on the optimal degrees of concentration as well as on relevant levels of intervention. But the eurocode words have by definition a very limited applicability outside the circle of Eurocrats. Now, the concept has spread out of the milieu of spatial planners and is even considered indispensable to the implementation of public policies [9].

It is also the point of view of Klaus R. Kunzmann, who produced the image of the European "bunch of grapes" as a metaphor for a polycentric Europe – the answer to the "blue banana" [17]. This metaphor offers an alternative representation of the ideal to be reached. It provides planners with a guideline and a spatial vision (literally "Leitbild" or "guiding image") that would be understood at first glance, facilitating the definition of strategies to be implemented. Thus polycentrism constitutes a "bridging concept" [21] filling the distance between both archetypes (*i.e.* the blue banana and the bunch of grapes). It is one of the bridges which could possibly lead to the desired spatial organization.

At the same time, polycentrism is described by the political analyst Beate Kohler-Koch (1999) as a "hegemonic concept", in the sense of Gramsci, *i.e.* as a simple concept designed to persuade decision-makers, and as an instrument for praxis. This was exemplified, among others, by a polycentric scenario put together in 1999-2001 – one which, although long-term and very hypothetical (2020), described a possible desirable outcome [2]. In fact, this story already participated in the construction of polycentrism by offering decision-makers the opportunity to view a desirable future representation and to claim it as their own [14]. Polycentrism thus constitutes the initial stage of the spatial vision. The remarkable spread of polycentrism in national policies of European planning led Simin Davoudi (2003) to describe these projects as a "normative agenda".

THE ISSUE OF SCIENTIFIC VALUE: AN INTERDISCIPLINARY DEBATE?

Nonetheless, polycentrism still attracts harsh criticism among academics. In particular, economists have highlighted the naive position of geographers, who – they point out – fail to

---

2. Délégation Interministérielle à l'Aménagement et à la Compétitivité territoriale.

take into account two common and ineluctable processes: polarisation and metropolisation. A report written by Laurent Davezies [8] estimates that *"giving money to Lisbon is thus a way to give money to Alentejo"*. The explanation is that *"the money spent in Lisbon induces more growth than the money spent in Alentejo"*. The polycentric ambition is thus mocked by a certain number of economists who emphasize, on the contrary, the advantages of concentration in a few poles. To invest somewhere other than in the major poles would be a waste. The polycentric project would consequently be a false good idea, which cannot be realistically implemented [1], and the ESDP *"a sort of Santa Claus letter mostly written by geographers focused on "territorial balance" and "quality of life" (...), all the while ignoring the economic advantages of territorial imbalance"* [4].

At this point in the debate, and given our current state of knowledge, we should admit that *"knowing with some certainty the comparative costs (...) of mostly monocentric or mostly polycentric territorial models is, even today, beyond reach"* [20]. This assertion is also confirmed by the foremost specialists in agglomeration economies [10] when they deal with the classic issue of city size: *"are big cities too big (...) or (...) too small (...)? The truth is that nobody knows, and nobody will know until there has been a lot of hard empirical work on the matter"*. Indeed, *"a complete theoretical characterization of a collective optimum in location does not exist, nor even a rigorous evaluation of the collective surplus of the metropolization phenomenon"* [11]. For Sven Illeris (2005), there is no empirical or theoretical argument that gives credit to the growth poles theory or to the idea that a capital city, seen as "an engine that pulls the rest of the country", could automatically attract a great proportion of foreign investments. Indeed what is verified from empirical studies is that foreign registered offices and finance services do not follow the same localisation processes as industry and services. By and large, we would also underline that the practical efficiency of polycentrism for the realization of greater spatial equity and cohesion remains to be demonstrated [13].

POLYCENTRISM: A SPATIAL IDEOLOGY FOR THE BENEFIT OF SPATIAL PLANNING

A system of representation

Such a lack of scientific certainty means that we are faced with two contradictory spatial ideologies. Spatial ideology is here understood as *"a system of organized and autonomous ideas and judgements, which is used to describe, explain, interpret or justify the spatial situation of a group or a local community. Largely inspired by values, it proposes a definite orientation through the historical action of this specific territorial unit"* [12]. Opposing "the concentration ideology" [7], polycentrism makes a stand as a "competing theory" [15], as a system of representation of explicit values (sustainable development, territorial balance...) implying societal choices and providing a "vision of the world" as an integrated "set of levers" [12].

In this case the ideological dimension of polycentrism – regardless of its poor scientific basis – is very useful, as it provides a reference for European development policies ensuring a common position among European policy makers. Consequently, polycentrism corresponds to a shared vision of a desirable future.

This shared vision, born of the conceptual weaknesses of polycentrism, also limits its operational scope. This could explain why polycentrism has disappeared in the Third cohesion Report, in favour of the territorial cohesion concept which aims *"to narrow the gap in the levels of development of various regions and allow less favoured regions to catch up"* (Amsterdam Treaty, art. 158). According to the Third cohesion Report *"this implies that no person should be disadvantaged because of where he/she lives in the Union"*. In September 2005, the European Parliament itself adopted a resolution on "The role of territorial cohesion within regional development" with a view to maintaining "equity towards all citizens throughout the territory" (2004/2256 (INI)). The same resolution describes the "polycentric development of the European territory", particularly that of "small and medium sized cities", as a "privileged vector" of territorial cohesion, without, nonetheless, sacrificing competitiveness – the other major Union objective.

A compatible cohesion and competitiveness strategy

Polycentric development policies do indeed aim for both territorial cohesion and competitiveness, something which can be summed up as follows *(Table I)*.

Table I. *Objectives and spatial strategies.*

Objective	Competitiveness	Territorial Cohesion	Competitiveness & cohesion
Spatial Strategy	Reinforce major poles	Reduce spatial disparities	Conciliate Gothenburg and Lisbon
Instrument	Growth Poles	Zoning	Polycentrism
Outcome	Efficiency, disparities	Solidarity	Territorial equity

The desire to strengthen national competitiveness leads each country to lean on its strong feature, usually its capital, whereas aiming for cohesion generally means zoning in favour of the less developed regions, via Community regional policy. To overcome this dilemma, polycentrism formulates objectives which are neither exclusively economic (such as competitiveness) nor socio-spatial (such as cohesion). In fact, the majority of corresponding policies aims explicitly at realizing the dual Lisbon-Gothenburg objective to the point where, in certain cases (France, Germany, Finland), "fostering cohesion and competitiveness is thus more or less the same" [22]. It is striking to note that according to the authors, the famous French "balancing metropolises" policy is regarded in the first instance as corresponding with the growth pole theory [15] and in the second instance with a polycentric policy [22].

Such an ambivalent perception indicates that the polycentric objective is not purely a matter of assistance but indeed a strategy taking into account the major role of urban dynamics in regional development, with the aim of increasing the potential of the economic and institutional resources of all towns, thus strengthening their assets. Regarding territorial cohesion, the polycentric project has the advantage of emphasizing how necessary it is to reinforce the lesser metropolised areas in order to ensure equal opportunities based on those towns' outstanding activities and competitiveness. The main interest of the polycentric strategy, then, is to highlight the necessity of balanced investments for the benefit of less favoured urban poles – not to allow these to seek compensation as such but in order to facilitate their convergence with more privileged centres in the long term. This naturally entails some selectivity and hierarchy, in accordance with French competitiveness poles. The question which frequently crops up is that of the optimal urban level at which to target public investment and the requisite thresholds to satisfy equity without losing efficiency, bearing in mind that the loss in global efficiency is liable to disadvantage even the least favoured.

An equitable project

We can however assert that the promotion of a polycentric organisation presents the advantage of favouring equity in the sense of John Rawls (1971), in so far as it first improves the well-being of the least favoured populations, from the most remote areas in the countryside to the disadvantaged suburbs. As Rawls' justice theory aims to strengthen social justice by maximizing the chances of the weakest, it becomes clear that a choice between efficiency and does not in fact have to be made. Indeed, the American philosopher proposes an ethic in which, in his own terms, "justice has priority over economic efficiency". And "the just has priority over the good" since, in any case, "a perfectly fair system is also effective". Now, in remote areas, the level of services – notably educational and cultural – is in fact very low, and cannot guarantee real equality of opportunity, so that it is fair to implement a policy which improves the situation of the less favoured. This is the case, for instance, of the future extension of the Louvre Museum in Lens, the heart of an old coal mining district where most of the population is made up of workers and low-income earners. Also, a spatial development measure which goes some way towards improving the well-being of more disadvantaged cities is fair, since the mobility which is supposed to remedy unfavourable situations – according to neo-classic economists – is more expensive in all senses of the term for the poorest populations [11]. The Community policy of territorial cohesion (Cohesion policy or Regional policy) aims exactly at reconciling considerations of equity with the objective of competitiveness.

Conclusion

Devised by spatial planners, the concept of polycentrism has smoothly asserted itself as a normative project for the European territory in spite of its vague definition and the criticisms it attracts. Polycentrism establishes an alternative development model which makes it possible to reconcile competitiveness and social cohesion objectives. Its implementation is, however, a long term process due to the inertia of urban systems and the dynamics of population settlement.

References

1. Bailey N., Turok I. Central Scotland as a Polycentric Urban Region: Useful Planning Concept or Chimera? *Urban Studies* 2001; vol. 38, n° 4: 697-715.

2. Baudelle G, Castagnède B (Eds). *Le polycentrisme en Europe*. La Tour d'Aigues : L'Aube, 2002, 269 p.

3. Clark GI. Vocabulary of the New Europe: Code Words for the Millenium. *Environment and Planning D: Society and Space* 2001; n° 19: 697-717.

4. Davezies L. Europe et solidarités territoriales: un couple improbable. In : *L'aménagement en 50 tendances*. Wachter S, *et al*. La Tour d'Aigues : L'Aube, 2002: 92-6.

5. Davoudi S. Polycentricity in European Spatial Planning: From an Analytical Tool to a Normative Agenda. *European Planning Studies* 2003; vol. 11, n° 8 : 979-99.

6. Di Méo G. *L'Homme, la Société, l'Espace*. Paris : Anthropos, 1991, 319 p.

7. Dumont GF. *Économie urbaine*. Paris : Litec, 1993, 295 p.

8. European Commission. *Economic and Social Cohesion in the European Union: the Impact of Member States' Own Policies*. Luxembourg: OPOCE, 1998, 237 p.

9. Faludi A, Waterhout B. *The Making of the European Spatial Development Perspective*. London: Routledge, 2002, 204 p.

10. Fujita M, Krugman P, Venables AJ (Eds). *The Spatial Economy: Cities, Regions and International Trade*. Cambridge (Mass.): MIT Press, 2001 (2nd ed.), 384 p.

11. Gérard-Varet LA, Mougeot M. L'État et l'aménagement du territoire. In : *Aménagement du territoire, Conseil d'analyse économique*. Paris: La Documentation Française, 2001 : 45-109.

12. Gilbert A. L'idéologie spatiale: conceptualisation, mise en forme et portée pour la géographie. *L'Espace Géographique* 1986 ; n° 1 : 57-66.

13. Gloersen E. Faut-il des visions spatiales pour construire une Europe polycentrique ? *Territoires 2030* 2005 ; n° 1 : 65-88.

14. Guigou JL. *Aménager la France de 2020*. Paris : La Documentation Française, 2002 (2nd ed.), 112 p.

15. Illeris S. *Regional Policy and Urban Systems: Growth Centres or Polycentricity?* University of Roskilde, 2005, 13 p.

16. Kohler-Koch B. EU Governance and the Role of Ideas. *Journal of European Public Policy* 1999; vol. 6, n° 8.

17. Kunzmann KR. La "Banane bleue" est morte! Vive la "Grappe européenne"! *Les Cahiers du Conseil*, Conseil général des Ponts et Chaussées, 2001 ; n° 2 : 38-41.

18. Lévy J, Lussault M (Eds). *Dictionnaire de la géographie et de l'espace des sociétés*. Paris : Belin, 2003, 1 034 p.

19. Rawls J. *A Theory of Justice*. Oxford: Oxford University Press, 1971, 667 p.

20. Saint-Julien T. Structure Polycentrique. In *A Critical Dictionary of Polycentrism, "The Role, Specific Situation and Potentials for Urban Areas as Nodes of Polycentric Development"*. Cattan N (Ed). ESPON 1.1.1., Working Package 1 (Theoretical and conceptual), 2003.

21. Waterhout B. Polycentric Development: What is Behind it? In *European Spatial Planning*. Faludi A (Ed). Cambridge (Mass.): Lincoln Institute of Land Policy, 2002: 83-103.

22. Waterhout B, Zonneveld W, Meijers E. Polycentric Development Policies in Europe: Overview and Debate. *Built Environment* 2005; vol. 31, n° 2: 163-73.

The ideo-centricity of urban poly-centricity

Niels Boje Groth, Søren Smidt-Jensen
Danish Centre for Forest, Landscape and Planning, University of Copenhagen, Denmark

Polycentricity has attracted much attention as a model for regional development. This is not surprising, since urban tissues get much stronger when joining complementary urban functions. Further, it seems to be in line with the goals of territorial cohesion to enhance the development of many medium-sized centres rather than just a few large centres. However, it also appears that the good intentions behind the concept have fostered a kind of ideological blindness to the contradictory qualities of the concept concerning scaling, potentials and political commitments. Thus, the CPMR[1] (2002) study indicated and the ESPON[2] 1.1.1 study [10] explicitly stated that the strategy needed to enhance polycentricity at the European scale is likely to favour the development of growth poles and hence to counteract the development of national polycentricities outside the European pentagon. Further, the ESPON 1.1.1 study showed that if polycentricity is to be enhanced generally in Europe, the centre rather than the peripheries of Europe would benefit the most, simply due to the fact that the urban tissue and, hence, the potentials for building relations between neighbouring cities, are more present in the centre than in the peripheries of Europe. Finally, it is often observed that the benefits of polycentricity are overshadowed by historically-rooted political commitments keeping cities from giving up their individual identities [12, 11].

In spite of these contradictory characteristics, polycentricity seems to survive in top-down spatial politics, probably because of the euphemistical attributes of the concept[3]. In this article, we shall change the perspective from top-down to bottom-up politics.

TWO PERSPECTIVES ON POLYCENTRICITY

Territory and actor

As we change the perspective from top-down to bottom-up politics, also the frame of reference for understanding urban relations changes from the territory to the urban actor.

---

1. The Conference of Peripheral Maritime Regions of Europe.
2. European Spatial Planning Observation Network.
3. For further analysis of polycentricity as a top-down concept see *e.g.* Faludi (2005) and Jensen and Richardson (2003), the application of which reveals a lack of conceptual consistency see *e.g.* Davoudi (2003 and chapter in this book) and Hague and Kirk (2003).

Based upon case-studies conducted in a number of medium-sized cities in the Baltic Sea Region, we shall discuss the relevance of the territorially based urban relations which the concept polycentricity is founded upon. We shall argue, that cities are involved in inter urban relations, the geography of which usually are not ruled by proximity. Rather, they are ruled by strategic relevance. An important background for understanding this situation is the change of the interplay between the state and the city. In the years after the Second World War medium-sized cities played the role as mediators of national programmes for development of the welfare state. Hierarchical systems of centres were planned as frameworks for an evenly distribution of welfare institutions over the national territories. This interplay between the state and the city has now changed due to the restructuring of the welfare state in its local urban settings [1]. Deindustrialisation and national institutional reforms have caused pronounced changes of the urban territories. In line with this development, cities have to meet the challenges by the initiation of locally defined actions aiming at the revitalisation of urban decline and urban change. Reconstruction rather than construction of the welfare state is on the agenda and enforces local governments to act as entrepreneurs of local change rather than as mediators of national programs [8].

In the role as entrepreneurs, the medium-sized cities make use of a palette of operational means, only one of which is co-operation with neighbouring cities. They cooperate with the most relevant and competent "players" in the market matching their goals and projects (G. Forssberg, mayor of Nyköping, Sweden, 2003: *"We cooperate with the best in the market"*). Matching partnerships, be they local or distant, with policies has become more relevant than matching policies with locally established partnerships. Thus, co-operation is not governed by proximity relations; it is not a function of aspirations of polycentricity. Rather, co-operation is ruled by new urgent needs for change in cities that have become more self-reliant.

In the territorial perspective, polycentricity is based upon cooperation between neighbouring cities on complementary assets, the idea of which is to form a larger and higher ranking polycentric "city". In this perspective, the territory is framing the strategies. In the urban actors' perspective, locally decided strategies are framing a variety of territories hosting each of its relevant urban network *(Figure 1)*.

In this paper, it is argued that polycentricity is but one of several action-oriented measures that medium-sized cities develop when they assume responsibility as initiators rather than just mediators of local development. This overall picture is modified as we shall see by the challenges and options for restructuring that confront cities in metropolitan, self sustaining and peripheral regions, respectively.

The role of polycentricity in urban strategies

In what follows, we shall examine examples revealing urban polycentricities from the actors' perspective. The examples are taken from the Medium-sized Cities in dialogue around the Baltic Sea Region (MECIBS), an Interreg IIIB project carried out by researchers and cities in the Baltic Sea Region *(Figure 2)* focusing on local strategies for urban transition [6].

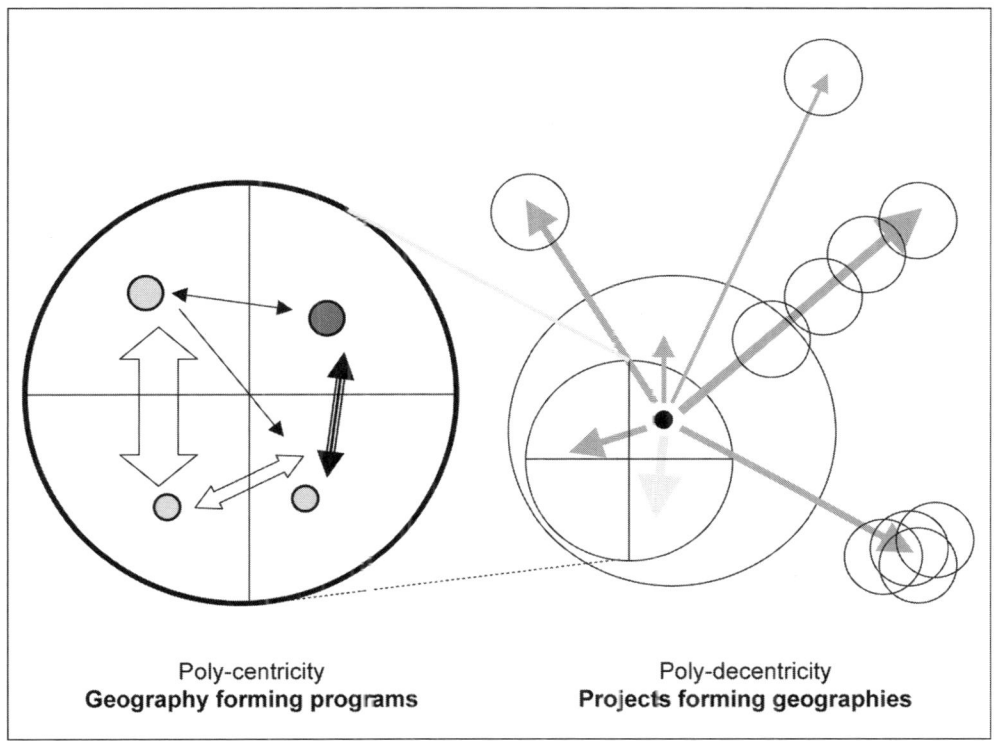

Figure 1. *Two perspectives on urban networking.*

The MECIBS project confirmed that in order to cope with urban transformation, medium-sized cities have developed a clear understanding of the need to carry out their own development strategies. Thus, most MECIBS cities have shown a distinct capability to form and conduct strategic action. The urgency of urban restructuring and the will for achievements have impelled the cities to try new paths that surmount bottlenecks of legal regulations, public opinion and traditions of political and administrative conduct. A shift of planning paradigms seems to take place. During urban growth, urban planning and policies were very much led by planning systems facilitating a public dialogue on where to go. Focus was on the goals, not the means. During urban restructuring, the goals for local planning and strategies are obviously set by the need to handle acute and obvious problems. The shortage is the lack of proper means to handle the situation. This is why local strategies for restructuring are leading cities to search for and try out new strategies which bring them into new areas of more risky decisions and to the edges of traditional urban conduct.

In what follows, we shall set up a model showing the elements of strategic conduct. Taking this model as the point of departure, we then examine the geography of the networks established by three cities to cope with urban restructuring. The observation is that proximity, although relevant, is not the guiding principle for choosing partners. Cities go for the best and most relevant partners, irrespective of their geographical location. Despite the differences, we can identify four elements characteristic of strategic action *(Figure 3)*.

Cities and networks in Europe – Polycentrism: What is behind the concept?

Figure 2. *Partners in the MECIBS project. The case studies selected for this article are from Herning (DK), Nakskov (DK) and Nyköping (SE).*

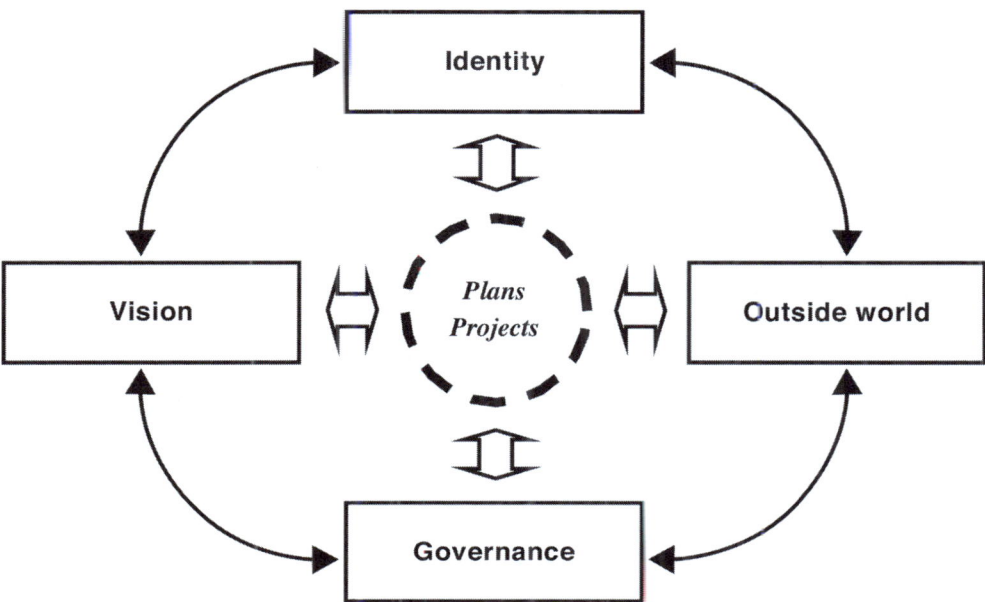

Figure 3. *The strategic circle.*

First, urban restructuring made several cities consider and reconsider explicitly their dependence on the outside world.

Second, several cities have realised that urban transformation deeply influences the position of the city in the regional urban system, the economic base and the symbolic representation of the city. These changes have forced cities to reconsider their identity and even to launch campaigns for branding new urban identities.

Third, urban restructuring forces cities to handle problems and to set up goals for action. However, restructuring often lays open new opportunities, as is the case when centrally located former industrial areas become obsolete and open themselves to development projects on attractive sites. This is why cities often engage in the creation of visions, trying to go beyond outdated development patterns and turn problems into options for new development.

Finally, urban restructuring makes cities inclined to attempt to widen the conventional scope of action. The concrete and specific impacts of urban restructuring call for initiation rather than regulation of development, as in the days of regulative urban planning. Therefore, cities are searching for new tools and new partnerships in urban governance.

Turning to polycentricity, the question is whether polycentricity plays a major role in forming these four elements of strategic action, as illustrated by *Figure 4*: as a step-stone to the understanding of the outside world, as the core of new urban identities, as the vision for urban development or as the principle for forming new urban partnerships? In what follows, we shall deal with these questions from the point of view of three cities.

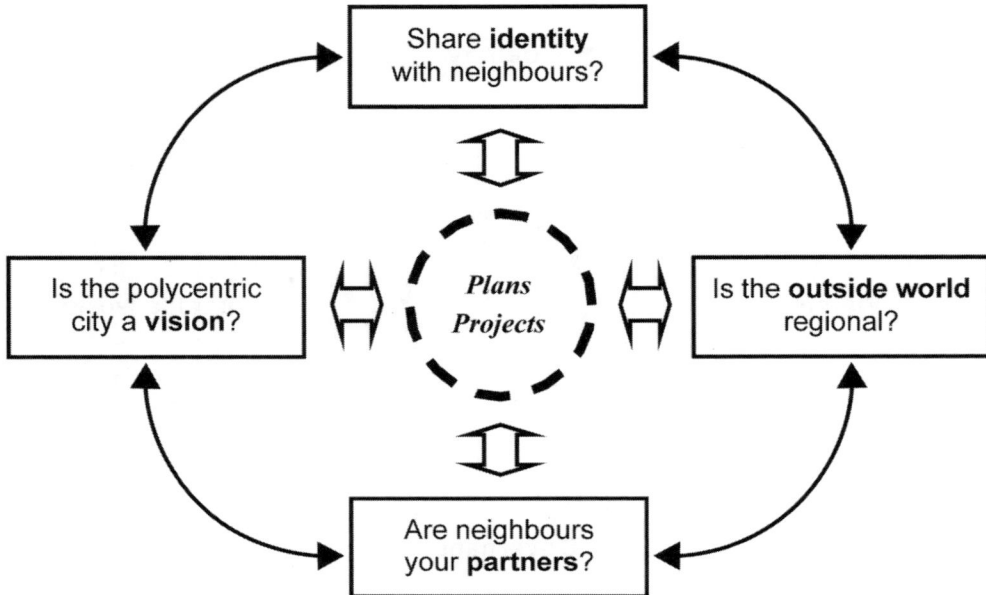

Figure 4. *Investigation into the influence of polycentricity on local development strategies.*

DEVELOPMENT STRATEGIES OF THREE MEDIUM-SIZED CITIES

In the peripheral region

Nakskov is a market town of about 15,000 inhabitants situated in the southern periphery of Denmark. The entire region has for long been a recipient of national and EU regional funds. By tradition, Nakskov was a working class city with important agro and metallic industries. In the late 1980s, the city was struck by the closure of some large old companies of which only Nakskov Sugar Factory is still operating. The closing of Nakskov's ship-building industry in 1986 was followed by a serious crisis in the city. Unemployment reached 35% for skilled and 40% for unskilled workers, and 10% of the municipality's inhabitants moved away in the period 1981-98. For several years, the city was paralysed. In 1997, however, a new mayor was elected and the municipality acquired a new chief executive and new director of the public utilities. That same year, Nakskov municipality approved a business strategy which generally broke with the idea of simply waiting for the economy to turn around. Due to the position as a recipient of national and EU regional funding the municipality had become accustomed to the idea that the situation could be turned around only by outside initiatives. Now, the municipality itself would take the initiative.

With Nakskov's favourable geographic location for contact to Eastern Europe, the city council decided to concentrate on the growth potentials of the environment and energy sector. The idea was to become a gateway for environmental exports to the East-European market. Unlike in many other harbour cities it was confirmed that the city had to find its way as an industrial city – and hence not to convert the harbour into a residential area. The former shipyard and adjacent land would instead be transformed into an industrial and environment park for new industries and a modern logistic harbour area.

Shortly thereafter, a kick off was facilitated by negotiations with the windmill factory VESTAS on building a subsidiary production plant for windmill wings in the former shipyard area. To follow up the strategy, Nakskov invested more than EUR 14 mill. to convert the area for production use. Today, Nakskov Industrial and Environment Park includes VESTAS, one of its subcontractors, a seed company, 3 pilot windmills, a biocleaning plant of the sugar factory, the municipal waste recycling station, a new district heating plant, the municipal waste-water treatment facility, a pilot area for biocleaning of harbour sludge and a logistic harbour area. Zoned land for agro-industrial production has been set aside in areas partly situated in the neighbouring municipality.

The formation and construction of the Nakskov Industry and Environment Park is a key element in Nakskov's development strategy. Accordingly, the core partners were those most crucial for developing the area, including: a local knowledge centre and the Danish Technical University in Copenhagen, which worked on a pilot project on cleaning of harbour sludge; the former Norwegian company Organic Power and the Swedish Rindi Energy AB, contracted to find the best suited technique for the new district heating plant; the Nakskov Sugar Factory for waste water treatment and the planning of a non-food agro-industrial area supplied by waste water from sugar beet cleaning. These and many other partners reveal relations between Nakskov and companies showing the most relevant expertise to carry out the concept of the Industrial and Environment Park.

Cooperation with local neighbouring municipalities has also taken place. A most specific cooperation is taking place with the neighbouring municipality of Rudbjerg on joint planning for the extension of the Nakskov Industry and Environment Park. Thirteen municipalities in the area have jointly formulated a development strategy. This cooperation, introducing a division of labour between the cities, resembles principles of polycentricity.

Nakskov's development strategy has focused upon revitalisation of the city on its own rather than regional competencies and assets. The analysis of the outside world has focused on the potentials for establishing a gateway position towards Eastern-Europe. Criteria for selection of key partners have been related to core competencies needed for specific projects. Thus, locally or regionally based polycentric partnerships have been given a low priority as compared to project relations and relations towards Eastern-Europe. The latter is further emphasised by the efforts to establish "Baltic Sea Solution", a cooperation of small- and medium-sized cities on out- and in-sourcing in the Baltic Sea Region. The purpose of the cooperation is to direct in-sourcing of companies and subsidiaries to the small and medium-sized cities rather than the regional and national capitals.

In the self-sustaining region

The city of Herning and its neighbour Ikast are situated in the centre of the Danish textile district. The two cities, with 58,500 and 23,000 inhabitants, respectively, are separated by just 3 km of rural land. The proximity was decisive for the decision in the early 1990s to start planning a linear city connection between the two cities. Thus, rather than building upon polycentricity, the idea was to merge the two cities at least physically into one city. An outcome of this planning strategy is the land use reservation of an industrial area "HI-Park" on either side of the municipal border. Accidentally, it happened to take place at the very moment of the opening of the borders between Eastern and Western Europe, the event that made possible the outsourcing of the Danish textile industry to Poland and Lithuania. In a few years, Herning and Ikast lost most of the manual jobs within the textile sector.

The idea of polycentricity, however, has played an explicit role in the region. In 2000, the Danish government for the first time appointed local networks of cities jointly as "national centres", the concept signifying the second highest ranking in the national urban hierarchy. Thus, Herning, Ikast and two other cities were jointly appointed as the national centre "Mid-West". The city network has acted as a powerful lobby towards the government on *e.g.* financing new motorways. Also, the network has shown potentials for achieving the critical mass needed for organising new regional institutions and projects, within the culture sector. However, the cities still operate individually. Thus, none of them have taken the opportunity to merge during the ongoing administrative and political reform where 275 municipalities have been amalgamated into 98 municipalities. If polycentricity was a core issue, one might expect that municipalities closest to each other would merge. However, Herning and Ikast did not merge, nor did Holstebro and Struer.

In spite of the outsourcing of the manual jobs within the textile industry, Herning and Ikast have succeeded in expanding the textile economy. This is due to a successful transformation of the former production companies into trading companies by upgrading competencies to higher levels in the value chain of production, such as branding, design, export, management and control.

A key instrument for modernising the textile industry was the provision of knowledge related to the economic base. The institutions facilitating this process are situated in the new Birk Centerpark, a cluster of new business institutions, schools and knowledge centres framed physically in high quality architecture and art. Two schools and four knowledge centres are specifically related to the local business milieu.

The Birk Centerpark is a showcase of two kinds of networking: local and professional. The local networking is focused upon joining local common interests in order to obtain a critical mass that could gain lobbying power against high level actors such as the national government. The professional networking is a result of cooperation among the most competent players in the field and reflects the need for institutional excellence. Local networking between business companies and local authorities was decisive for the establishment of most institutions of the Birk Centerpark, whereas professional networking has been crucial for the standard and further development of several institutions. As an example, the local business and engineering school, HIBAT, was formed in a merger of two local schools. But it was further developed in cooperation with the Copenhagen Business School and has now merged with the University of Århus.

In the metropolitan region

Nyköping, a town of about 50,000 inhabitants situated 100 km south of Stockholm was once one the largest industrial cities in Sweden. Deindustrialisation began early in the city and today most of the industrial companies are gone. So is the military airport, which was closed in 1980. But the city was not left without opportunities. The proximity to Stockholm was an important lever for the conversion of the former military airport into a commercial airport and for integration into the greater Stockholm labour and housing market.

Facing these drastic changes, Nyköping began forming its own development strategy, according to which it was decided fully to exploit the options of becoming a residential city in the archipelago of the Stockholm region and to make use of the logistic potentials given by the combined proximity to national main roads and rails, a deep harbour at the shore of the Baltic Sea and the new commercial airport in Skavsta. Thus it became a vision to develop Nyköping as an attractive living environment and as a logistic hub. Several concrete projects were planned and organised: Branding and housing campaigns, new housing areas close to the sea shore and the city centre, education facilities, a sports and event centre and strategic plans for developing the infrastructure projects.

The visions for the development of Nyköping are very much a product of the city government. However, the implementation is carried out in close cooperation with a number of authorities and agents. A brief overview reveals a variety of networking geographies, each of which is logically suited to the strategies and projects in question. At a very general level, Nyköping has cooperation arrangements with 48 municipalities and 5 counties for developing and promoting the Stockholm-Mälardal region. The strategy of developing Nyköping as a logistical hub involves at least four different networks. In cooperation with 34 municipalities, cities and counties from Stockholm and Gothenburg via Ellsinore and Copenhagen to Hamburg, Nyköping is lobbying for the high-speed connection "Europe Corridor" to the central part of Europe. A local part of the Europe Corridor is crucial for improving commuting between Nyköping and Stockholm. The five municipalities and two counties involved have formed a jointly owned company to promote this part of the rail connection, called Östlänken. The most local elements of the hub strategy are carried out by ONYX, an organisation formed by Nyköping and the neighbouring municipality, Oxelösund. ONYX hosts one of the cornerstones in the hub-concept, an ice free harbour with direct connection to the Baltic Sea. Finally, the conversion of the former military airfield into Stockholm-Skavsta airport involved cooperation with the national building agency, a major engineering company and a British real estate firm. The potential for marketing Nyköping in a wider European context is being exploited in cooperation with Ryan Air and with those European cities linked by Ryan Air's direct connections.

The composition of partners may be illustrated by focusing on the education sector. In the middle of Nyköping, a "house of knowledge" hosts a number of nonacademic training centres within electronics, nursing, logistics, management, law and business economy. Co-operation is taking place between these centers and universities and high schools from Stockholm and a number of regional capitals, including Linköping, Gävle, Trollhjättan and Örebro. This way of establishing "knowledge corridors" between the medium-sized city and the universities bears great resemblance to the corridors established at the HIBAT school in Herning.

In this metropolitan region, the variety of urban policies generates partner networks in different geographical settings, from the international Ryan Air cities network to the local Nyköping-Oxelösund network. Thus, policy fulfilment seems to be main driver of networking rather than a search for synergies based upon local urban complementarities.

A typology

The missing link in most empirical studies of polycentricity is the relational dimension. Due to lack of data, most empirical studies are restricted to the morphological aspects. In this empirically-based study, we have tried to exploit the geography of the networks established by medium-sized cities facing urban restructuring. The study is a result of three years' cooperation among 17 cities, three of which were chosen as case studies focusing on networking activities. What the study lacks in statistical validity is compensated by qualitative observations showing that polycentricity follows the logic of policies, which only coincidently coincide with the logic of space. When policies are dictated by requirements of professional excellence, cities transcend their geographical boundaries and search out the most competent partners, a process we may characterise as tentacular networking. The logic of space is at stake when neighbouring cities jointly strengthen local urban tissues in order to reach thresholds and critical mass for lobbying, institution building and local promotion. The tissue- and tentacle-developing networks may coincide, but they rarely do.

Another conclusion is that the different geographical positions of the cities seem to call for different kinds of networking *(Table I)*. In the peripheral regions, the impacts of deindustrialisation are specific and concrete. The scope for change is restricted, as are the options for changing role and identity. Cities are cooperating with professional agents on specific projects, rather than on long term strategies. Cities situated in self-sustaining regions with a solid economic base are usually focused upon sustaining the economic base and competencies of the region. The strategy is to modernise their economy and hence, to clarify the essential features of the role and identity of the city. Cities situated in such regions may be inclined to strengthen regional tissue-developing networks, and hence, to exploit regional polycentric potentials in order to build a stronger regional identity. At the same time, these cities are deeply involved in sustaining the local economic bases by establishing specialised professional tentacular networks.

Finally, the scope of action for cities in the metropolitan regions seems to be more open than in the above-mentioned regions due to the fact that the expanding metropolitan labour and housing markets have created possibilities for these cities to change their role from centres of their own to "metropolitan suburbs". To these cities, joint networking with neighbouring cities is focused mainly upon metropolitan infrastructure, whereas strategies for changing the urban identity are core strategies of the city themselves.

Table I. *A regional typology of strategies for urban restructuring.*

Position of the city	Scope of action	Role and identity	Strategies and polycentricities
Metropolitan region	Optional	Changing	"Suburbanisation" Strategy-oriented "polycentricities"
Independent region	Focused	Clarifying	Modernising economy Economy-oriented "polycentricity"
Peripheral region	Restricted	Reniewing	Restoring impacts of change Project-oriented "polycentricities"

Conclusion

This article has argued that ideo-centricity characterised the mainstream understanding of polycentricity and that this ideo-centricity stems from the priority given to the territorial understanding of the concept. With a background in case studies of several medium-sized cities, three of which are highlighted in this article, we have approached polycentricity in the perspective of the city in its capacity as a strategic agent, and we have argued that networking based upon professional, institutional and political competencies is usually more relevant in urban strategies than networking based upon territorial proximity. Cities simply need more than morphological polycentricity to cope with urban transition.

REFERENCES

1. Brenner N. Urban governance and the production of new state spaces in western Europe, 1960-2000. *Review of International Political Economy* 2004; 11: 447-88.

2. CPMR. *Study on the construction of a polycentric and balanced development model for the european territory.* Conference of Peripheral Maritime Regions of Europe, 2003.

3. Davoudi S. Polycentricity in European Spatial Planning: From an Analytical Tool to a Normative Agenda. *European Planning Studies* 2003; 11: 979-99.

4. Faludi A. Polycentric Territorial Cohesion Policy. *Town and Country Planning*, TPR, 2005; 76: 107-18.

5. Forssberg G. *Interview 04 Nov. 2004.* MECIBS project, 2003.

6. Groth NB, et al. *Restructuring of Medium sized Cities – Lessons from the Baltic Sea Region.* Frederiksberg: Danish Centre for Forest, Landscape and Planning, KVL, 2005.

7. Hague C, Kirk K. *Polycentricity Scoping Study.* Edingburg: School of the Built Environment, Heriot-Watt University, 2003.

8. Hubbard P, Hall T. The Entrepreneurial City and the New Urban Politics. In *The Entrepreneurial City.* Hall T, et al. (Eds). Wiley & sons, 1998: 1-23.

9. Jensen OB, Richardson T. Being on the Map: The new Iconographies of Power over European Space. *International Planning Studies* 2003; 8: 9-34.

10. Nordregio. *ESPON 1.1.1: Potentials for Polycentric development in Europe.* Stockholm: Nordregio, 2004, rev. 2005.

11. Romein A. *Spatial planning in competitive polycentric urban regions: some practical lessons from Northwest Europe.* Chicago: Paper submitted to City Futures Conference, 8-10 July 2004.

12. Turok I, Bailey N. The Theory of Polynuclear Urban Regions and its Application to Central Scotland. *European Planning Studies* 2004; 12: 371-89.

Polycentricity, equity and competitiveness: The Dutch case

Wil Zonneveld, Bas Waterhout
Delft University of Technology, OTB Research Institute, The Netherlands

Over the years the concept of polycentric urban development has appeared in many disguises in the literature [2]. During the 1990s the concept also appeared in political discussions on the development of the EU territory. The concept became widely known through the European Spatial Development Perspective (ESDP) of 1999, prepared and adopted by the (then 15) Member States of the European Union and the European Commission [1]. Very briefly the concept states that economic prosperity and good economic performance should not be limited to a relatively small part of the European territory, often referred to as the pentagon, defined by the cities London, Paris, Milan, Munich and Hamburg. Other areas within the European Union, albeit at a smaller scale, should also become economically competitive at the European and global level [11]. As such the "makers" of the concept – which is currently known by its short version: polycentricity – have tried to strike a balance between competitiveness and cohesion. In the process of making the ESDP competitiveness was interpreted as pointing to those areas and places which economically perform at the highest level. Cohesion was interpreted as the struggle for equal economic opportunities and welfare across the European territory. Competitiveness was identified with the concept of a core area, cohesion with the periphery [15].

The makers of the ESDP tried to avoid identifying which areas outside the pentagon could form Europe's polycentric structure. Politically this is a highly sensitive issue because identifying areas often means selecting cities and regions which are eligible for certain policy measures. Territorial designation also means the branding of spaces which is also a highly sensitive issue even when there are no strings attached. The appearance of a city or a region on a political map always means the attachment of a kind of label, either positive or negative.

This is proven by the Dutch case. Here traditional regional policy focussing on backward regions has been traded in for a new spatial-economic policy aiming at strengthening the Dutch spatial economic main structure and therewith trying to contribute to the overall competitiveness of the country. Although the term polycentricity has not been used in this policy turnaround, the role of cities and urban regions were at the centre of political discussions. Compared with all other EU member states [10, 17], in our view there is no other country where recent political events have led to such a strong emphasis on the competitive potential of urban regions and the dropping of the policy objective of territorial cohesion. The aim of this contribution is to unravel the policy changes in the Netherlands. In doing this we in particular emphasise the political sensitivities in interpreting and reinterpreting the concept of polycentricity. The following section discusses the late 1980s/early 1990s when the issue of competitiveness was gaining weight in Dutch spatial-economic policies to the detriment of distribution and cohesion. The section thereafter discusses the introduction of a new policy concept, breaking away from the idea of cities on their own and instead emphasising the regional dimension of urban and economic development. This section is followed by a section focussing on the latest changes in Dutch national-economic policy, getting rid of the last remnants of cohesive thinking.

THE EMERGENCE OF A COMPETITIVENESS DISCOURSE IN DUTCH SPATIAL ECONOMIC POLICIES

Like in so many other Western European countries the Dutch post-war welfare state had a territorial dimension: to change the distribution of the population and the economy over the country. Regional policy was directed at the integration of weak regions into the national economy and at equal opportunities for people living in different parts of the country. The main instruments were subsidies for companies to relocate and government investments in the general business environment: infrastructure but also the soft sector of education. Budgets mounted to hundreds of millions of guilders per year in the seventies. During the 1960s and 1970s an extensive programme to relocate central government back offices from the seat of government (The Hague) to other parts of the country was also carried out. The emphasis was put on areas outside the economic core area of the country and in particular on the north of the country.

During the early 1980s national government started to revise this cohesion policy which was sparked off by a deep economic recession following the oil crisis. Cities, in particular in the west of the country, were badly hit by unemployment. The government also wanted to bring down budget deficits so national policy had to become "cheaper". The 1983 Structure Sketch for the Urban Areas introduced the new approach. The new credo was that in future optimal use would be made of the economic potential of the Randstad, being the core area of the country [4]. Other regions had to exploit their own potential without relying on dispersal policies pursued by national government. With a proper sense of the power of rhetoric this was called "Regions on their own" *(Regio's op eigen kracht)*.

These developments appeared to be particularly influential when, in 1988, government published the Fourth Report on Spatial Planning. Previously such national reports had focussed almost exclusively on urbanisation policies and above all on the various ways to reach urban containment. By restricting urban development national spatial policy was becoming accused of being one of the causes of the economic downturn the country was facing during the 1980s. The higher echelons of the department responsible for designing national spatial policy, together with the minister, decided that this policy should become more focussed on the issue of economic development instead of urban development, in order to remain politically relevant. So the new 1988 report coined the term "spatial-economic main structure", referring to those areas, urban regions and transport axes playing the most important role when it comes to the competitive position of the country as a whole.

An important role in this spatial-economic main structure is played by so-called urban nodes: a limited number of cities selected to play an important role in the expected increase in competition between countries and regions in Europe. Central government should be strengthening the position of these urban nodes by concentrating investments in, for instance, education, culture and accessibility, in these nodes. Initially nine such urban nodes were distinguished. Several more "objective" criteria were used for the selection of these nodes, like service level, external accessibility and economic structure. Also a more fluid criterion was used, opening the way for fierce political debates on the selection of urban nodes (see below) in terms of their distribution over the country. Although the issue of economic competitiveness was crucial in the selection of urban nodes, this also meant that some sort of cohesion or equity principle was in force. One can interpret the pattern of urban nodes as polycentric, a term not used but implicitly present.

The concept of the urban nodes seemed to steal the limelight [4]. There was a general feeling that a considerable transfer of funds would accompany the urban node concept. The label "urban node" was also considered to have marketing value, nationally and internationally. So, whilst being supported by "their" provincial government and other parties (like chambers of commerce), several municipalities who were not selected fought heavily together with members of Parliament to acquire this promising label.

Critics of the new policy approach emphasised in particular that only one city in the north of the country was selected, while this part of the country was traditionally the focus of regional policy. Also the southern part of the country was passed over. Whilst for several decades the Randstad was said to form the economic core of the country, the makers of the Fourth Report concluded that throughout the years the economic core had been extended and now also encompassed areas in the middle and the south of the Netherlands. Planners called this area the Central Netherlands Urban Ring [3]. It is a somewhat misleading spatial concept due to the use of the ring metaphor, whereas in fact the area is not one continuous urban zone (like this metaphor suggests) but more an urban network. The ministry of Economic Affairs, at that time still responsible for regional-economic policies and feeling threatened by the economic turn spatial planning was taken, claimed that it was more of a network than a ring, and proposed the concept of a Central Economic Network [14].

The difference between a "Ring" and a "Network" is more than a mere linguistic difference. The opposing views of the ministry of Economic Affairs and the ministry for Housing, Spatial Planning and the Environment are more of a fundamental nature. The main objection of the ministry of Economic Affairs was that the new spatial policy was far too selective about those areas and cities having the strongest competitive position internationally. Market forces would determine this, not central government. And thus, according to Economic Affairs, there was absolutely no reason to designate urban nodes or to select just the western part of the Randstad (Amsterdam, the Hague and Rotterdam, including the main port of Rotterdam and Schiphol Airport) as the most competitive region of the country, the core of the core (Central Netherlands Urban Ring) so to speak.

According to the legal procedures surrounding central government reports on spatial planning, Parliament has the final word on their content. It did accept the concept of urban nodes but also decided there should be thirteen of them instead of the original nine, thus changing the level of polycentricity! Thirteen instead of nine urban nodes was more than the government had anticipated. The principle of selectivity, however, was maintained by dividing the urban nodes into several categories with, of course, corresponding budgets (see the smaller circles in *Figure 1*). The four additional cities form the category of so called regional urban nodes, which is just a different way of saying that they are of lesser importance *(Figure 1)*.

Whereas spatial planning is a well established policy domain in the Netherlands, it nevertheless strongly depends on policy instruments in the control of sectoral departments. And it is here where it all went wrong with the concept of urban nodes. The urban node did not exactly "program" government investments in the subsequent years. Spending departments

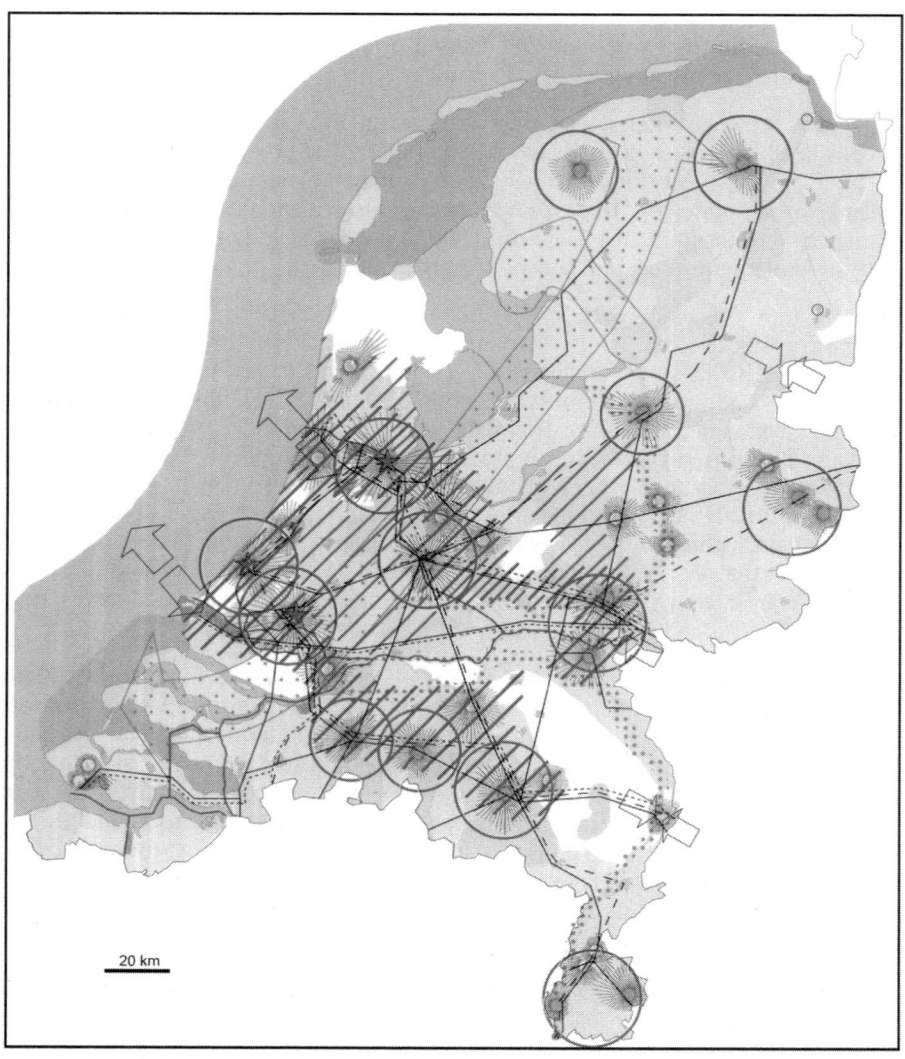

Source : MVROM 1993

Figure 1. *The thirteen "urban nodes" as decided by parliament.*

still followed their own investment rationales. During the second half of the 1990s the urban node concept became entirely obsolete. With hindsight its most important function is seen as making local government aware of the competitive edge of cities and regions [13]. Williams (1996) calls this spatial positioning: the capacity to conceptualize or think about one's location or situation within the spatial structure of a large area. The question is, though, whether this by itself made a concept like urban node necessary.

FROM NODES TO A VAST SYSTEM OF URBAN NETWORKS

In 1998, after prolonged political and professional debates on the necessity of a new national spatial planning policy the government then in power, a centre-left government, started a so-called key decision procedure [16, 4] which ultimately should have produced a new report on spatial planning, the fifth since 1960. The government did indeed publish a first version of this Fifth Report in 2001. It comprised a new interpretation of the Dutch urban system, a national network made up of urban networks at the sub-national (the Randstad, renamed as Deltametropolis) and regional level. Concepts like the urban node and the Central Netherlands Urban Ring were dropped. This course of events suggests that spatial structures can be interpreted in different ways irrespective of the political viewpoint.

The concept of urban networks meant the return of polycentricity in the thinking and policies on spatial planning for urban areas. The new element, which marked the Fifth Report as a watershed in nearly three decades of national urban policy, was that, from now on, the entire territory of the network city would form the search area for new urban developments. The watchword was no longer "concentric" urbanization (the "centre" located in individual cities). Moreover, the urban network as a whole – rather than the individual cities – would be self-sufficient in terms of urban functions.

The concept of the urban network is not just a policy concept on urbanisation though. Urban networks are also expected to play a major role when it comes to the competitive position of the Netherlands as a whole. Six so-called national urban networks are considered particularly important. Eight "regional" urban networks are also identified, with the possibility of an even larger number in the future. More or less the same mechanism worked here as in the case of urban nodes about a decade earlier. The promise of government funds and grants stimulated lower levels of government to lobby for their appearance on the policy maps of the Fifth Report, with some results. The course of events meant that the polycentricity concept is now being deployed at two spatial levels: the national level, where the competitive edge of the country is the main issue, and the regional level, where local governments are expected to flesh out future urbanisation policies through co-operation, which, if successful, will be financially rewarded by national government. The Fifth Report strikes a delicate balance between competitiveness and cohesion. The policy map of the report is speckled with urban networks. Almost 65 cities are recognised as being part of a regional, national or international urban network *(Figure 2)*. Several town councils supported by their provincial councils fought hard to be recognised in this way. The budget they could expect from these territorial designations was not particularly big, especially in the case of regional networks. The important issue here is "being on the map" [5].

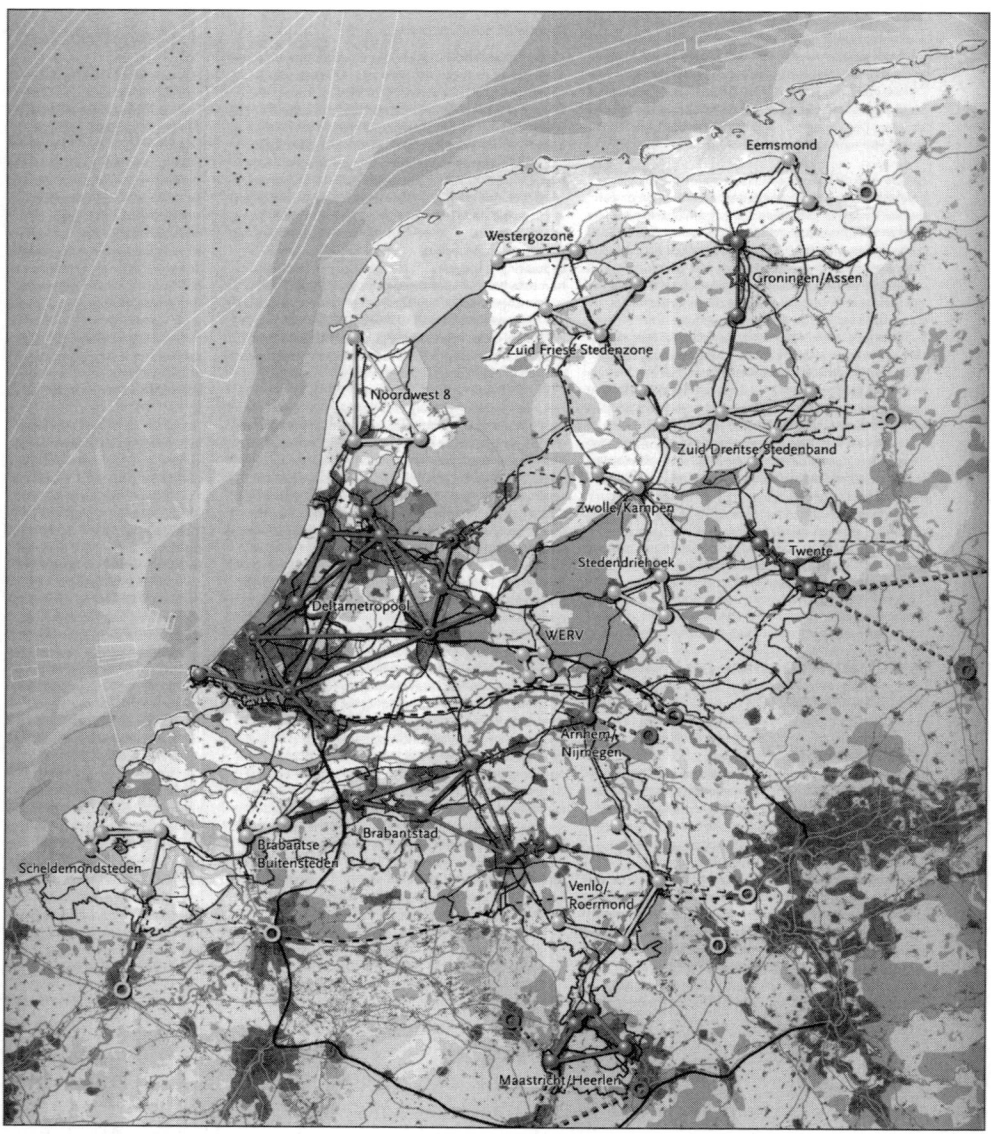

Source : MVROM 2002

Figure 2. *An intricate pattern of urban networks identified in a draft government policy report on spatial planning.*

COMPETITIVENESS AT THE TOP OF THE AGENDA

April 2002 saw the collapse of the centre-left coalition government responsible for the Fifth Report. The new, centre-right government, which took over in the same year, appeared to be pursuing a new "philosophy of governance"; it had a different vision of its role in relation to the provinces and municipalities and envisaged "fewer rules and regulations dictated by central government, more scope for local and regional considerations, more development planning and less development control" as one can read in the National Spatial Strategy issued March 2004 [6]. It is particularly protective of the so-called "national spatial structure", a system of networks and regions which is regarded as nationally important and which would form the main focus of government investment (ibid: 6). In Dutch the new integrated policy document still carried the word "Report" in its title ("Nota Ruimte"), but the English title better reflects its real ambitions: "National Spatial Strategy". While a report is basically a pile of paper, strategy has the connotations of things happening. Also the subtitle of the new policy document is meaningful: "Creating Space for Development", development here clearly meaning economic development. Compared with the Fifth Report this means far less emphasis on spatial quality and a far less restrictive attitudes to where urban development is allowed to take place, the latter being the hallmark of national spatial planning of the 1990s.

In terms of the espoused spatial-economic doctrine two matters are particular striking. In contrast with the Fourth Report this time Economic Affairs was certainly not ill-disposed towards territorial designations. As the reader will remember, about fifteen years previously the department had heavily resisted spatial planning approaches being selective about areas and cities having the strongest competitive position internationally. Market forces would determine this, not government. In 2004, though, a whole string of policy concepts and territorial designations were committed to paper. The second striking event is that the present government wants to shake off the last remnants of cohesion policies. Let us now look at these two issues, which are not unrelated: the new policy designations were "needed" to get rid off the classical spatial thinking directed at stimulating economic development in weaker regions.

The six national urban networks, as identified in the Fifth Report, survived in the National Spatial Strategy. The National Spatial Strategy partly adopts the approach of the preceding Fifth Policy Document and partly rejects it. For example, it neatly adopts the definition of urban networks from the Fifth Policy Document. However, the Strategy refuses to outline the composition of each of the six urban networks it identifies (*i.e.* the cities belonging to a network). This clearly reflects the governance philosophy embraced by the Strategy, that central government wants to take a step backwards in favour of allowing the local authorities, and in particular the provinces, to play a key role. This means that national policy should not be strict on the composition of urban networks. The maps bear this out. All that we see is a rough indication of the location and the boundaries (see the shaded patches in *Figure 3*). In the same way the idea of regional urban networks is dropped. It is not up to national government to identify such networks. If lower levels of government want to coordinate policies within such networks they are happily invited to do so but national government does not play a role here.

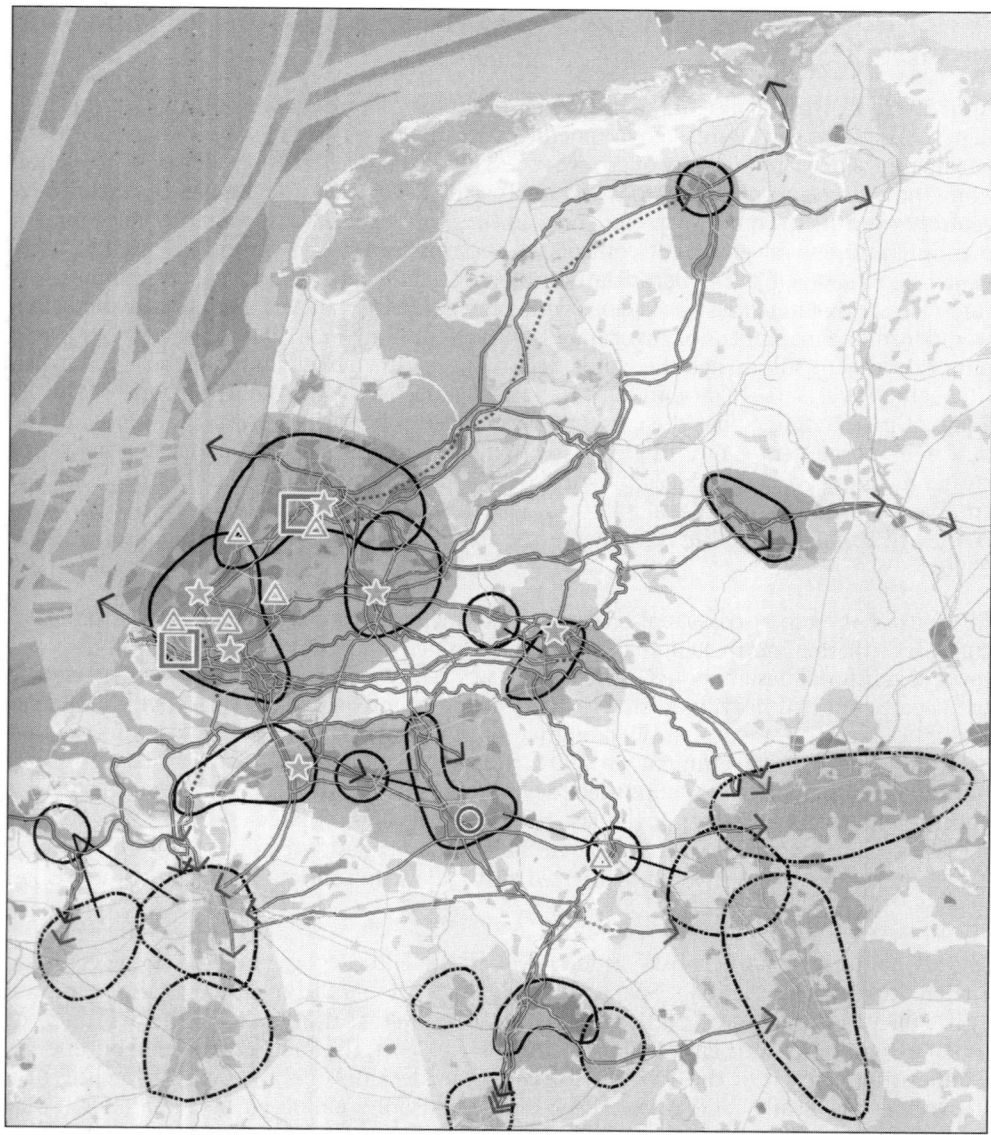

Source : MVROM 2006

Figure 3. *Urban networks and economic core areas forming a cornerstone of the current National Spatial Strategy.*

The makers of the Spatial Strategy deemed it necessary, however, to coin a second urban concept: the economic core areas, thirteen in total (see the outlined circles in *Figure 3*). Again, extensive lobbying went on by local governments feeling passed over. As a result the medium-sized cities of Zwolle and Leeuwarden (both located in the North of the country) were awarded some sort of policy label. However, the lobby appeared only partly successful. While these two cities get the same financial treatment as some of the recognised urban networks they will not be featured on any map! Obviously, the government primarily focuses on those areas with the highest potential and highest chance of value for money. That such an approach can lead to a certain degree of polarization does not frighten the government. In fact, it explicitly argues the need for selectivity and concentration in order to sort out effects. Interestingly, in Spring 2006 the Dutch government and the European Commission were quarrelling over the question of where to spend the Structural Funds, with the government in favour of the regions designated as economic core areas and the Commission arguing for the weakest regions even if a relatively small proportion of the country's population is living there. This is certainly interesting, seen from the perspective of interpreting broad principles like competitiveness and cohesion.

Clearly, with the present government a new phase of spatial economic thinking has been introduced. Efficiency and effectiveness, or in other words, value for money, are the key words now. Never has there been a government that so consistently dares to advocate a territorial competitiveness discourse and therewith a concentration of efforts and investments in the Randstad in order to keep this region on an even keel with international metropolitan regions. The spatial allocation of the budget of the Ministry of Housing, Spatial Planning and Environment gives a clear indication of this. Of the total budget of 6,504.3 million euro of this ministry for the period 2000-10, 71% (4,619.5 million euro) will be spent on projects in Randstad cities and towns[1]. The four Northern provinces, Friesland, Groningen, Drenthe and Overijssel, where 17.2% of the population live, will receive 7.8% or 506.1 million euro. Note that some of the ministries, like Transport & Water and Management, Interior and Economic Affairs, have larger budgets and also spend according to the principles outlined above.

Conclusion

Fostering economic development in certain regions and certain places always goes hand in hand with some sort of territorial selectivity. This is true for the early phases of Dutch regional policy, characterised by the support given to the economic development of economically weaker (employment, welfare) regions and industrialisation centres located within these regions. This is also true for the current phase in Dutch regional-economic policy, focussing on the economically strongest regions of the country. Whatever the prime goals of policy – competitiveness or cohesion – the level of selectivity has come under attack. The result was always that the original level of territorial selectivity proposed by national government weakened when it came to the definite drafting of policy. In relation to the present period this is quite surprising given the territorially rather balanced pattern of economic development and given the fact that currently the budgets for regional-economic support are rather small. The whole debate about prolonging the support to the North of the country turned around an annual budget of roughly 60 million euros, a fraction of private investments in the area. So in a fairly polycentric and egalitarian country as the Netherlands even relatively small budgetary shifts in government spending cause political turmoil.

---

1. Own calculations based on figures on: www.vrom.nl (*"investeringskaart"*)

The Dutch case also shows the often weak empirical base of such policy. The concept of urban nodes put forward in the 1988 Fourth Report presumes that a limited number of cities form the driving force of Dutch national economic development. Moreover, the concept of the urban node only focussed on just the central city of an urban region whilst ignoring the regional dimension of economic development. More recently the empirical base of some of the current spatial concepts came under attack by research carried out by the National Institute of Spatial Research. The claim is that spatial-economic development shows highly complicated patterns that contradict the fairly simple policy concepts like economic core areas. An important conclusion to be drawn here is that the use of a notion like main spatial-economic structure, which forms a pillar under the current Dutch National Spatial Strategy, is risky. It forces the identification of fairly simple spatial categories that are not necessarily in line with actual spatial patterns and processes. If the empirical foundations of policies are questionable it is difficult to imagine that these policies can be effective.

References

1. Committee on Spatial Development (CSD). *European Spatial Development Perspective: Towards Balanced and Sustainable Development of the Territory of the EU*. Luxembourg: Office for Official Publications of the European Communities, 1999.

2. Davoudi S. Polycentricity in European spatial planning: From an analytical tool to a nvormative agenda? *European Planning Studies* 2003; vol. 11, n° 8: 979-99.

3. Duinen L. van. *Planning Imagery: The Emergence and Development of New Planning Concepts in Dutch National Spatial Policy*. Amsterdam: PhD, University of Amsterdam, 2004.

4. Faludi A, Van der Valk A. *Rule and Order: Dutch Planning Doctrine in the Twentieth Century*. Dordrecht/Boston/London: Kluwer Academic Publishers, 1994.

5. Jensen OB, Richardson T. Being on the Map: The New Iconographies of Power over European Space. *International Planning Studies* 2003; vol. 8, n° 1: 9-34.

6. Ministry of Housing, Spatial Planning and Environment (MHSPE). *National Spatial Strategy – Creating Space for Development* (Summary). The Hague: MHSPE, 2004.

7. Ministerie van Volkshuisvesting, Ruimtelijke Ordening en Milieubeheer (MVROM) [Ministry of Housing, Spatial Planning and the Environment]. *Vierde Nota over de Ruimtelijke Ordening Extra; Deel 4: planologische kernbeslissing nationaal ruimtelijk beleid [Fourth Report on Spatial Planning Extra; Part 4: Spatial planning key decision]*. Den Haag: Sdu Uitgevers, 1993.

8. MVROM. *Ruimte maken, ruimte delen, Vijfde Nota Ruimtelijke Ordening; Deel 3: Kabinetsstandpunt [Fifth Policy Document on Spatial Planning; Part 3: Governmental Decision]*. Den Haag: MVROM, 2002.

9. MVROM et al. *Nota Ruimte: Ruimte voor ontwikkeling; Part 4: tekst na parlementaire instemming [National Spatial Strategy: Creating space for development; Part 4: Final text after parliamentary consent]*. Den Haag: MVROM, 2006.

10. Nordregio et al. *ESPON 1.1.1: Potentials for polycentric development in Europe; Project report*. Stockholm/Luxembourg: Nordregio/ESPON Monitoring Committee, 2004.

11. Waterhout B. Polycentric Development: What Is Behind It? In *European Spatial Planning*. Faludi A (Ed). Cambridge Mass.: Lincoln Institute of Land Policy, 2002: 83-103.

12. Williams RH. *European Union Spatial Policy and Planning*. London: Paul Chapman Publishing, 1996.

13. Zoete PR. *Stedelijke knooppunten: virtueel beleid voor een virtuele werkelijkheid? Een verkenning van de plaats van indicatief rijksbeleid in de wereld van gemeenten*. Amsterdam: Thesis Publishers, 1997.

14. Zonneveld W. Naar een beter gebruik van ruimtelijke planconcepten. *Planologische Verkenningen* 64, Amsterdam: Planologisch Demografisch Instituut Universiteit van Amsterdam, 1992.

15. Zonneveld W. Discoursive Aspects of Strategic Planning: A Deconstruction of the 'Balanced Competitiveness' Concept in European Spatial Planning. In *The Revival of Strategic Spatial Planning*. Salet W, Faludi A (Eds). Amsterdam: Royal Netherlands Academy of Arts and Sciences, 2000: 267-80.

16. Zonneveld W. In search of conceptual modernization: The new Dutch 'national spatial strategy'. *Journal of Housing and the Built Environment* 2005; vol. 20: 425-43.

17. Zonneveld W, Meijers E, Waterhout B (Eds). Polycentric Development Policies across Europe. *Built Environment* 2005; vol. 31, n° 2: 97-173.

Brussels: Polycentricity as "images on the map", not in reality

Mathieu Van Criekingen*, Pierre Cornut**, Sarah Luyten***

* Free University Brussels (ULB), Fonds National de la Recherche Scientifique (FNRS), Human Geography Laboratory
** Free University Brussels (ULB), Institute for Environmental Management and Territorial Planning
*** Katholieke Universiteit Leuven, Social and Economic Geography, Belgium

Until the 1990s, the concept of polycentricity has been thought as an analytical tool to explore changing metropolitan or regional patterns of settlements. It has been notably used to describe changing intraurban geographies of economic activities that significantly alter the relevance of the classic monocentric model of metropolitan organisation. At this scale, polycentricity refers to the growth of a series of clusters of economic activities composing new sub-centres within metropolitan areas. These new urban forms have received particular attention in the US context under the "edge city" header [5][1]. Moreover, polycentricity has been applied to the inter-urban scale to refer to regional settings wherein neighbouring but historically and politically distinct cities have developed significant functional interconnections between them [8]. In Europe, the Randstad (Amsterdam – Rotterdam – The Hague – Utrecht), the Rhine-Rhur region (Bonn – Köln – Düsseldorf – Essen – Dortmund) and the Flemish Diamond (Brussels – Ghent – Antwerp – Leuven) are very frequently mentioned examples of such (alleged) "polycentric urban regions".

Today, polycentricity has become central to debates on spatial planning and regional policies in Europe. As Davoudi (2003 and chapter in this book) has argued, a fundamental shift has occurred in the last fifteen years with the emergence of a normative approach to polycentricity, that is, the concept is now widely used as a guiding principle for European spatial planning. The preparation and adoption of the European Spatial Development Perspective (ESDP) have played a key role in this shift. Implementing polycentricity in planning measures and policy actions is assumed throughout this document to be highly beneficial in economic, social and environmental terms at multiple geographic scales, from the regional one to the EU level [13].

In this new context, attempts by planners to design a polycentric image for a metropolitan area or a region are more and more common. It is therefore important, from an analytical point of view, to cautiously (re-) compare alleged polycentric structures designed in planning and policy documents to the actual degree of functional integration between the multiple centres. As some recent works on polycentric urban regions in Europe have indicated [1, 10],

---

1. See Philippe *et al.* (1999) for an analysis in Europe.

polycentricity as a "geographical image on the map" [9] should not be automatically conceived as reflecting the actual existence of strong functional ties between multiple centres.

In this contribution, we will consider the actual relevance of the concept of polycentricity as a morphological and functional reality in the case of Brussels. Two geographic scales will be analysed successively. First, at the inter-urban scale, Brussels is often considered today as part of two polycentric urban regions, that are, the "Flemish Diamond" and the "Walloon Triangle". Both these regional planning visions endorse broader goals of developing diverse network city arrangements as favoured frameworks for meeting the requirements of the informational economy, while avoiding diseconomies of large (monocentric) agglomerations and related environmental or social problems. However, many contributions to the literature are quite sceptical about the reality of the functional interconnections between cities in such alleged polycentric urban regions [1, 10].

Second, at the intraurban scale, it is necessary to assess the extent to which recent suburban developments in Brussels are signs of an emerging polycentric agglomeration. Decentralization of service activities in European agglomerations, and the development of diverse out-of-core (sub-) centres are now well-documented trends [12]. However, while many urban governments endorse the development of such decentralized centres in order to control and structure suburbanization, such coordinated planning strategies are very much hindered in politically fragmented metropolitan areas.

Both the inter-urban (or regional) and intraurban (or metropolitan) scales are of particular importance as far as the governance of Brussels is concerned since they both imply dealing with a fragmented political context. Since 1989, Brussels is a federated region on its own within the federal configuration of Belgium, formally named "Brussels Capital Region". Actually, the boundaries of the Brussels Capital Region correspond to the extension of the core city (1 million inhabitants). About 1.4 million inhabitants live in the rest of the metropolitan area (*i.e.* in Flanders or in Wallonia), among whom about 400,000 are daily commuters to the core city (60% of the workforce employed in the Brussels Capital Region). Hence, the existing spatial and functional extension of the metropolitan area is divided between the three regions. This truncation of the Brussels' metropolitan area has been confirmed as a mean of political pacification between the Dutch– and French-speaking communities during the country's federalisation process. Enlarging this territory is now a political taboo for the Flemish majority at national level since it would mean the conversion of a part of Flanders (which still has a significant French-speaking minority in the first-ring of suburban municipalities around Brussels) into an area with an officially bilingual status [7].

THE "FLEMISH DIAMOND" AND THE "WALLOON TRIANGLE": TWO MARKETING PROJECTS?

The concept of polycentricity is now integrated in regional planning documents in Flanders and in Wallonia, with references to Brussels as a core element in both these regional strategies. By contrast, planning strategies of the Brussels-Capital Region, whose territory is limited to the core part of the agglomeration, deal almost exclusively with the internal organisation of the city, without much attention to trans-regional issues. Moreover, there is no national or federal vision of polycentricity in Belgium since spatial planning is an exclusive competence of the regional authorities and there is no political or administrative structure at federal level designed for supra-regional coordination, unlike in some other federal states in Europe (*e.g.* Germany). Therefore, two separate regional polycentric visions cohabit in Belgium, one in Flanders and one in Wallonia, both of them including Brussels. Nevertheless, the concept of polycentric urban region has been interpreted differently by Flemish and Walloon regional authorities [16].

Regional planning policies in Flanders have incorporated the concept of inter-urban polycentricity since the mid-1990s, that is before the adoption of the ESDP. The "Flemish Diamond" (Vlaamse Ruit) is a key element in the "Ruimtelijke Structuurplan Vlaanderen" [11]. Through strong emphasis put on this alleged polycentric urban region formed by Ghent, Antwerp, Leuven and Brussels *(Figure 1)*, planners have shifted from a traditional hierarchical conceptualisation of the regional territory towards a logic of urban network at the regional scale. The objectives of this new planning approach are twofold. First, the regional authorities aim at reconcentrating population and activities in existing urban nodes. In response to the very strong trend towards urban sprawl in Flanders in past decades, regional authorities are now particularly aware of issues such as control of the suburbanisation process and land preservation. Secondly, promotion of polycentricity in Flanders endorses the creation of an integrated urban network that would be a match for a larger metropolitan region able to compete with neighbouring large urban areas such as Paris, London, the Randstad in the Netherlands or the Rhin-Rhur region in Germany.

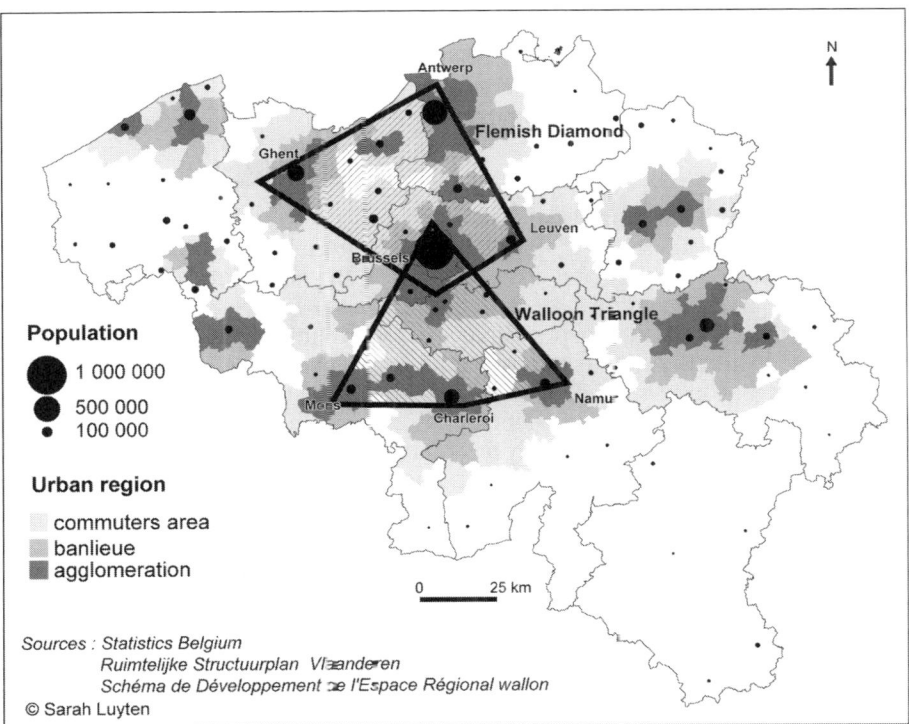

Figure 1. *The Flemish Diamond and the Walloon Triangle*.

However, the extent to which cities in the Flemish Diamond are actually linked to each other through strong economic interconnections and networking practices is a contested issue. While some authors support this assumption, others are quite sceptical about it [1]. For instance, Cabus and Van Haverbeke (2006) have shown that companies in the Flemish Diamond have more interactions with companies located outside the Diamond than with companies within it. Moreover, Vandermotten et al. (2006) have stressed that the labour pools of the four cities in the Flemish Diamond remain largely independent from each other. For these authors, the Flemish Diamond should be merely understood as an "image on the map" with a strong marketing function: what is at stake is to "sell" to international investors a prime geographic location in Europe, in a dense urban environment concentrating a vast array of high-level tertiary functions and close to a first-order international pole (Brussels).

In Wallonia, the integration of the concept of polycentricity in planning practices and documents is more recent, globally weaker and associated with a different signification than in Flanders. Polycentricity is thought here to foster the development of strong links between Walloon cities and agglomerations in neighbouring regions (Brussels) or countries (Germany, The Netherlands, Luxemburg and France) where advanced business services activities are generally more developed. In this way, polycentricity is thought as a way to endorse a post-industrial economic redevelopment for Wallonia, a region severely hit by deindustrialization in the last decades. Accordingly, the main regional spatial planning document (*i.e.* the "Schéma de Développement de l'Espace Régional Wallon" – SDER) is largely structured around the "Eurocoridor" concept, that is, privileged axis of transnational cooperation like *e.g.* Western Hainaut – Lille, Liège – Maastricht – Köln, Arlon – Luxemburg [6]. The SDER has also introduced the concept of the "Wallon Triangle" (Brussels – Mons – Charleroi – Namur) as an area for active inter-regional cooperation *(Figure 1)*.

It is only later, though, that the Walloon government has launched a research project aimed at exploring the actual polycentric character of the Walloon Triangle. The research project showed eventually that the Walloon Triangle does not function as a polycentric network [3]. On the one hand, the area is very heterogeneous, opposing affluent Brussels' residential suburbs in its northern part (*i.e.* Walloon Brabant) and depressed areas in the old industrial Walloon axis in its southern part (in the Hainaut province). Both these parts clearly show opposite figures in terms of economic performances, demography (structures and evolutions) and consumption patterns of their inhabitants. On the other hand, collaborations or cooperation between the poles of the Triangle are scarcely considered – or even desired – by public or private actors interviewed in Brussels and the Walloon cities. Competition and concurrence between municipal, provincial and regional authorities were found largely predominant in daily practices. These elements lend credibility to the idea that the Walloon Triangle has been merely introduced as a response to – or in imitation of – the development of the "Flemish Diamond" concept in Flanders.

In sum, the conceptualization of the Flemish Diamond and the Walloon Triangle in separate regional planning documents seems to correspond first to competing territorial marketing strategies. This reflects the fragmented political context in Belgium, and the absence of any federal vision of polycentricity. However, the actual emergence of cooperative networks between cities in other, less fragmented national contexts in Europe is also far from evident. Often, polycentric interrelationships are more evident between (sub-) centres within urban agglomerations. In the next section, we explore the relevance of polycentricity at the intraurban scale in Brussels.

NEW DEVELOPMENTS IN THE SUBURBS OF BRUSSELS:
SIGNS OF AN EMERGING POLYCENTRIC AGGLOMERATION?

Compared to most European countries, urban sprawl is rife in Belgium. This process is rooted in a long-standing commuting tradition but has been strongly reinforced after the Second World War as the spatial expression of the Fordist economic growth model in a context of loose spatial planning constraints. Suburbanization of middle-class households remains a dominant mode of urbanisation today. However, since the 1980s, a similar trend has also become prominent for service activities. Not only household services activities bounded to local demand (*i.e.* health, education, retail, leisure) or place-consuming activities (*e.g.* logistics) are now suburbanizing, but also business services activities traditionally very concentrated in the core parts of large urban areas. In Brussels, evolutions suggest that a very significant part of the intrinsic growth of the business services sector at the scale of the whole metropolitan area is captured by suburban areas, hence outside the territory of the Brussels Capital Region [15]. As far as the spatial distribution of these service activities is concerned, the dominant pattern is one of concentration on particular spots in the suburbs rather than one of spatial spread *(Figure 2)*. In particular, the Zaventem-airport area, at the intersection of the motorways to Antwerp and to Liège with the Brussels' ring road, is very appealing for a wide range of firms in business services (*e.g.* accountancy, consultancy), transport and communication (*e.g.* ICT firms), high-technology industries or corporate headquarters. Significant developments are also noticeable, although to a lesser extent, in more distant peripheral locations, especially in Leuven and Louvain-la-Neuve. In both these cities, development in business service activities is related to the presence of large universities.

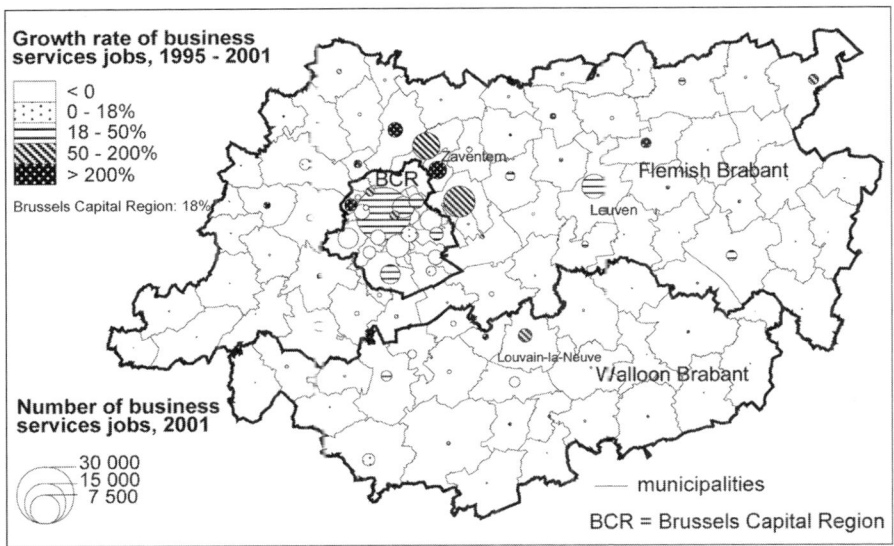

Figure 2. *Suburbanization of business service activities in Brussels.*

Such developments in the Brussels' periphery clearly echo similar trends towards the emergence or consolidation of new concentrations of service activities in the suburbs of large European metropolises. Such trends, however, do not mean that central cities are soon to be abandoned by firms and activities. In Brussels, the central city remains by far the largest concentration of service jobs in the metropolitan area and peaks of land value for office spaces remain located in the CBD [16]. The Brussels Capital Region concentrates today 80% of the total added value produced in the agglomeration. Over the last decades, a wide range of highly specialized activities (*e.g.* lobbies, NGOs, international law or consultancy firms, etc.) have increasingly clustered in the inner city in order to take advantage of direct proximity of influent public institutions, the European Commission most notably, and extended opportunities for face-to-face contacts with EU officials or persons in other specialized firms [14]. The current trend towards suburbanization of some advanced service activities in Brussels should then be better analysed as an expression of the enduring importance of agglomeration economies. For those firms that are not tied to an inner-city location (for reasons of direct proximity with the EU or prestige, for instance), cheaper and up-to-date office spaces in suburban business parks, close to motorways and the airport are very attractive location factors. Inquiries carried out in the framework of the POLYNET research programme report that firms located in Brussels' suburbs (hence on the territory of the Flemish or the Walloon region) consider themselves as being located in Brussels and that these firms are not back-offices or branches of companies whose headquartered in the inner city [16].

In sum, the economic geography of the Brussels' metropolitan area is progressively moving towards a more polycentric form, with new significant concentrations of service activities growing in out-of-core locations. However, this evolution should not be associated with a trend towards the emergence of a functional polycentric structure at the metropolitan scale. Spatial competition – for jobs, activities and population – rather than cooperation between the core (*i.e.* the Brussels Capital Region) and the periphery (in Flanders or Wallonia) are predominant in daily political practices. Coordination efforts at the supra-regional level regarding cross-border issues remain very seldom, single-purposed and very much constrained by Flemish or Walloon political agendas. This context strongly limits the development of any metropolitan-wide urban vision for Brussels.

Conclusion

While polycentric forms can be drawn on maps at both intraurban (metropolitan) and inter-urban (regional) levels, evidence of functional integration between the core city and (sub-) centres in the Brussels' metropolitan area or between Brussels and other cities in the Flemish Diamond or the Walloon Triangle is very scarce. In other words, polycentricity as "geographical images on the map" does not translate today in functional realities, at both scales. On one hand, the emergence of a polycentric configuration in the Brussels' metropolitan area is still a recent and ongoing process. Nevertheless, the concomitant emergence of "polycentric thinking" in planning practices and documents is very much hindered by the political fragmentation of the agglomeration. On the other hand, potential for functional polycentric development at regional level is largely underexploited today, with polycentricity mainly thought of as a territorial marketing tool in both Flanders and Wallonia.

In the context of a politically fragmented metropolitan area such as Brussels, the emergence of a polycentric model of spatial planning could offer the opportunity for local and regional authorities to redefine current modes of governance of the city. Obviously, a host of cross-boundary issues could be more efficiently tackled if more cooperative governance frameworks could be implemented, hence limiting spatial competition between regions (*e.g.* fiscal concurrence). However, given the increasingly tight political context in Belgium, with more and more trans-regional conflicts remaining unsolved, we are pessimistic about the actual possibility to implement cooperative planning strategies. Moreover, the potential efficiency of spatial planning actions in fostering the emergence and consolidation of collaborative functional interrelationships between territories should not be overstated, at least over short-term time periods [4].

REFERENCES

1. Albrechts L. How to proceed from image and discourse to action: as applied to the Flemish Diamond. *Urban Studies* 2001; 38, 4: 733-45.

2. Cabus P, Van Haverbeke W. The territoriality of the network economy and urban networks, evidence from Flanders. *Entrepreneurship and regional development* 2006; 18: 25-53.

3. CPDT. *Thème 3, aires de coopération.* Ministère de la Région Wallonne, Conférence Permanente du Développement Territorial, 2002, cpdt.wallonie.be.

4. Davoudi S. Polycentricity in European Spatial planning: from an analytical tool to a normative agenda. *European Planning Studies* 2003; 11, 8: 979-99.

5. Garreau J. *Edge City: life on the new frontier.* New York: Doubleday, 1991.

6. Gouvernement Wallon. SDER – *Schéma de Développement de l'Espace Régional, Synthèse.* 2000, 66 p.

7. Kesteloot C, Saey P. Brussels, a truncated metropolis. *GeoJournal* 2002; 58, 1: 53-63.

8. Kloosterman RC, Musterd S. The polycentric urban region: Towards a research agenda. *Urban Studies* 2001; 38, 4: 623-33.

9. Lambooy J. Polynucleation and Economic Development: The Randstad. *European Planning Studies* 1998; 6, 4: 457-67.

10. Lambregts B, Zonneveld W. Polynuclear urban regions and the transnational dimension of spatial planning. Proposals for multi-scalar planning in North West Europe. *Housing and Urban Policy Studies* 2003; 26, Delft University Press.

11. Ministerie van de Vlaamse Gemeenschap. *Ruimtelijk Structuurplan Vlaanderen.* Brussel, 1997 and 2004.

12. Philippe J, Léo PY, Boulianne L (Eds). *Services et métropoles : formes urbaines et changement économique.* Paris: L'Harmattan, 1999.

13. Turok I, Bailey N. The theory of polynuclear urban regions and its application to Central Scotland. *European Planning Studies* 2004; 12, 3: 371-90.

14. Van Criekingen M, Decroly JM, Lennert M, Cornut P, Vandermotten C. Local Geographies of Global Players: International Law Firms in Brussels. *Journal of Contemporary European Studies* 2005; 13, 2: 173-86.

15. Van Hamme G, Marissal P. *Les causes de la faible croissance économique de la Région de Bruxelles-Capitale.* Brussels: unpublished research report, IGEAT-ULB, 2000.

16. Vandermotten C, Roelandts M, Aujean L, Castiau E. Central Belgium: polycentrism in a federal context. In: *The polycentric metropolis: learning from megacity regions in Europe.* Hall P, Pain K (Eds). London: Earthscape, 2006, chapter 11.

Networking Italy.
Polycentrism and networks in Italian regional policies

Francesca Governa, Carlo Salone
Dipartimento Interateneo Territorio, Politecnico e Università di Torino, Italy

The concept of polycentrism, with other quite heterogeneous topics, is one of the main goals of spatial planning at EU level [15] and, according to Cremaschi (2005), seems to have consolidated a sort of common wisdom in European policy-making. The aim of this paper is to discuss the theoretical and empirical foundations of the concept of polycentrism on the basis of changes occurring in the Italian institutional framework and of urban and territorial policies, in particular at regional level. Currently, the Italian institutional framework is changing towards strong devolution of power to local and regional authorities. In Italy, the EU objective of polycentrism stimulates innovation in territorial policies at local and regional level rather than changes at national level or in the general planning system [12]. To describe such changes, we refer to a number of regional planning applications in which the regional territory is considered in some ways innovative, also inspired by the principles of European Spatial Development Planning (ESDP).

POLYCENTRISM AND SPATIAL COHESION: OPPORTUNITY AND AMBIGUITY

According to Davoudi (1999), "one of the most central yet least clear concepts in the ESDP is that of polycentricity". The relevance of the concept of polycentrism in the ESDP depends on its coherence with the political options for the development of European space and on its capacity to address the three main objectives of ESDP, namely economic and social cohesion, conservation of natural resources and cultural heritage, and a more balanced competitiveness of the European territory. Actually, in the ESDP and other guideline European official documents, the concept of polycentrism is not used to explain any existing or developing situation, but rather as a regulatory agenda for achieving two policy goals which are often conflicting. ESDP promotes polycentrism at European level in order to ensure a more regionally balanced development across the EU and to enhance the Community's economic competitiveness in the world market (balanced competitiveness). The notions of balanced territorial competitiveness and economic and social cohesion mirror some of the crucial challenges facing the EU today. Supporting polycentrism may be a strategic answer to the currently unbalanced structure of European space [2].

Nevertheless, the concept of polycentrism is and remains problematic for a lot of reasons. Despite its widespread usage and its long history, the precise meaning of polycentrism has remained elusive: it "means different things to different people" and also" different things when applied to different spatial scales" [7]. Therefore, there is a sort of indifference to the territorial scales of polycentrism and that induces the idea that local and European problems can be faced in a coherent and homologous way at all territorial levels [5]. From a political point of view, the objective of polycentrism testifies to an" idealistic approach" to spatial planning [13] highlighting a theoretical and practical gap. In other words, it is not clear what kind of policies have to be implemented to reach it and, in more general terms, whether polycentrism really is a panacea for the European spatial, economic and social structure.

Like polycentrism, also territorial cohesion appears, therefore, a rather ambiguous concept [10], fluctuating between a "therapeutic" way of intervention on regional disparities and a proactive approach to the valorisation of regional and local resources [9]¹. In short, European Spatial Planning documents seem to give polycentrism a preparatory role to territorial cohesion, as the *condicio sine qua non* to guarantee a more balanced development across Europe [14].

THE SPECIFICITY OF THE ITALIAN CONTEXT: THE CHANGES OF THE 1990'S

In Italy, "territorial planning is virtually non-existent at national level, it merely consists in a guideline at regional level, and is implemented at local level" [4]. This situation has not changed in recent years, despite some efforts by the authority in charge of spatial affairs (*i.e.* the Ministry for Infrastructures). The weakness of the national planning process does not facilitate the elimination of asymmetries between North and South that traditionally characterize the Italian spatial, economic and social structure. In addition, the relationship between actual economic development dynamics and institutional guidelines has been highly asymmetric. This situation has recently changed.

The trend towards devolution and gradual reform of local government started around the mid-1980s and accelerated in the early 1990s, during a period of deep crisis in the Italian institutional and political systems. The main changes in the institutional order consist of simplification, reorganization at the centre, legislative and administrative devolution, institutional cooperation and competition, public capacity building, local and regional financing. These are the issues that characterized one of the most important reform processes in Italian institutional history, through the introduction of major innovative legislation and the adoption of a constitutional reform. These innovations influence the general framework of centre-periphery relations (*i.e.* the introduction of public-private partnerships or inter-institutional relationships) more than the actual amount of power transferred to local authorities, and owes probably more than is commonly attributed to the European Union. Actually, Italian urban and territorial policies do try to apply the "key principles" of the EU policy approach,

---

1. In the 1997 EU Treaty of Amsterdam a "territorial" declension of the concept of cohesion appears for the first time. After this, the expression is largely illustrated in the Second Report on Economic and Social Cohesion (2001), in the text of the European Constitution and, finally, in the Third Report on Economic and Social Cohesion (2004).

i.e. local authorities autonomy, subsidiarity, accountability, adequacy of public structures to discharge responsibilities assigned to them, flexibility in inter-institutional relationships, citizen participation in collective decisions, and streamlining the bureaucracy [11].

Obviously, the relevance of these changes, over and above initial requirements, must be verified in practice. The innovations introduced after the 1988 reform of Structural Funds are a good test of this [11]. Naturally, this experience has good as well as less agreeable points, as testified by the wide debate recently primed to verify actual implementation, unfulfilled promises and potential for change. In this debate, heavy criticism of some aspects is set against calls to rethink Italian regional policies, emphasizing the gap between European key principles and their translation in Italian practices [1]. Moreover, documents produced to define strategic guidelines for regional policy, through which Italy plans to manage the resources of EU cohesion policies and national funding for the period 2007-13, recognise the need to introduce changes to the previous period, especially as regards some of the key principles of the new regional policies.

LOCAL TERRITORIAL SYSTEMS AS ACTORS OF LOCAL AND REGIONAL POLICIES

Recent research carried out in Italy highlights the importance of the territorial dimension in the processes of development, and of the policies for its promotion [8][2]. Such attention differs from the traditional approach of Italian research to the dynamics of industrial districts, also on account of the evolution of contemporary international debate. Starting from the by now established characterization of the role of agglomeration in benefiting local economic development and providing significant competitive advantage to local production facilities, reference to the territorial aspect in the processes of development is made increasingly more complex especially by the contribution of institutionalist perspective and the so-called cultural turn in economic geography. Within this framework, the territorial dimension plays the double role of space for localization of actions and activities, and of place of connection between identity dimension, political dimension, economic dimension, symbolic dimension and temporal dimension.

According to an extensive international literature, territory is a complex concept. It could be seen as a political and economic "fact", a "social construction" deriving from the collective action of groups, interests and institutions, a complex set of values and resources, a common good of fixed assets, material and immaterial, an exhaustible resource. In short, at various geographical levels, territory is no longer seen as static and passive space, but as a dynamic and active context, as a proactive subject rather than a passive object of policies, as an actor itself in the development process on the basis of the collective action taking place within it.

---

2. For a deeper discussion of the various theoretical and methodological approaches on the role of territory in globalisation, local territorial systems and governance processes, see Dematteis and Governa (2005).

This theoretical debate could be translated into operational tools applicable to territorial policies referring to the model of "local territorial systems" [8][3]. As a preliminary definition, a local territorial system may be considered as a local network of players who, starting from their relationships with each other and with the specific features of the local milieu in which they work and act, in certain circumstances behave as a *de facto* collective actor. Each local territorial system has more or less capacity of self-representation and self-designing: the geography of the local territorial systems describes the potential geography of self-organized local capacity and interactions with the territorial milieu and supra-local levels. According to Dematteis and Janin (2006), local territorial systems are the nodes of the lowest hierarchical level upon which the idea of European cohesion, based on a polycentric model, is grounded. According to this view, networking of local territorial systems is the starting point of European polycentrism for promoting territorial cohesion at various levels.

POLYCENTRISM AND NETWORKING IN ITALIAN TERRITORIAL REGIONAL PLANS

As a consequence of enhancement of the devolution process in the institutional framework, over the last decade Regions have renovated their spatial planning laws producing documents variously referring to the main issues of European spatial planning. Here, the key concepts of polycentrism and cohesion have been attributed a spatial dimension.

Spatial policy-making by Italian regions is little differentiated throughout the country, in terms of both technical tools and quality and content of planning activity. Many Regions are redefining their territorial plans according to a strategic approach; others combine prescriptive aspects referring to land use, carefully addressing the problem of co-ordinating policies and programmes of different sectors. In short, recent regional territorial plans are based on three sets of models as follows:

1. A "compulsory regional plan", in which the relationships among local plans, landscape-environmental planning and economic programming are arranged according to a hierarchical layout;
2. A "structural regional plan", more or less prescriptive in its relations with local and sectoral plans;
3. A "strategic regional plan", in which the relationships between different local and sectoral plans are redefined in terms of spatial design and coherence between the various project scales.

Inspirations and explicit or implicit references to polycentrism, networks and local territorial systems are traceable mostly in the third family, which includes documents and plans such as those of Campania, Emilia-Romagna and Piedmont.

---

3. The model of "local territorial system" was investigated by a research team from Dipartimento Interateneo Territorio of the Turin Polytechnic and University, in co-operation with other Italian geographers, and applied to empirical research projects on local development and territorial policies on behalf of public authorities.

Regional plan of Campania: "A plural Campania" *(Una Campania plurale)*

The example of the Campania Region is the most advanced in terms of both its application, as proven by official approval from the Regional Council (in 2004), and of coherence with an "operational" declension of polycentrism.

The first element of interest is the attempt to bring economic programming and spatial planning close together, via Regional Operational Programmes (Programmi Operativi Regionali) for EU Objective 1, and spatial planning. This is particularly evident in the "interconnection" issue, to be addressed in terms of both physical-functional links (infrastructures for transport and logistics) and relations between local actors (decision-making networks based on inter-municipal agreements, which constitute local territorial systems). The second aspect is the explicit mention of polycentric dimension as a desirable configuration for regional space. Deconcentration in Naples, one of the most densely populated metropolitan areas in the country, necessitates a better distribution of urban values (public functions, collective facilities in education, culture and leisure), in order to counter the dominance by the central municipality. The third point is the systematic breakdown of regional territory due to various forms of inter-municipal co-operation (also extended to nongovernmental actors, such as businesses, employers' associations, etc.) experienced over the last decade and very close to the concept of local territorial systems: areas in which integrated development programmes are implemented, protected natural parks, Comunità Montane (Mountain Communities) and industrial districts officially acknowledged *(Figure 1)*. The territorial dimension of these elements define the so-called "territorial systems of development", the very cornerstones of the plan and its implementation.

Despite, or because of, its "enlightenment" structure this document reveals some weaknesses, the most evident of which is to cover the entire regional territory. The complexity of regional space makes this aim rather simplistic, for two basic reasons:

1. As the Region has so far witnessed traditional difficulties in tackling spatial issues, it could be desirable and more strategic to target specific crucial nodes (*e.g.* functional decongestion of the metropolitan area and some environmental issues);
2. Regional development involves unbalanced mechanisms, which differ throughout the region, and as such necessitate selecting local systems to be focused.

Regional plan of Emilia Romagna: "Governing by city networks" *(Governare per reti di città)*

In 1997 the Emilia Romagna Region published a report titled "Scenarios and Strategic Options for Updating the Regional Development Plan". After that, a Development Perspective of the Regional Territory (Schema di Sviluppo del Territorio Regionale) was approved in 2005. With these documents the regional government tries to restore historical regional polycentrism *(Figure 2)*. The aim is to encourage the creation of an "opportunities differential" (measured in terms of real estate, public services, commerce, junction points, etc.) to the benefit of medium-sized cities. Moreover, actions aiming to devise new centralities are envisaged: new cities have come into being in the region – or rather, old cities' boundaries have changed considerably, and the role of some inner cities is tapering off because of the altered relationship between centre and periphery. Redevelopment of abandoned areas, upgrading of areas around railroad stations and other transport junctions, siting of certain functions requiring

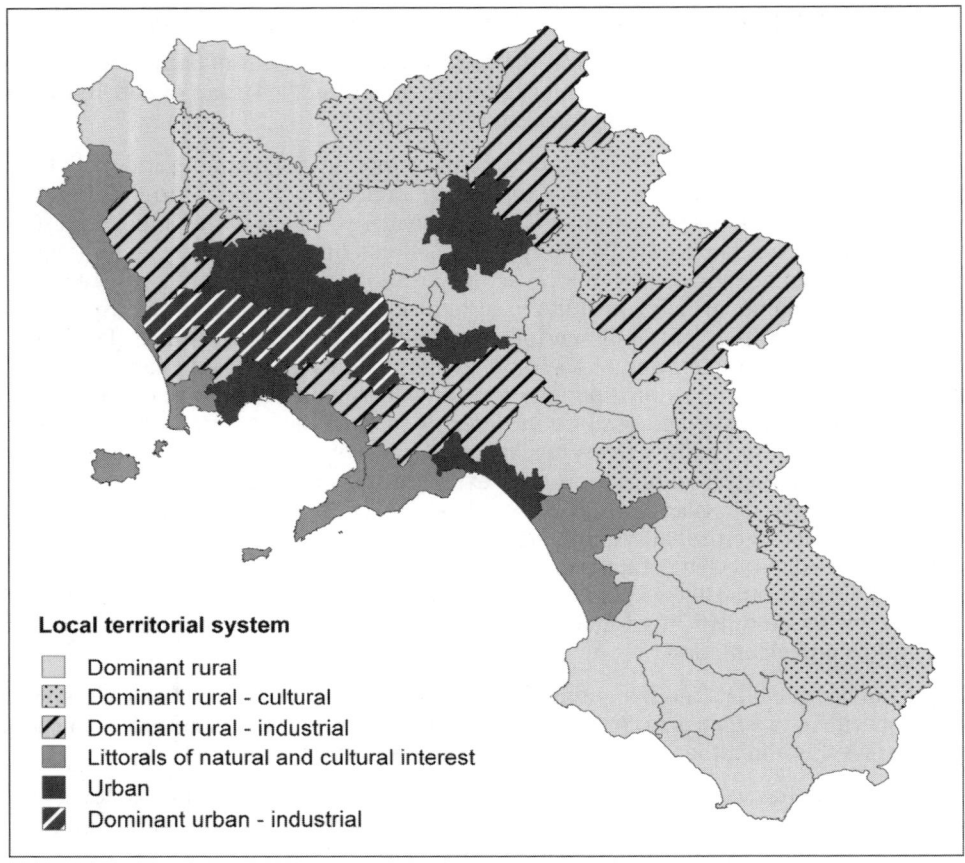

Source : Campagna Region, 2004

Figure 1. *Territorial systems of development according to Campania's Regional Plan.*

easy access – all these should be seen as opportunities to work towards an urban design that brings order to the "new" cities. As a minimum, such a policy promotes actions for improving service networks of a polycentric base, according to a logic of competitiveness imposed by the relevant global network. Indeed, global networks should be evaluated not only as competitive frameworks but also in terms of their potential for developing regional functions (*e.g.* in the fields of transportation, business services, scientific and technological research).

References to ESDP policy options and a clear awareness of the concept of polycentrism in EU policy documents are frequent in regional policy discussions. The Region's political élites and decision-makers have been exceedingly receptive in the debate about the adoption of ESDP in Italian spatial policies, within the Regions' Conference. This is because of at least two reasons, namely historical polycentrism of Emilia-Romagna's regional structure, which is considered a positive factor, and the high level of its political and technical élites, usually open to cultural innovation and receptive to new policy messages from EU.

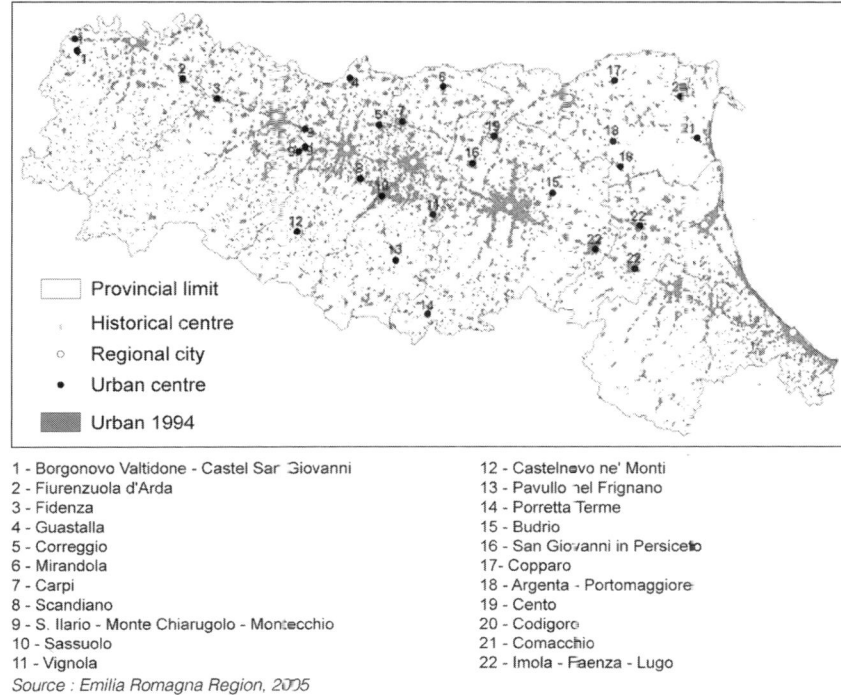

Figure 2. *Urban hierarchy in Emilia Romagna.*

Regional plan for Piedmont: "Integrating economic and spatial planning"

At the end of 2005, Piedmont's regional government approved and published the methodological report "For a New Regional Territorial Plan" (*Per un nuovo piano territoriale regionale*). The document is highly coherent with ESDP "philosophy", in which polycentrism plays a significant role. Simultaneously, polycentric development is evoked as a current phenomenon and as a policy objective. Polycentrism must develop at several levels, *i.e.* European, regional-interregional, metropolitan (in the Turin regional capital area) and urban-rural level.

The basic components of the regional mosaic are the local territorial systems, coalitions of municipalities, economic and social actors sharing a common set of objectives for a given territory. They are assumed to be the outcome of "social and institutional self-identification of local communities", transcending historical and administrative boundaries *(Figure 3)*. This approach is clearly influenced by the positions emerged from academic research in Italian geography, particularly that of the Turin scholarship which is directly working to the new regional plan (see § 5)[4]. Furthermore, significant contributions have been provided by the Turin school about the network

---

4. At both institutional and advising level: the current head of Territorial Policies for the Regional Government is an academic geographer from Turin University, with many geography and planning scholars serving on the technical advisory board.

urban systems in Piedmont in the early 1990s, with a focus on the rise of new polycentric spaces, particularly in the southern part of the region (for an overview, see [3]). The current challenge for the Piedmont regional territorial plan is to bring regional planning and economic programming together, looking for convergence of the future Plan and the activities underway for the preparation of a new Cohesion policy for the period 2007-13.

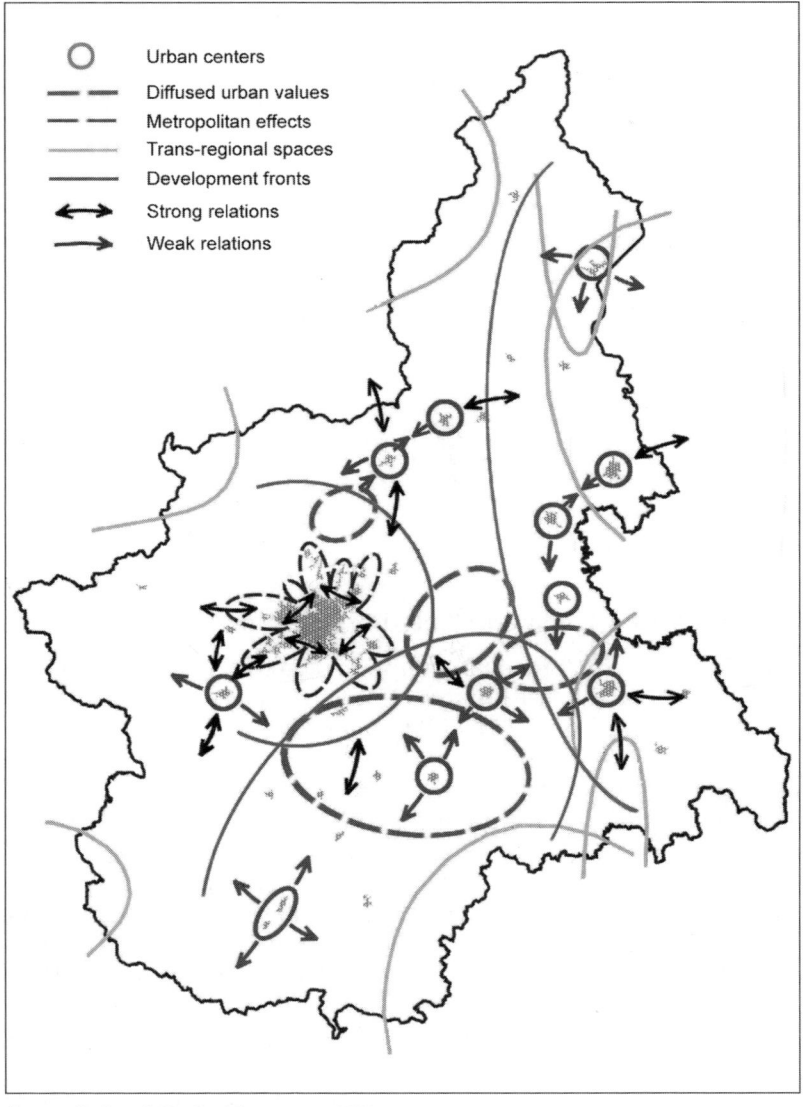

Figure 3. *Spatial components of Piedmont regional space.*

Conclusion

A number of contractual and governance projects were implemented in several Italian regional contexts during the last fifteen years, often based on EU experiments and influence. The main principle was that of "integration", stated in terms of multiple forms of action integrating various sectoral policies, trying to connect economic and social objectives, co-ordinating various institutional levels and public and private actors.

So, it is possible to identify a progressive evolution towards the explicit adoption of a contractual approach, as well as towards the concrete integration of various forms of action. The Italian version of polycentrism in urban and territorial policies is nowadays focused on increasing centrality of the role of actors and organizations aiming for common goals through networking activities. Italian network policies are the outcome of a bottom-up process, in which localities themselves define their developmental directions, although they do so within a legal framework set out by central government.

The reform of public sector administration, which reinforces vertical subsidiarity in central government, regions and local authorities, plays a positive role in strengthening territorial cohesion and polycentrism. The transfer of power to regional government, especially in the area of industrial policy, has helped to increase the competitiveness of the territorial systems. It also helped the development of new forms of regional partnership and contractualization involving private and public players, thereby increasing the efficiency of regional and local government. Both a central government effort in planning and inter-municipal collaboration are present in many Italian Regional plans described earlier. They are based on a strong attitude to inter-communal co-operation, in which networking has become the most usual way of interaction. These networks produce social capital which can also be applied to other forms of collective action. Local collaboration, public – private partnerships and so on are the most innovative features in a sector traditionally dominated by an authoritative and all-encompassing approach to planning activities. Such process brings with itself the evolution of new territorial levels at which relationships are established and within which actions are carried out, thereby multiplying territorial subdivisions and places where policies are implemented and where actions take place. On the one hand, this is in accordance with the growing inclination of European countries to devolve competencies and powers away from the centre. On the other one, it testifies to a new (or renewed) centrality assumed by reference to the local territory in theoretical reflections on development processes and on urban and territorial governance models.

REFERENCES

1. Barca F. *L'Italia frenata. Paradossi e lezioni della politica per lo sviluppo*. Roma : Donzelli, 2006.

2. Baudelle G, Castagnède B (Eds). *Le polycentrisme en Europe*. Paris : Editions de l'Aube-Datar, 2002.

3. Camagni R, Salone C. Network urban structures in northern Italy: elements for a theoretical framework. *Urban Studies* 1993; 30, 6: 1053-64.

4. Commission of the European Communities (CEC). *The EU Compendium of Spatial Planning Systems and Policies: Italy*. Regional Development Studies, Brussels/Luxembourg: CEC, 2000.

5. Cremaschi M. *L'Europa delle città. Accessibilità, partnership e policentrismo nelle politiche comunitarie per il territorio*. Firenze Alinea, 2005.

6. Davoudi S. Making sense of the European Spatial Development Perspectives. *Town and Country Planning* 1999; 68, 12: 367-69.

7. Davoudi S. Polycentricity in European spatial planning: from an analytical tool to a normative agenda. *European Planning Studies* 2003; 11, 8: 979-99.

8. Dematteis G, Governa F (Eds). *Territorialità, sviluppo locale, sostenibilità: il modello SLoT*. Milano: FrancoAngeli, 2005.

9. Dematteis G, Janin Rivolin U. For a South-European and Italian perspective in the "next ESDP". In *The process of territorial cohesion in Europe*. Pedrazzini L (Ed). Milano: FrancoAngeli, 2006: 103-17.

10. Faludi A. Territorial Cohesion: A Polycentric Process for a Polycentric Europe. *Aesop Congress* 2004; 1-4 july, Grenoble.

11. Governa F, Salone C. Territories in action, territories for action: the territorial dimension of Italian local development policies. *International Journal of Urban and Regional Research* 2004; 28, 4: 796-818.

12. Governa F, Salone C. Italy and European Spatial Policies: Polycentrism, Urban Networks and Local Innovation Practices. In "Southern Perspectives on European Spatial Planning", Faludi A, Janin Rivolin U (Eds). *European Planning Studies*, special issue, 2005; 13, 2: 264-83.

13. Krätke S. Strengthening the Polycentric Urban Systems in Europe: conclusions from the ESDP. *European Planning Studies* 2001; 9, 1: 105-16.

14. Meijers E. Polycentric urban regions and the quest for synergy: is a network of cities more than the sum of the parts? *Urban Studies* 2005; 42, 4: 765-81.

15. Waterhout B. Polycentric development. What is behind it? In *European Spatial Planning*. Faludi A (Ed). Cambridge, MA: The Lincoln Institute for Land Policy, 2002: 83-104.

Part III
Networking: What potential for the polycentrism?

Cities as nodes of research networks in Europe

Francesca Silvia Rota
Dipartimento Interateneo Territorio, Politecnico di Universitá of Torino, Italy

Over the last decades, a number of important changes have taken place in the way the urban phenomenon is interpreted. Cities are no longer identified as mere physical entities, where activities and individuals cluster, but as economic players. Furthermore, they are more and more identified with what flows through them rather what stays in them [10]. This interpretative shift is certainly linked to the extraordinary progress in communications and mobility that has affected developed economies since the 1980s. In particular, the increasingly frequent, varied and far-reaching relations connecting urban players – especially those in large metropolitan areas – have led to the metaphor of cities as nodes of supra-local networks, placing the issue of analysing the structuring and restructuring of inter-urban relationships at the heart of the debate on urban studies [7].

In this context, the aim of this study is to investigate a specific type of relations, *i.e.* inter-urban research networks, with an attempt at detecting their spatial logic and dynamics in Europe. The analysis of these specialised linkages will also allow me to introduce some reflections about the placement of several European cities in terms of their behaviour within international scientific partnerships.

RELATIONAL APPROACH AND RESEARCH NETWORKS

Theorisation and representation of urban networks

In the theorisation of cities as nodes of supra-local networks, a number of approaches may be identified. From the 1970s to the 1990s, for example, many efforts were directed towards studying cities as units of larger urban systems [7]. European cities, in particular, were examined according to different functional criteria; so, those with comparable performances in one function (for example tertiary services or innovative potential) were thought to have analogous roles and control over the rest of the system. Many hierarchies and taxonomies were thus produced[1]. But most of this literature is based on "stock" parameters, *i.e.* without

---

1. For a review see, for example: the "Review of comparative studies on the networks of European towns and cities" prepared by Denise Pumain, Thérèse Saint-Julien, Marianne Guérois, Peter Hall, Simin Davoudi and Stead Dominic for the 1999 Meeting of the Study Programme in European Spatial Planning (Stockholm, 22-24th February), and Cetri and Rota (2004).

considering flows between cities [1]. Some images submitted by geographers to represent the uneven development of the European territory (the European pentagon, the golden triangle, the blue banana, etc.), provide a relational, yet far from quantitative, approach where somewhat "classic" paradigms (based on urban assets and proximity) lead to the identification of a central area of strong urbanization (the "core") juxtaposed with several weaker surrounding area (the "periphery").

More recently, some efforts have been made towards achieving a relational approach to urban networks. From both a theoretical and practical perspective, inter-city relationships are explicitly considered on different geographical scales and analysed according to their spatial models and rationale. On the one hand, network externalities have been recognised as key factors of a city's success [3], while on the other hand, a growing number of empirical studies have addressed the analysis of supra-local flows, considered as valued links between the nodes of a network [11]. Many of them give substance to the European Commission's efforts to create a polycentric and coherent European territory [4]. Nevertheless, even though advanced statistical techniques are introduced to evaluate nodes and networks, direct measurements of relationships (intangible ones in particular) remain somewhat hampered by the scarcity of data and sources [12]. Moreover, in most of these analyses the time factor is ignored as an irrelevant variable in network analysis. These limits have a dramatic effect on the quest for a new praxis to represent current hyperconnected urbanisation and its dynamics. To discuss this framework, I deal with inter-city research relationships, *i.e.* co-participations in projects, in Europe.

Co-participation in projects

At the heart of my analysis are the cooperative relationships originating from the participation of different urban players in the same research projects. According to Cattan and Saint-Julien (1998), these are specialised networks, characterised by spatial logics that are distinct, for example, from those of cultural, economic or financial networks. One might then hypothesize that some relational factors, such as cultural and socioeconomic conditions, intervene to influence the way urban players define research agreements at supra-local level[2]. In other words, the spatial organisation of the research network would not only reflect gravitational or critical mass circumstances – *e.g.* the availability of infrastructures and capital – as suggested by a large part of the literature [9], but also urban specialisation, institutional frameworks and local policies. Moreover, as variety is a recognised condition for innovation and development, research networks between cities are likely to modify and expand in the medium to long term.

For the European context, the following questions are then formulated: what is the spatial organisation of the research network? Centred? Polycentric? Which is the rationale used to describe the urban structure? Are national patterns relevant? Is the network hierarchically organised?

In particular, I questioned whether the European research network is influenced by "classic" variables (population, GDP, and research assets), or is influenced by relational place-specific (possibly noneconomic) endowments or attitudes. This latter hypothesis matches in fact that part of literature that says that urban players interact with others in a territorialized way [7].

---

2. According to Cattan and Saint-Julien (1998) other logics, beside relational ones, are those based on resources and national administrative divisions.

Data and methodology

Data on inter-urban co-participation in projects were obtained from the Cordis database, *i.e.* the online portal set up by the European Commission to provide easy access to information on research and innovation. In particular, all the projects of the 5th and 6th Framework Programmes (FPs) were considered. Each FP contains all the Research and technology development (RTD) projects financed by the European Commission in the corresponding funding period (from 1999 to 2002 the 5th FP; from 2002 to 2006 the 6th FP). The projects are identified by an acronym (based on content) and related to a set of information regarding investments, results, partners (above all research centres), and their location (city, region and country), that were freely available at the time of the query (September 2005). Geographical information concerning research partners in particular has been used to reconstruct inter-urban relationships in a GIS environment.

Cities with 200 or more RTD projects were assumed (48 cities according to the 5th FP) as nodes of the research network. Then, for each pair of cities, the number of projects involving players located in both cities was considered (co-partnership as defined by [2]). The resulting links were assumed in relative terms, in order to enable comparisons between different data sets (the 6th FP was in fact still in progress at the time of the query) and organised into two adjacency matrixes both symmetric and valued.

The analysis of the network has been based on social network analysis (SNA) methods. To describe the prominence of nodes in the network, the SNA measurements of centrality degree (the number of incident edges on a node) and betweeness (the sum of all pair-dependencies resulting from computing the length and number of shortest paths between all pairs are calculated for the abovementioned matrixes and for the sub-matrixes obtained by separating capital cities from the rest of the sample. According to Besussi and Alves (2005), these measurements are in fact designed to be the most appropriate to represent patterns of monocentrism or polycentrism in the European space. Betweeness centrality, in particular, is traditionally considered crucial to measure the interconnection of the network and detect gateways[3] as it describes the extent to which a network depends on a node to connect otherwise isolated parts of its structure.

Finally, some qualitative considerations on the territorial organisation of the network are pursued via the GIS visualization of the graph representing the inter-city relationships.

CONCENTRATION AND CENTRALITY IN THE EUROPEAN TERRITORY

The participation of cities in RTD projects is analysed by comparing the number of their projects (*i.e.* project size). Not surprisingly, the strongest values correspond to national capitals (especially Paris and London), where major players and assets converge (namely universities and public research centres). Nevertheless, there is also high participation in projects

---

3. Following Besussi and Alves (2005), "considering a matrix $G = (V; E)$, where V is the set of nodes (vertices), and E is a set of undirected edges, degree centrality is [...]: $N(v) = \{i \in V(G) : (i, v) \in E(G)\}$ and it is usually normalised by the total number of possible incident edges. [Instead,] betweenness centrality can be written as: $C_B(v) = \sum_{i, j: i \neq j, i \neq v, j \neq v} \frac{g_{ivj}}{g_{ij}}$ where g_{ivj} are the shortest paths from i to j through v" (p. 177).

from some non-capital cities such as Munich and Milan, where place-specific endowments are probably key factors in explaining city networking. In the case of Milan, for example, most of the city's RTD projects are undertaken by private and public universities. In Munich, on the other hand, a particularly diverse local innovative milieu (made up of many research centres and scientific and technological poles) is responsible for most of the projects.

From a geographical perspective, the result is a rather different picture of the European urban system from the ones proposed by classic centre-periphery models and urban hierarchies. According to the 6th FP, for example, there emerges a concentration of cities with relevant masses in at least three main areas *(Figure 1)*: the first stretching from London to Rome, and is bow-shaped; the second extends to Paris, which is involved in 10% of the projects considered (6.8% of the total of projects in the 6th FP); the third is along the corridor connecting Lisbon to Budapest.

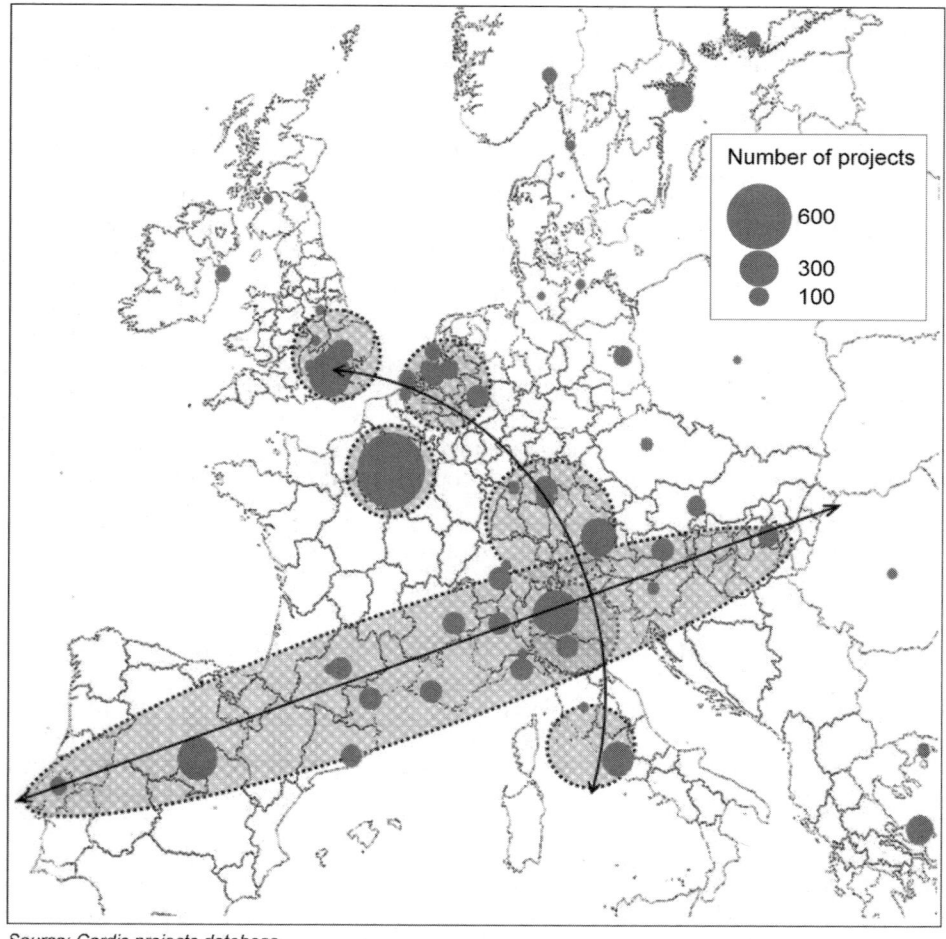

Figure 1. *Cities' project size (6th Framework Programme)*.

Network analysis metrics are then used to verify this circumstance, *i.e.* the cities' mutual positioning in the European research network, not only according to stock data (projects) but to relational data (co-partnerships) as well. What results is that the project size and the centrality of cities are not always correlated.

According to the 5th FP, for example, Vienna is more "central" than cities with higher project masses such as Milan and Munich; Budapest outdoes Stuttgart; Turin is more central than Oxford *(Figure 2)*. These differences probably mean that Vienna, Budapest and Turin are involved in a large number of research projects within the selected set of European cities, while Munich, Stuttgart and Oxford – which are less central than one might expect from their project size – are likely to establish partnerships either with few cities in general (with whom they have in any case many agreements), or cities not included in the data-set (as they do not reach the quota of 200 projects). For example, Munich and Stuttgart establish many relations with many cities, above all German ones (respectively 32 and 15 co-partnerships with Cologne and Karlsruhe). Conversely, Oxford frequently has partnerships with the most important economic and financial centres of the European system (especially Paris, London and Munich), but few with the other cities in the network, included those of the United Kingdom.

Next, variations based on the FP lead us to some considerations on the dynamism of the research system. From 2002 to 2005, for example, Paris and Munich registered an increase in centrality far higher than that of any other city. In the case of Graz, the city's greater centrality corresponded to a dramatic increase in its participation in EU projects, driven by regional cluster policies. But the opposite is also true. London, for instance, lost 20% of its centrality, while Warsaw maintained low values of centrality (it occupies 25th place in both the 5th and 6th FP) despite participating in many projects.

This seems to confirm the hypothesis that, especially in the case of non-capital cities, regardless of the number of contracted projects, other factors enhance (or impair) the capacity of cities to establish supra-local relationships. In my perspective, these factors (that are still to

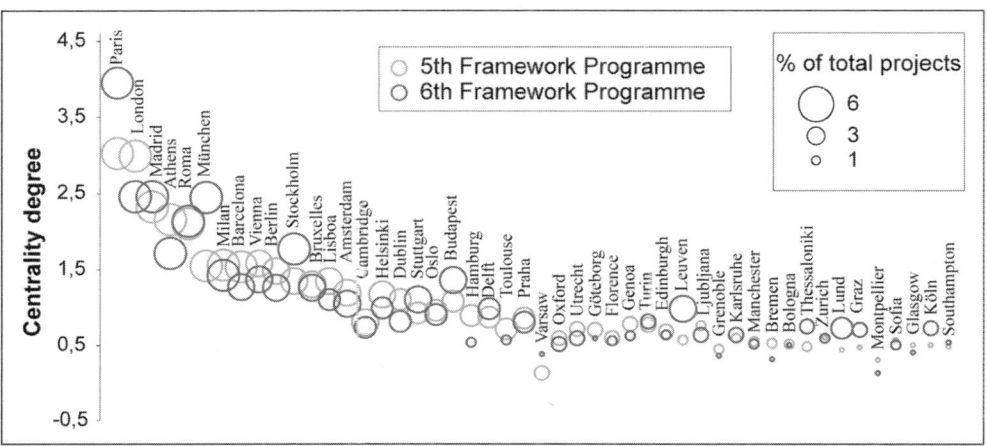

Source: Cordis projects database

Figure 2. *Centrality degree and project size.*

be clearly identified) are influenced by local institutional, cultural, and policy circumstances, such as the Federal organisation of the German research scene[4] or the UK R&D and Innovation Policy[5]. These have a substantial modifying power (at least in the medium term) in large and medium cities' skill to enter into partnerships.

To complement this first analysis, I analysed also the cities' betweeness degrees in order to point out the aptitude of cities acting as network gateways. As with centrality, it resulted that betweeness is related to project size just partially. As *Figure 3* shows, the largest cities with the highest masses have betweeness values of nil, while some medium cities – such as Graz (according to the 6th FP) or Prague and Utrecht (5th FP) – are characterised by high betweeness. In other words, these cities – more than larger ones – take part to many independent research teams and networks, that enable them to act as research gateways.

This mismatch is probably due to the fact that European hubs such as Paris, London and Madrid conduct research relationships with all the cities in the sample, while cities like Graz and Prague particularly attract relations from some peripheral urban nodes, which would otherwise be isolated from the rest of the network. Prague, in particular, has intense ties with Eastern cities such as Warsaw, Ljubljana, and Sofia.

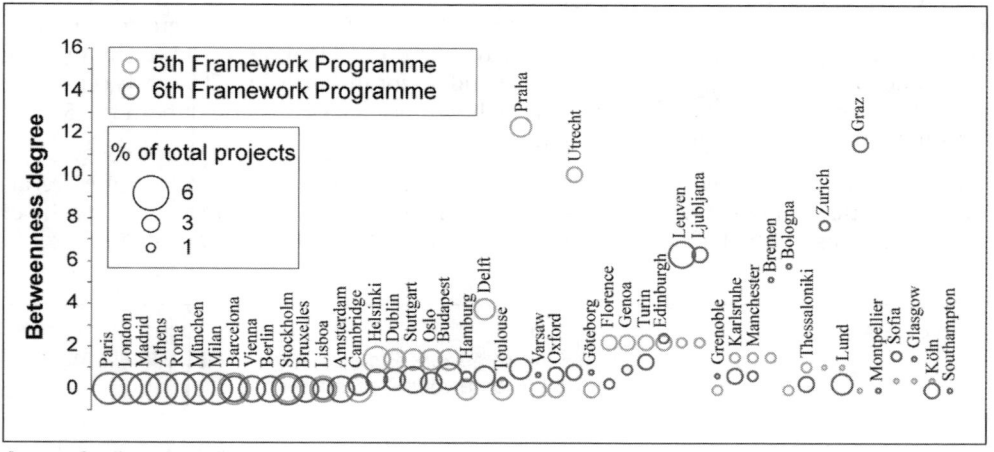

Source: Cordis projects database

Figure 3. *Cities betweeness and project size.*

---

4. In Germany the Committee on Education, Research and Technology Assessment drafts decisions of the German Bundestag in the field of education and research policy. In the field of research policy in particular, the Committee deals with support mainly for collaborative projects involving participation by several German and European players (business enterprises or scientific institutions) who share responsibility for the projects and promote the transfer of knowledge and technology.
5. In 2004, the UK Government published its Science and Innovation Investment Framework 2004 -2014. The UK aim is to create new prosperity by attracting both in Europe and throughout the world highly skilled scientists, engineers and technologists as well as the companies which have the potential to innovate and to turn innovation into commercial opportunity.

Moreover, betweeness degrees vary even more significantly than centrality depending on time: from 2002 to 2005 Graz rose from 43rd to 1st place; Prague has fallen from 1st to 11th place; Utrecht from 2nd to 14th. This is a very important result as it supports the idea that, regardless of the number of projects they are involved in, cities can strengthen their role as network gateways by simply varying the panel of cities with which they interact. Moreover, this variable is crucial for evaluating the polycentrism of the network: as cities with positive betweeness in 2002 are fewer than in 2005, this means that the number of gateways increased, paving the way for a more polycentric spatial organisation of the urban system. This depends not only on the comprehensiveness of the links (the condition of connecting each node with the highest possible number of other nodes) but also on their relative spatial position. The geographical distribution of nodes and its strongest ties (50 and more co-partnerships) are thus considered in terms of a geo-referenced representation of the network[6] *(Figure 4)*.

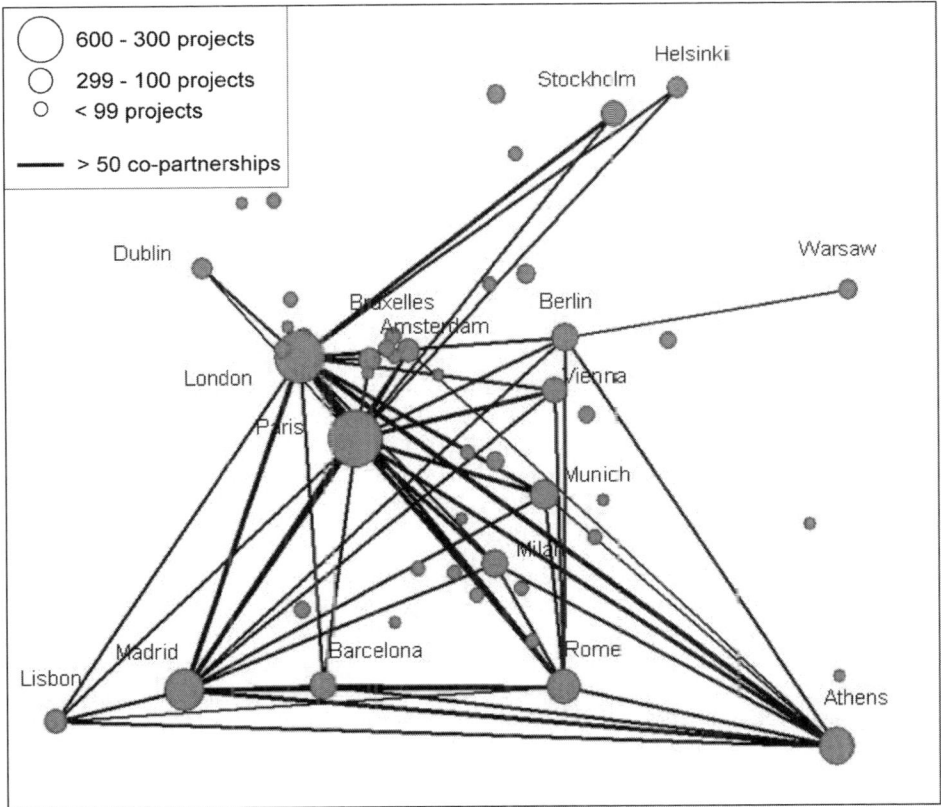

Source: Cordis projects database

Figure 4. *Main research co-partnerships (6th Framework Programme).*

---

6. Via the graph visualization software NetDraw 2.3.

Paris and London emerge as structuring poles of the research network, along with a number of other cities, namely capitals such as Athens, Rome, and Madrid, acting as important attractors in research networking. From this representation thus emerges that hierarchical logics are a better and more useful mean of describing the European urban system than the centre-periphery model.

This result must, however, be moderate because it is clearly subject to the limitations of an oversimplified representation that considers a narrow sample of cities. In the next section of this paper a complementary approach is thus proposed, based on the investigation of research sub-networks [8].

SUB-NETWORKS, GATEWAYS AND POLYCENTRISM

In order to detect all the various spatial models shaping the European research network, capital cities are separated from non-capital (or regional) cities. The co-partnerships developed inside these two groups of cities are then analysed individually.

National capitals

As for centrality *(Table I)*, Paris confirms its role as prevailing hub (1st place both in 2005, with centrality degree 41.5; and 2002, with 45.8). Next come London and Madrid. European Western capitals, in particular, are more "central" than Eastern ones, however with some exceptions: Budapest, for example, performs better than the majority of the cities of the so-called European "core". Analogously some of the most "peripheral" cities such as Stockholm, Athens, and Vienna, appear more central than "core" capitals such as Brussels. In other words, the hypothesis of the geographical structuring of the European territory according to a centre and periphery is one more time addressed from a sceptical point of view (see paragraph II). Furthermore, one can notice that "traditional" hierarchical logics as those mentioned when describing the network of cities with 50 and more co-partnerships *(Figure 4)* overlap with those resulting from centrality rankings just in correspondence with their highest segments, while the correlation diminishes proportionally to the rank of the cities.

From a dynamic perspective, in the period 2002-05, all the nodes of the sub-network, with the only exceptions being Budapest, Paris and Stockholm, lost centrality. Although this result might be interpreted as evidence of a polycentric transformation of the network (less centrality of nodes meaning less interconnectivity and thus space to the development of independent sub-networks tied together by gateways), in actual fact the betweeness values (all nil according to both FPs) contradict this hypothesis: the research network of the capitals remains highly hyperconnected in all its parts.

Differences can be at least introduced according to the intensity of cities' co-partnerships: according to the 6th FP *(Figure 5)*, for example, capitals at the heart of the most intense relationships are Paris, London, Madrid, Rome and Athens; dramatic relationships are also those of Vienna, Berlin, Brussels and Budapest; while links of Lisbon, Stockholm, Helsinki, Oslo, Prague, Sofia, Ljubljana, Warsaw are less intense. Again, the graph reproduces a gravitational logic (the largest cities have the most intense relationships), while geographical proximity is

Table I. *Cities' centrality*

	Centrality degree	
	5 FP	6 FP
Paris	41.5	45.8
London	41.1	31.2
Madrid	33.3	31.1
Rome	30.6	27.3
Stockholm	19.4	22.0
Athens	31.9	21.1
Budapest	17.7	17.9
Vienna	24.5	17.2
Berlin	21.7	15.7
Brussels	19.9	15.5
Lisboa	20.5	14.9
Helsinki	19.2	14.6
Oslo	15.1	12.9
Dublin	17.1	11.1
Praha	14.2	10.2
Ljubljana	12.6	8.7
Sofia	9.8	7.1
Warsaw	2.4	5.6

Source: Cordis projects database.

not a key variable. Moreover, from 2002 to 2005 just some slight changes occurred in the graphs (for example, increases in the co-partnerships of Oslo and Eastern cities), eventually supporting the literature that describes European high-level cities as "fixed entities" in an inherited and relatively stable hierarchical structure.

Regional cities

Among non-capital cities Munich registers the highest centrality degree *(Table II)*, followed by Milan, Barcelona and Stuttgart, while (quite surprisingly) Cambridge, Oxford, and Manchester occupy the last places. In 2005, for example, Turin resulted more central than Zurich, Cologne, and Cambridge. In this case, gravitational criteria (which consider renowned research assets and institutions as mass functions attracting co-partnerships) do not serve to

Cities and networks in Europe – Networking

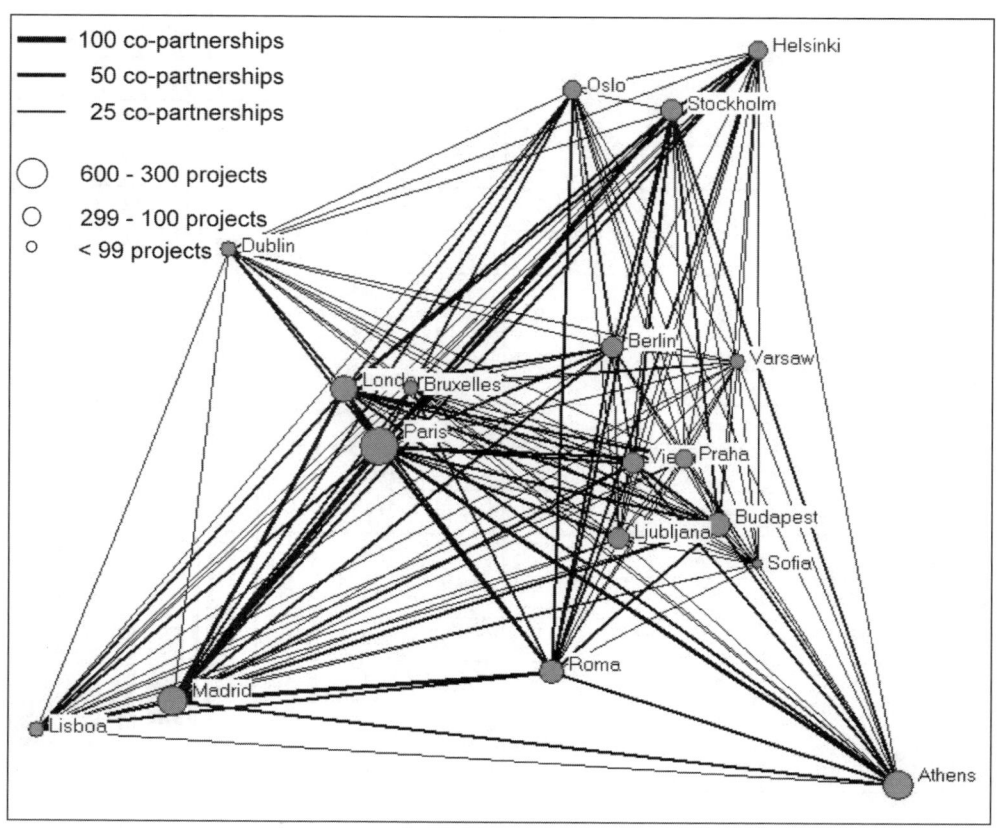

Source: Cordis projects database

Figure 5. *Research co-partnerships between capital cities (6th Framework Programme).*

explain centrality. Other factors, not necessarily linked to other mass variables, significantly influence networking among regional cities.

The sub-network of regional cities is also more dynamic than the capitals' one: from 2002 to 2005, cities such as Munich, Leuven and Thessalonica gained centrality; some others lost it, *e.g.* Milan, Barcelona and Amsterdam; others maintained it, *e.g.* Cologne. But above all it is the betweeness factor that saw the clearest changes: in 2002 no cities had betweeness values, while in 2005 there were 23 valued at over 30. The network thus went from a compact structure to a more "dispersed" one, *i.e.* with many gateways. As I already explained, a too hyperconnected system does not have in fact the space (namely, holes, and missing/loosing ties) that are instead essential to create a polycentric network structure.

Figure 6 shows that, despite strong links connecting Munich with Leuven, Milan, Barcelona, Cambridge and Amsterdam, the overall resulting impression is that these non-capital cities tend to form quite an equipotent network.

Table II. *Cities' centrality and betweeness*

	Centrality degree		Betweeness		Centrality degree		Betweeness
	5 FP	6 FP	6 FP		5 FP	6 FP	6 FP
Munich	45.0	49.9	0.0	Genoa	22.8	12.6	0.4
Milan	41.5	27.1	0.0	Karlsruhe	16.1	12.5	0.3
Barcelona	42.1	24.5	0.0	Zurich	16.9	11.8	2.1
Stuttgart	27.8	22.1	0.1	Utrecht	19.0	11.7	0.3
Leuven	15.4	20.1	2.3	Toulouse	22.2	11.2	0.0
Amsterdam	32.7	19.4	0.0	Florence	15.8	11.2	0.1
Delft	23.3	19.2	0.1	Southampton	15.0	11.2	0.0
Turin	23.9	16.7	0.6	Hamburg	27.1	10.8	0.1
Cambridge	23.7	15.6	0.1	Manchester	15.3	10.2	0.3
Lund	13.5	15.4	0.1	Oxford	17.4	9.8	0.2
Köln	15.3	15.3	0.0	Bologna	14.6	9.3	1.6
Graz	12.9	14.9	3.1	Glasgow	15.0	8.1	1.1
Thessaloniki	12.5	14.6	0.1	Grenoble	12.9	7.3	0.3
Edinburgh	18.8	13.3	1.0	Bremen	14.6	6.3	1.4
Göteborg	23.2	12.6	0.3	Montpellier	9.4	2.1	0.0

Source: Cordis projects database

In other words, Munich excluded, it is not possible to identify a system of hubs (as in the case of Paris, London, Madrid, Rome, and Athens) attracting all the most intense co-partnerships. Not every city in the network is strongly interconnected with all the other cities of the sample, and this is a positive element with respect to the issue of polycentrism.

Conclusion

This paper proposes a "thematic" and dynamic approach for the analysis of research co-partnerships in European RTD projects. The database that has been used, moreover, represents the innovativeness of the information it contains; while the adoption of SNA methodology and geo-referenced graphs matches certain recent efforts in urban studies.

The study leads to two main conclusions that can be put forward to the current debate on European spatial development and planning.

Firstly, the need for a more critical approach to "classic" spatial models and hierarchies clearly emerges. Using the European context as the geographical scale, the exercise conducted empirically shows how core-periphery and gravitational models vary according to the selected

Cities and networks in Europe – Networking

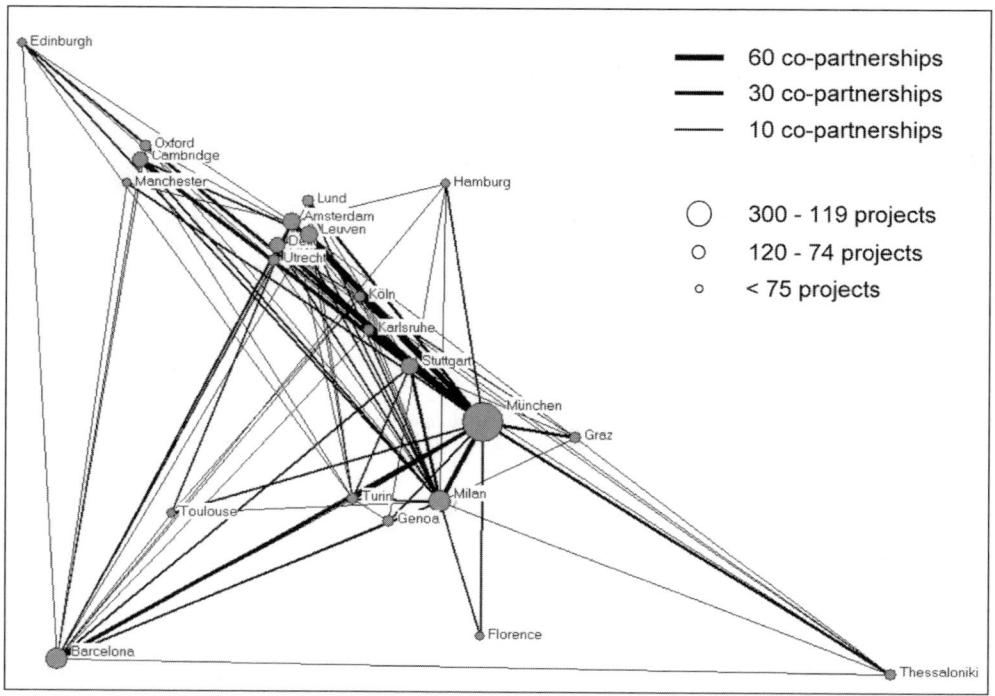

Source: Cordis projects database

Figure 6. *Research co-partnerships between regional cities (6th Framework Programme).*

sample of cities. In particular, when distinguishing between capitals and non-capitals, important differences emerge both in the network structure and in its spatial organisation (as shown by geo-referenced graphs). In the capital cities networks, Paris, London, Madrid, Rome and Stockholm form a sort of highly interconnected networking "platform," characterised, however, by a relatively polarised and hierarchical spatial logic. As far as regional medium-sized cities are concerned, a co-presence of different rationales tend to emerge: i) polarisation of relationships with major urban areas (especially Munich) where there is a cluster of higher-level research assets and knowledge; ii) a system of regional gateways (such as Graz, Leuven, Zurich and Bologna) favouring the connection of peripheral cities with major poles. These specialisations and other place-specific factors seem to play a more critical role in enabling networking than size variables. In particular, the fact that UK cities lack co-partnerships may be interpreted as a consequence of certain determinants probably related to the existence of national and institutional patterns.

Secondly, the study shows that network hierarchies are not as fixed as suggested by "traditional" urban analysis. In particular, the sub-network formed by non-capital cities is characterised by a degree of dynamism far higher than in capitals. This unevenness in the spatial organisation of research relations would thus imply some important consequences in territorial praxis. It particularly urges the need for supra-local territorial policies to focus on regional cities, rather than capitals. Even though cities such as Berlin and Vienna (favoured by their position as well as by past and present development paths) are important gateways for their hinterlands, capitals are rather static in their networking. Thus the European Commission's intention to pursue polycentricism by concentrating decentralised activities and favouring a network of centres of excellence as catalysts for backward areas, appears to be potentially more effective than the distribution of research functions from congested capitals to corridors and gateways, since the principle of deconcentration is in conflict with the fixity and tendency towards polarisation of capitals. The analysis points to this polarisation in Paris and London, for example. To resist this trend, medium-sized cities (hopefully favoured by national and community policies) may exploit their intrinsic dynamism to impose competitive tactics, by strategically selecting their partners. The positive effects of this policy orientation will be seen both at continental and regional level.

REFERENCES

1. Beaverstock JV, Smith RG, Taylor PJ. World City Network: A New Metageography? *Annals of the Association of American Geographers* 2000; 90, 1: 123-34.

2. Besussi E, Alves JS. *Geographic Patterns and Flows of Knowledge in Europe*. ESPON working paper, 2005.

3. Capello R. The City-Network Paradigm: Measuring Urban Network Externalities. *Urban Studies* 2000; 37, 10: 1925-45.

4. Cattan N. Les réseaux urbains en Europe. Des vecteurs d'intégration territoriale. *CNRS Thema* 2003 ; 1 : 83.

5. Cattan N, Saint-Julien T. Modèles de l'intégration spatiale et réseau des villes en Europe Occidertale. *L'espace géographique* 1998 ; 1 : 1-10.

6. Dematteis G. Spatial Images of European Urbanisation. In: *Cities in Contemporary Europe*. Bagnasco A, Le Galés P (Eds). Cambridge: Cambridge University Press, 2000: 33-47.

7. Dematteis G. Shifting Cities. In: *Postmodern Geography: Theory and Praxis*. Minca C (Ed). Oxford: Blackwell Publishers, 2001 113-28.

8. Ietri D, Rota FS. Reti di relazioni tra città: un metodo di indagine. In: *I numeri per Torino*. Russo G, Terna P (Eds). Torino: Otto editore, 2004: 107-41.

9. Sassen S. *The Global City* (2nd ed.). Princeton University Press, NJ, 2001.

10. Smith RG. World City Actor-Networks. *Progress in Human Geography* 2003; 27, 1: 25-44.

11. Storper M. Territories, Flows, and Hierarchies in the Global Economy. In *Spaces of Globalization. Reasserting the Power of the Local*. Cox KR (Ed). New York: GuilfordPress, 1997: 19-44.

12. Taylor PJ, Catalano G, Walker DR. Measurement of the World City Network. *Urban Studies* 2002; 39, 13: 2367-76.

Students mobility, gender and polycentrism in Europe

Nadine Cattan
CNRS – Géographie-cités, Paris, France

The issue of territorial organization in Europe is not something new, neither are cities interacting in networks. Study conducted over the last few years made it possible to develop several functional urban models that have interesting features. However, because they are always positioned within a logic of competition in interpreting territorial dynamics, the models are restricted to a hierarchy of "poles" in which only processes of wealth generation are taken into account. Indeed, the great majority of existing researches seeks to produce knowledge on the cities themselves, to evaluate their strengths and weaknesses, and to estimate their growth rates. Consequently, this means that a large majority of studies constantly produces and reproduces urban typologies, reducing the patterns of territorial integration in Europe via city networks to two classic representation models, which are the centre-periphery model and the hierarchic network model for national urban systems. In these acceptations, the European space is seen in a dichotomous manner. In the first case there is a predominant centre to which dependent or isolated peripheral areas are more or less well connected; in the second, there are major poles which have secondary, less prominent or visible centres as satellites.

Yet in many current analyses the functionality of a network of relationships is rarely taken into account. The reasons given by many scientists to explain that it is difficult to take the realities of mobility into account consistently relate to material or technical contingencies, ranging from lack of access to relational data to the methodological complexity of using such data. It is true that these limitations are considerable. However the debate is incomplete, while any attempt to give meaning to space and to populations, in terms of linkage and interdependence rather than in terms of zone and distribution, meets resistance in various forms: symbolic, ideological, and institutional. Peter Taylor (2002) denounces the paradox of researches on the world cities in the following way: whereas the essence of world cities is their relations to each other, studies continue focusing on case and comparative studies neglecting *ipso facto* intercity relations.

The objective of this study is to provide a necessary counterweight to the dominant visions and perceptions of the researches on the European cities networking. By viewing, on the one hand, the territories and the cities in the way they articulate one to another, *i.e.* in terms of functional relationships, rather than principally in terms of locality, i.e. of spatial distribution of the nodes, the study highlights the fact that deeper consideration should be given to the flows as a factor of producing territory. By focusing, on the other hand, on the students' mobility whereas the majority of work on urban networks focuses on what is known as structuring flows, such as financial flows, commercial exchanges, freight or commodity flows, this paper underlines the interests to pay attention on the flows which are usually considered as less structuring, such as cultural exchanges, scientific cooperation and information relationships.

Box 1. The data

This study was made possible by the individual data on student migration for the year 2000 provided by the French SOCRATES/ERASMUS programme centre.

A process of aggregation of university establishments was performed to develop a database corresponding to inter-urban student migrations in Europe. The spatial aggregation of university establishments by city is based on the coding of these establishments as given in the ERASMUS database *i.e.* mainly at the municipality level. This way of doing can be criticized for the fact that it does not group certain university establishments located in the immediate outskirts of large metropolises with the establishments in the centre of these metropolises. However, apart from the fact that there is no official delimitation of urban areas in Europe, the main reason for the choice was to preserve a visible distinction in the large metropolises, in particular for France, between the central and the peripheral university offer. This differentiation is particularly suited to the aims of the present study. In addition, this aggregation problem only concerns a few large cities, London and Paris in particular, and has very little or no effect elsewhere.

This study explores the way in which today inter-urban students' mobility in Europe provides scope for a reappraisal of the patterns and representations we entertain concerning spatial integration. In the information-based society, access to knowledge is a factor in competitiveness that is as vital as the access to transport infrastructures. Today, universities, by positioning themselves in relevant partnership networks, are active agents in territorial dynamics. Inter-university cooperation and the way in which it directs relationships between different places is therefore a major issue, both for the cities themselves and for the regional territory as a whole. Very few studies have explored the spatial aspects of student mobility in Europe and those that have observed this mobility at the infra-national level from city to city are extremely rare. Student exchanges are a particular migratory phenomenon, because the migrations occur within a time scale that is relatively shorter than that of other migratory flows, and because the decision to migrate results from personal decision even if the destination could be in part conditioned by cooperation agreements established between universities. Thus students mobility can be considered as representative, even if only indirectly, of society models, lifestyles and representations that the students entertain on the European space. The present work analyses student exchanges taking place within the ERASMUS programme *(Box 1)*. Every year more than 110,000 students stay for a period of three to twelve months in a town or city other than that in which they normally study.

THE POLYCENTRIC NETWORK OF STUDENT MOBILITY

The main student inter-urban migrations show a polycentric connected Europe *(Figure 1)*. Most of the metropolises, whether they are political or economic capitals, in southern Europe

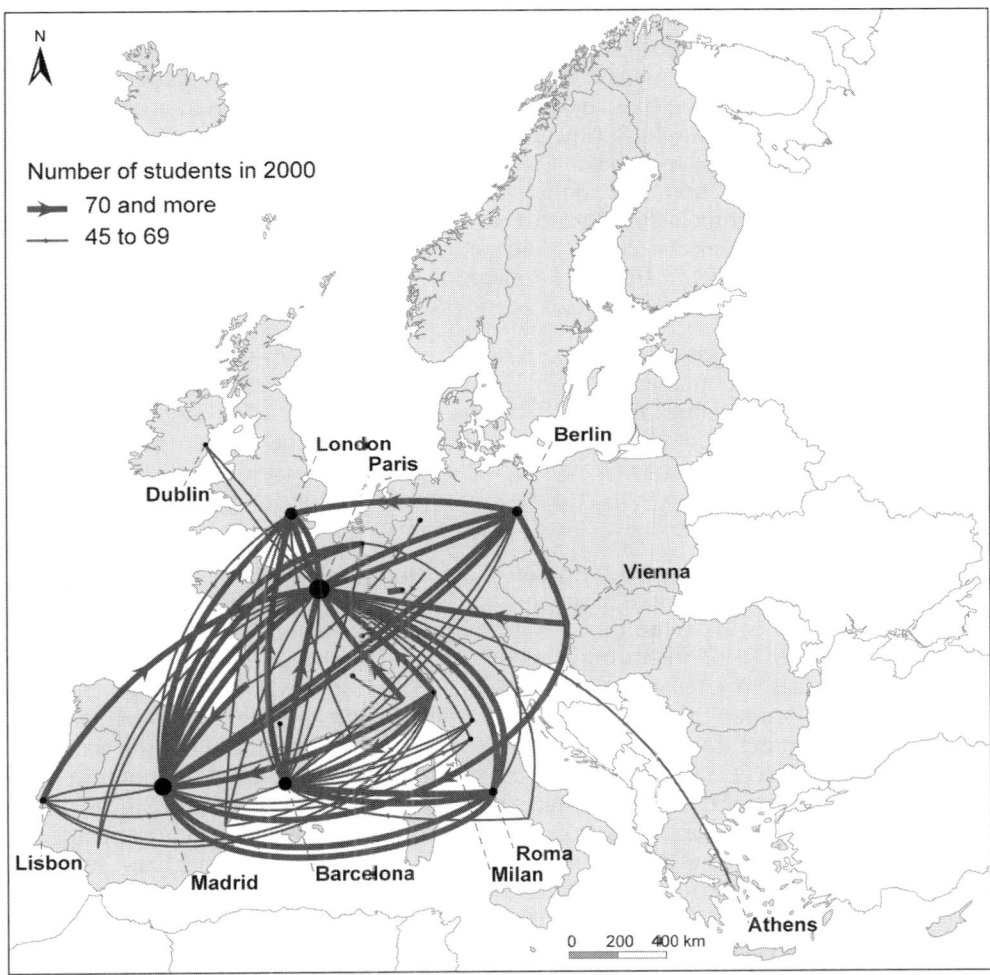

Source: Socrates - Erasmus

Figure 1. *Erasmus students mobility*.

(*e.g.* Lisbon, Madrid, Milan and Rome) and in northern Europe (*e.g.* Dublin, London, Paris, Brussels) exchange more than 45 students a year. To the east, only Berlin is part of this main network. Vienna, which sends more students to Paris, Berlin and Madrid than it receives, is in a position of relative dependency in this migratory network.

In the networking processes of the European territory, this "capital city" effect is not surprising: work has been done by several researchers on this metropolitan structuring of the spatial integration dynamics through inter-urban exchanges [6, 5, 8]. Student mobility, however, is a case apart. In most previous work, the network of capital cities always emerges as a second-order structuring in spatial integration dynamics in Europe. It is the centre-periphery model that always appears dominant in the networking processes of the European space. With student migration, the metropolitan network of European capitals forms the major structure in the interdependency of the territories. This leading position is probably connected with the long-standing academic tradition of the capitals, characterized by the presence of several university centres enjoying prestige over the territory as a whole. But there is another originality of the spatial organization of student migration in Europe that couldn't be explained by this structural factor. Indeed, unlike a large number of inter-metropolitan connections which are dissymmetrical, oriented and often highly polarized, student mobility is balanced, symmetrical and non-oriented. No city or pair of cities dominates the network of exchanges, and metropolises of different size and in very different locations exchange equivalent numbers of students. This is the case for instance between Dublin and Paris, Madrid and Paris, Barcelona and Rome, and Lisbon and Madrid *(Figure 1)*.

Whether this networking is targeted as a result of agreements between partner universities or as a result of a more spontaneous process is not the question. The above observations make it possible to describe the organization of the main network of student mobility in Europe with regard to polycentric development issues [3]. More than other types of exchanges, the students mobility points to a reticular configuration of the European territory where there is greater diversity in the connections. This type of organization is a powerful vector for integration of the European space.

This result does not mean that the imbalances are removed nor that the integration of the European territory is taking place in an equalitarian manner. It merely suggests that systematic and exclusive consideration, in a large volume of research work, of the same type of exchange considered to be structuring elements, distorts the view and that the work over the last fifteen years has enclosed discourse and representation in this dominant logic. Students mobility, because it questions, more than other types of exchange, the dual centre-periphery model and the hierarchical network structuring of the European area, opens the way to reviewing the excessively static representations of the European territory. It shows that the mode of organization of the European territory is in reality much more diversified. On the one hand, territorial organization is supported by specialized networks of cities as defined by common patterns of either material or nonmaterial production. On the other hand, territorial organization takes place through networks of cities that are either economic or political capitals. Freed from the constraints of distance, from the urban hierarchies and from political boundaries, the integration processes vis-à-vis student mobility tends to contribute to a change in perspective, providing an alternative to the metropolization and to the centre-periphery model. Rather than polarized and pyramidal, the spatial dynamics of the European integration is viewed in terms of interconnection and reticulation.

THE RETURN OF MEDIUM-SIZED TOWNS FROM THE EUROPEAN "FRINGES", AND THE EFFECT OF GENDER

The multipolar organization of student migration is confirmed by the attractivity of cities according to the total number of students received by each city. It is indeed observed that the differences in attractivity from one city to another are not very great. The number of students received decreases regularly among the four cities receiving the largest numbers: Paris, Madrid, London and Barcelona *(Figure 2)*. If the gap is greater with Berlin which receives nearly 1,000 students less than Barcelona, the decrease in the number of students received then becomes very regular, showing no threshold and no abrupt break. The regularity of the decrease extends well beyond the twenty most "attractive" cities. This means that the migrant students distribute themselves across the European urban system in a relatively homogeneous and balanced manner, and that they are not particularly sensitive to the structuring effects of a hierarchy or of some form of centrality, which hence lose a certain degree of their credit. Among the fifty cities receiving more than five hundred students, amounting to 40% more than the mean number of students received per city in Europe overall, half are "peripheral" cities. If, not unexpectedly, a "capital city" effect is observed, with metropolises such as Madrid, Dublin, Rome, Lisbon or Vienna, towns of relatively moderate size are also found in the category of "attractive peripheral" cities, for example Valencia, Granada, Seville in Spain. Edinburgh in Scotland, and Rennes and Bordeaux in France. These not very large cities account in fact for nearly one third of the fifty top attractor cities in Europe. It is however the overall balance in inter-urban exchanges, *i.e.* the migratory inward and outward flows of a city, that provides the most markedly multipolar picture of the students mobility networking. Indeed, in inward and outward migrations, with the exception of Paris, London and Berlin, it tends to be peripheral cities and medium-sized towns that show a markedly positive balance, with the largest numbers of students in excess *(Figure 3)*, for instance the towns of Galway in Ireland, Aberdeen and Newcastle in the UK, Toulouse and Montpellier in France, Salamanca and Saragossa in Spain, and Jönköping in Sweden. Conversely, capital cities and economic capitals considered to be integral parts of the centre receive far less students than they send out. This is true in particular for Leuwen, Milan, Turin, Frankfurt, Munster and Freiburg. The migratory balance therefore clearly questions the classic views of a vast majority of work on European cities. In a typological vein, partly as a result of institutional and social demands, and

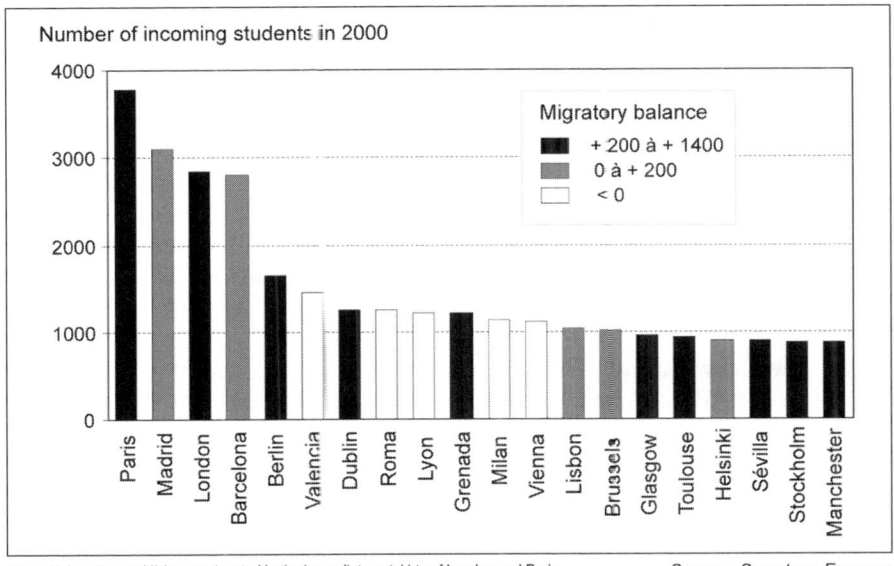

Figure 2. *Most attractive European cities for Erasmus students.*

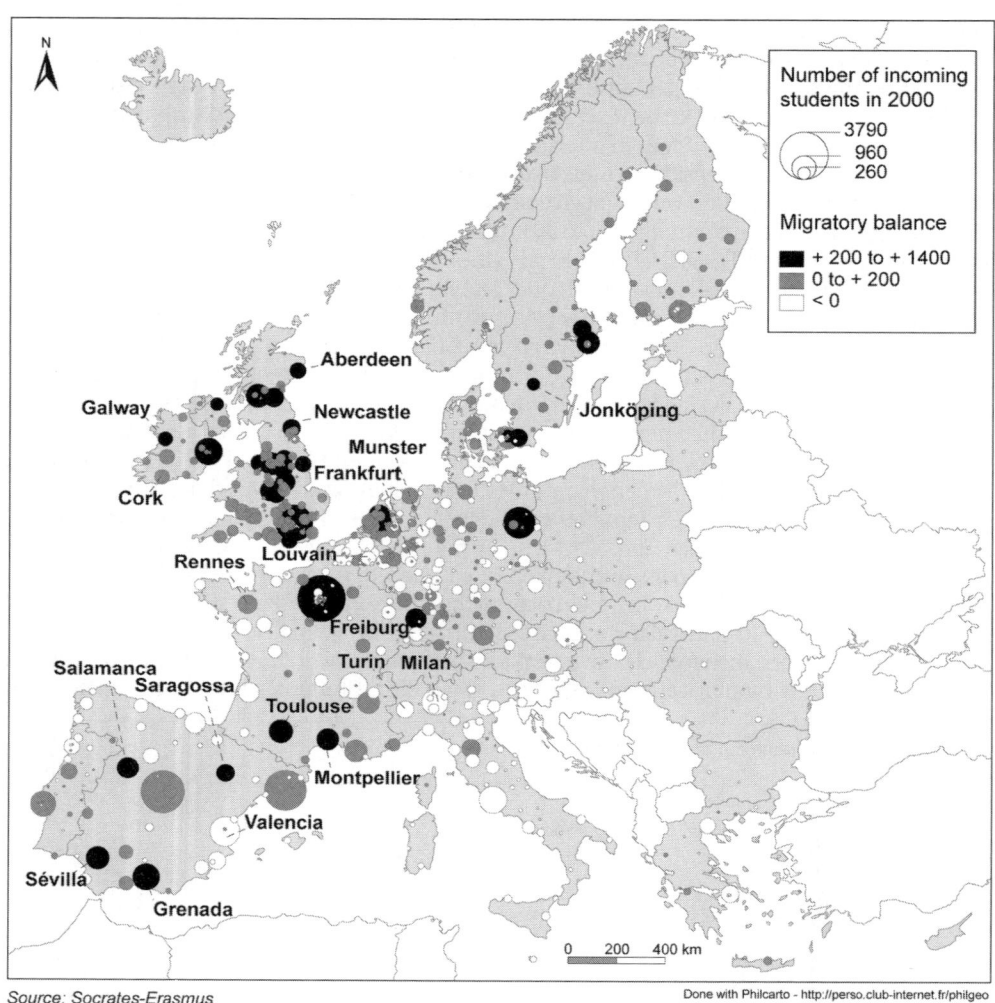

Figure 3. *Erasmus students migratory balance.*

in line with the binary categories of contemporary modes of thought, these approaches nominate "top" or "winning" cities, often large central metropolises, and "losers", often medium-sized peripheral towns. Student migrations, by restoring the image of some of these "peripheral" cities provide an alternative, less static image of the European space and its integration dynamics. In a European context where 61% of migrating students are female it is logical to wonder about the role of gender in these urban networking configurations. In a recent work, I showed that medium-sized towns are a majority choice for female students and that most predominantly female flows are not markedly polarized and generate an eclectic network in which the most frequent associations correspond neither to a particular urban theory nor to a specific spatial logic [3]. In the absence of socioeconomic surveys, it is only possible to hypothesize explanations for the different motivations in these female migratory patterns. On the negative side, it is possible to suggest reluctance or fear in relation to the large city. Conversely, medium-sized cities may exert positive attraction, since they are often viewed as being more human in dimension, and thus may meet expectations of quality of life, living environment and lifestyle that women students may involve in their decisions to a greater degree than the men. In these spatial choices by female students, is it possible to see the emergence of "a new model of migrations" where female migrations would be linked to "postmodern values" [12].

Alongside these urban patterns, student migratory behaviours also evidence specifically national and macro-regional spatial configurations. The national effect is spectacular, in particular in the UK where all cities show a positive balance which means that the numbers of students emigrating in the ERASMUS programme are much lower, whatever the city considered, than the numbers of students migrating into UK cities from cities in other European countries. Conversely, in Italy, the universities do not make up the departures of their own students by arrivals of students from other European countries. On this point, Italy is in line with the profile of most central and east European counties, where all cities show an overall deficit in the migratory balance, underlining the strength of territorial "belonging" and the persistence of a macro-regional pattern still at work today.

Consideration of these elements overall suggests that it is well worth devoting further study to a case study centred on a particular country that underline explicitly the gender spatial differentiation in students migrations. The choice here is to focus attention on student migration linking France to the other European countries because France constitutes the second most attractive destination for students and receives 65% female students (against the European average of 61%).

FEMALE STUDENTS FROM THE REST OF EUROPE PREFER FRENCH REGIONAL CAPITALS AND MEDIUM-SIZED TOWNS WHILE MALE STUDENTS PREFER PARIS METROPOLITAN AREA

On average, French cities receive twice as many female as male students. Almost half of these cities have a gender ratio[1] that is above this average. Among the cities that receive significantly more female than male students, there are large regional metropolises like Marseille, Bordeaux, Rennes and Strasbourg *(Figure 4)*. But the large majority of these preferred destinations for women students are medium sized towns such as Avignon, Pau, Cortes or Perpignan in the south of France and cities in the Great Paris basin situated at about an hour's travel from Paris, such as Amiens, Reims, Orleans, Caen, Angers, Poitiers and Dijon.

Conversely, one fifth of French cities receive relatively more male than female students in relation to the national average. Cases in point are, on the one hand, large cities like Nancy, Metz or Grenoble where the university offer is in science and technology, and which stand out in the French university offer by way of the presence of an Institut National Polytechnique,

---

1. Number of women received over the number of men received.

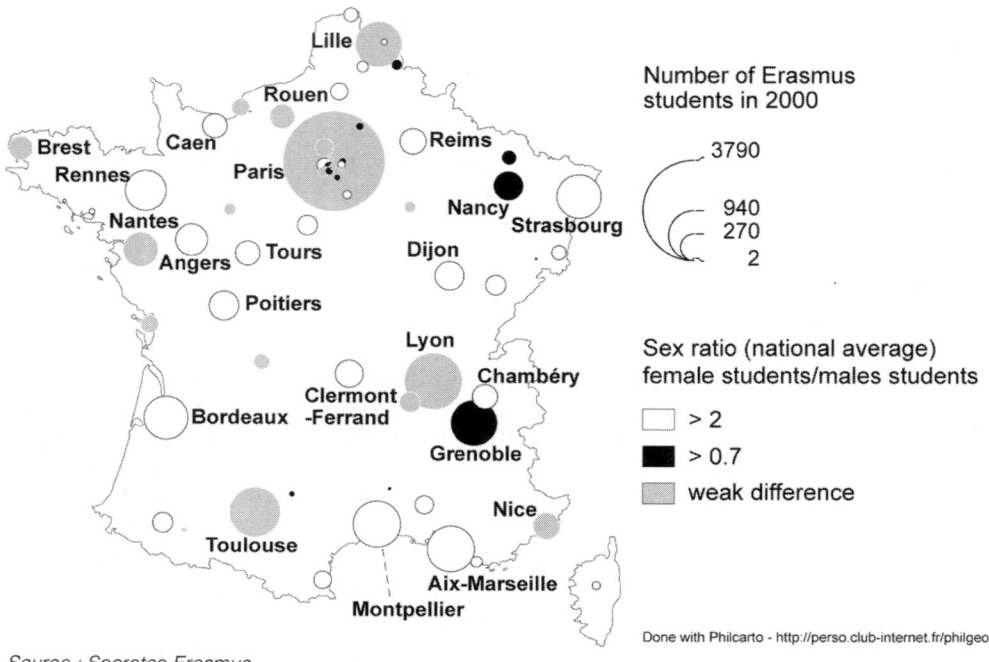

Figure 4. *Attractivity of French cities for Erasmus students.*

and, on the other hand, towns or municipalities in the wide suburban area around Paris ("francilian" region) which houses universities with a markedly professional bias, and *"grandes écoles"* (in France these are the seats of academic excellence in science and technology), such as Evry, Jouy-en-Josas, Gif-sur-Yvette, Palaiseau, and also the town of Compiègne *(Figure 4)*.

These urban preferences that are markedly gender-differentiated show more pronounced dispersion of female migrant students among receiving cities. Measurement of the concentration of student numbers according to gender over urban centres confirms this observation: while 28% of female students from Europe migrating into France choose Paris or Lyon, which are overall the two most attractive French cities for all ERSAMUS students, 30% of male students make this choice. If a larger number of receiving cities is taken into account, it can be seen that the five most attractive cities receive 42% of the female students, as compared to 46% of the male students, and the proportions are 62% and 66% respectively for the first ten destinations.

Whatever the reasons for choice, scope for alternative forms of territorial development can be seen in this gendered attraction among urban destinations. This result suggests that the lights of the large cities do not attract women, while men are more inclined to be drawn. It means that migratory preferences of female students go further to questioning the neo-classic models of spatial mobility than do those of male students[2].

FEMALE MOBILITY AS A WAY OF HIGHLIGHTING "ALTERNATIVE" SPATIAL FUNCTIONING

The previous hypothesis is reinforced by the migratory itineraries preferentially engaged in by female students. By positioning the gender migratory networks in a more explicit relational approach, focusing more on "space of flows" rather than on "space of places" [7], this section highlights a more expressive illustration of the lesser degree of polarization in the female migratory network. The evaluation of the number of inter-urban links required to total respectively a given proportion of female students and male students migrating toward France show that 32 links between a European town and a French town are required to total 30% of male migrations towards France while 41 links are needed to give an equivalent proportion of female migrations. Differences in behaviour according to gender are even more visible when the migratory behaviours of a larger number of students are considered. Indeed, half the male students migrating towards France are concentrated on 74 links, while half the female students are distributed over 90 links. Finally to account for 80% of the male migratory behaviours towards France, 184 interurban links are required, as compared with 220 links to reach the same proportion for female migratory behaviour. Thus it can be said that male student migrations towards France are concentrated on a smaller number of links than female migrations. This means that male students have migratory patterns involving smaller numbers of departure and arrival points, while female students use a wider variety of places.

One can synthesize these figures in saying that the ten main flows of female students towards French cities represent 15% of the total number of female students migrating to France and 18% of the total of male students. When the fifty strongest flows are considered, the gender difference is slightly larger: 37% of female migrations and more than 41% of male student movements. That means that the migrations of the male students are concentrated on a more restricted number of interurban connections than the migrations of the female students.

The combination of the lower attractivity of the large French cities for European female students and the less marked polarization in the network of female migration towards France means that female mobility participate more actively than male migration in the territorial recomposition in progress and in the construction of alternatives to metropolization. These female migrations patterns could indeed reflect more flexible spatial configurations in which more polycentric, more reticulated and possibly fairer territorial development patterns can form.

---

2. A remark however is required: it would be worth examining the gender attractivity of cities in relation solely to migrations between universities, *i.e.* excluding migrations arising from other higher education training institutes and the "grandes écoles". Although the latter account for only a small proportion of student migrations, they have specific features. Indeed, these establishments run courses that include compulsory times abroad as an integral part of the course, which is not the case in universities; in addition, these establishments have markedly different populations in respect to gender.

Conclusion

This study shows that student mobility between European cities forms a polycentric urban network in which interconnection and integration patterns are both reticular and symmetrical. By questioning the dual centre-periphery pattern and the hierarchical network structure more profoundly than is the case with other types of exchange, student migrations make it possible to envisage reappraisal of the terms and representations of integration processes taking place at different geographical level within the European space. Student mobility also made it possible to go beyond certain overstatic images of the organization of the European territory where solely wealth-generating processes are taken into account.

The use of student migrations towards French cities, and differentiation of these behaviours according to gender, shows that it is female more than male spatial behaviours that contribute to spatial reorganization and constructions providing an alternative to metropolization and polarization. Whatever the reasons and motives behind the decision to migrate towards a particular destination, an alternative for territorial development can be seen in these student migrations, in particular among women. In debate in the scientific and territorial development communities on metropolization, multipolarity, sustainable development and recomposition of living spaces, the gender differentiation of the exchanges with regards the territorial attractivity and the networks organizations can no longer be ignored. The mobility of students and in particular of female students leads us to review our static, two-way representations of the integration of the European territory, and also to reconsider the spatial theories and processes that underpin such representations.

References

1. Brunet R. L'Europe de réseaux. In *Urban Networks in Europe*. Pumain D, Saint-Julien T (Eds). Montrouge: John Libbey Eurotext, 1996.

2. Camagni R. Organisation économique et réseaux de villes. In : *Espace et dynamiques territoriales*. Derycke PH (Eds). Paris : Economica, 1993.

3. Cattan N. Genre et mobilité étudiante en Europe. *Espace, Populations, Sociétés* 2004 ; 1 : 15-27.

4. Cattan N (Ed). *Critical Dictionary of Polycentrism. European urban networking*. Annex report A, ESPON 1.1.1 Potentials for polycentric development in Europe, 2004 http://www.espon.lu/online/documentation/projects/thematic/index.html

5. Cattan N, Saint-Julien T. Modèles d'intégration spatiale et réseau des villes en Europe occidentale. *L'espace géographique* 1998 ; 1 : 1-10.

6. Cattan N. La dynamique des échanges aériens internationaux entre les grandes villes européennes. *Revue d'Économie Régionale et Urbaine* 1993 ; 4 : 649-60.

7. Castells M. *La Société en Réseaux. L'ère de l'information*. Paris: Fayard, 1996.

8. Dematteis G. Towards a unified metropolitan urban system in Europe. In : *Urban Networks in Europe*. Pumain D, Saint-Julien T (Eds). Montrouge: John Libbey Eurotext, 1996.

9. Jallade JP, Gordon J, Lebeau N. *Student mobility within the European Union: a statistical analysis*. European Commission, DGXXII, 1997 http://europa.eu.int/comm/education/erasmus/statisti/index.html

10. OCDE. *Regards sur l'éducation, Les indicateurs de l'OCDE*. Paris : OCDE, 2001.

11. Raulin E, Saint-Julien T (Eds). *La mobilité géographique des étudiants des universités*. Paris : Rapport de recherche CNRS-MENRT-DATAR, 1998.

12. Sanchez MJA. Intra-European migrations: from North to South. Paper presented at the Third European feminist research Conference *Shifting bonds, shifting bounds: women, mobility and citizenship in Europe*, University of Coimbra, Portugal, 1997 July.

13. Taylor PJ, Walker DRF, Beaverstock JV. Firms and their global service networks. In :*Global networks, linked cities*. Sassen S (Ed). London: Routledge, 2002.

The network of transnational cooperation programmes in North West Europe and in the Atlantic area

Grégory Hamez*, Guillaume Lesecq**
* CEGUM, University of Metz, ** UMR Géographie-cités, Paris, France

Numerous studies on polycentrism focus on the spatial organisation of cities from a morphological point of view, in terms of describing the urban hierarchy. Only a few tackle the relational side of polycentrism, *i.e.* the way cities are connected as a network. This lack may be partly explained by the chronic scarcity of data on flows, as well as by the conceptual and methodological challenges of analysing the relationships. Nevertheless such studies deserve a great interest in terms of displaying unusual spatial organisations. In this paper a particular kind of city networking is analysed, through the relational patterns of cities cooperating in the Interreg IIIB programme. In other terms the data on Interreg partners and projects are used and aggregated at the city level in order to grasp the spatial logics of interaction.

Two contrasted Interreg IIIB areas are compared: the densely populated and economically developed core of Europe (North West Europe) and the Western low density periphery (Atlantic Area). The internal coherence of these areas in terms of polycentric networking is questioned, first by presenting the spatial patterns of cooperation, secondly by analysing the integration processes. The integration processes settled by partnerships take into account the spatial proximity, the urban hierarchy and the sectoral proximity. The results show noticeably different processes which are segmented in North West Europe and balanced in the Atlantic Area.

THE SPATIAL PATTERNS OF TRANSNATIONAL COOPERATION

The Interreg Community initiative is guided towards a specific representation of territorial organisation, balanced and polycentric. Europe is seen as a whole territory, in which border regions often correspond to gaps or weaknesses in its urban network. So the European Commission designed transnational cooperation as an instrument to implement the aim of balancing EU territory putting the emphasis on the reinforcement of the links between regions. Here we analyse the genesis and the actual morphology of the Interreg cooperation networks to understand the way it contributes to the strengthening of such an approach of territorial development in Europe.

A comparable framework for the both areas

Three strands shape the Interreg cooperation programmes. One of them, the transnational strand, results from a new point of view characterized by a change of scale in the EU territorial cooperation policy. Indeed, when it was launched in 1991, Interreg community initiative included only cross-border and sectorial programmes. Due to a lobbying work from several organisations such as the Conference of the Peripheral Maritime Regions (CPMR), transnational cooperation projects progressively developed and received specific funds. These punctual projects gained significant frame after 1997 through the creation of the transnational strand of Interreg: the Commission defined macro regions, within which actors and territories could gather and build financially supported cooperation programmes at a transnational level.

The definition and delineation of transnational cooperation areas have been designed regarding the existing experiences and networks. This paper focuses on two macro regions: the central and densely populated North West Europe (NWE) and the peripheral Western low density Atlantic Area (AA). Comparing NWE to AA leads us to question the autonomy of the regional partnerships in building the cooperation programmes. Moreover the overlapping between both macro regions allows us better understanding of their actors as regards their belonging and networking strategies. Our interest in NWE lies in its centrality in Europe: though most of the cooperation areas are peripheral, due to the influence of the CPMR on the creation of this strand, North West Europe includes the most urbanized areas and the main capital cities in the European Union. NWE population is more than twice the AA population for a smaller surface *(Table I)*.

Regarding these various regional characteristics, large differences could be expected between the cooperation projects proposed by the two areas since the only EU contractual requirements consist in gathering partners from at least two countries and displaying transnational features. Surprisingly the mean size of projects happens to be very close in both areas in terms of total number of stakeholders, implied cities or the average number of projects per city *(Table I)*. Thus these figures show a comparable situation in both areas, except for the funding, which is higher in the NWE, due to the presence in this area of bigger organisations. However, taking into account the demographic and urban structures of the two areas, these figures mean a relatively stronger cooperating dynamism in the AA than in NWE. Indeed the density of partners per inhabitant is by far higher in the peripheral area than in the central one.

Regarding the concerned themes, both areas actually respect the guidelines of the Interreg III[1] defining four main priorities plus a technical assistance funding[2] *(Figure 1)*. The first priority concerns spatial development strategies, confirming the assimilation of the concept of poly

---

1. Communication of 28 April 2000 (2000/C143/08) from the commission to the member states laying down guidelines for a Community Initiative concerning trans-European cooperation intended to encourage harmonious and balanced development of the European territory.
2. The guidelines in fact mention a fifth priority, which doesn't concern our two areas: integration of outermost regions.

Table I. The size of the Interreg IIIB areas and networks.

	North West Europe	Atlantic Area
Area (km^2)	787,400	856,420
Population (millions)	171	76
Total funding (millions €)	655	206
Funding per inhabitant (€)	3.8	2.7
Thematic priorities	5	4
Projects	83	76
Stakeholders	568	540
Implied cities	300	267
Stakeholders per project	7.8	8.0
Projects per city	2.16	2.25

Source: Inforegio (funding), Interreg secretariats. Total funding includes provisional European and national contributions for the 2000-06 period

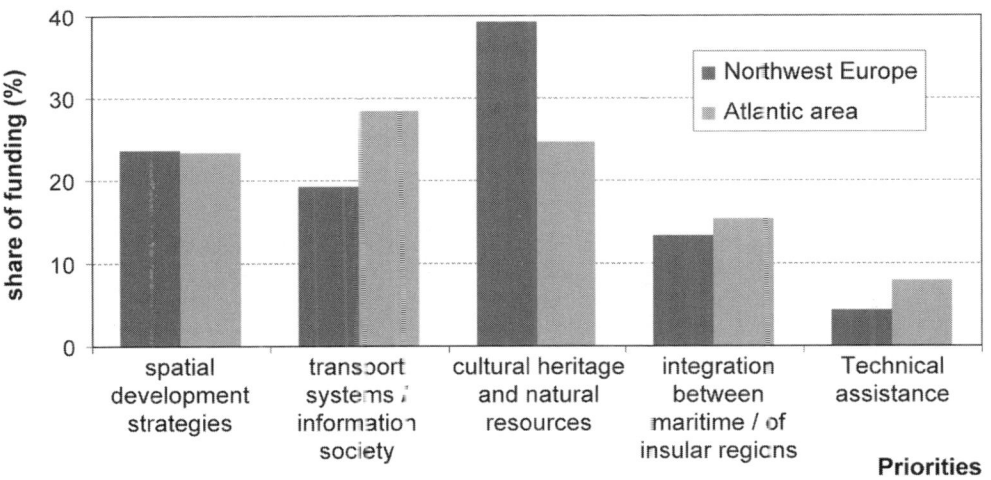

Source : Programme complements (provisional European and national contributions for the 2000 - 2006 period)

Figure 1. *Thematic priorities of the Interreg IIIB programmes.*

centric development by the applicants to the programme. Inside this first priority, the urban concern is more explicit in Northwest Europe with a specific measure, representing 14% of the total funding. The second priority is organised in the same way in both areas, although the AA financial effort in transport and communication is stronger. The third priority has been split up in two priorities in the NWE in order to emphasize the particular concern of the partners about water and flood management. The last priority relatively appears of secondary concern in both areas (10 to 15% of total funding), but the projects seem more centred on cultural and patrimonial perspective in the Atlantic Area and on economic and port concerns in the NWE. Beyond the common framework of cooperation, the proportions of the thematic priorities highlighted in *Figure 1* also show that each area keeps a relative freedom concerning the integration of its own choice and objectives in the projects undertaken.

Another sign of similarity between the cooperation strategies of each area is provided by the involvement of the city in a project. A rank-size analysis shows that the differences are quite tight between the two areas. One could however notice that on the one hand concerning the top of the urban hierarchy, Santiago de Compostela in the AA is more "hegemonic" than Brussels in the NWE, and on the other hand Atlantic Area medium-sized towns are more implied in the cooperating process than NWE medium size-towns *(Figure 2)*. These urban hierarchies do not fit the classical hierarchies, based on population or international functions: in our case the administrative function (national or regional capital) seems predominant and has a direct impact on the transnational cooperating dynamism. Thus, in the NWE, Brussels and Den Haag are more involved than Paris, London and Amsterdam (that doesn't even appear in the top ten). All the same, in the AA, Santiago de Compostela, the capital of Galicia, is much more involved than La Coruna and Vigo, the two biggest cities of this region whose population is more than twice Santiago one. This result actually highlights the overrepresentation of institutional partners in the transnational cooperation networks [8]. However the strong implication of administrative capitals traditionally considered as second-rank cities suggests that these cooperation's networks partially cast off some traditional urban polarisation effects. A deeper analysis of the geographical distribution of involved cities reveals that the urban polarisation acts in another way, by marking the networks according to specific spatial organisation patterns: a "megalopolitan" pattern for Northwest Europe and a "polycentric" pattern for Atlantic area.

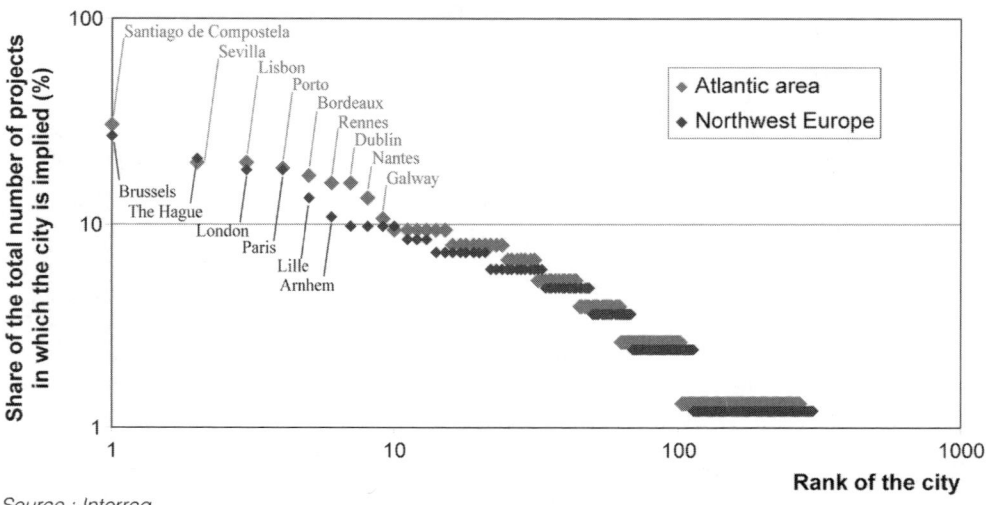

Source : Interreg

Figure 2. *The urban hierarchy of transnational cooperation.*

Two specific spatial organisation patterns

North West Europe: A rather "megalopolitan" organisation

In North West Europe, the geographical distribution of Interreg stakeholders seems far from the strict hierarchic patterns. In this densely populated area the distribution of the cities involved in a transnational cooperation project rather evokes a metropolis continuum and the urban density gradient in the whole EU territory. Indeed it partially fits in with the "Blue Banana" scheme, with a high concentration on Netherlands and Belgium (except the Ardennes region), extending towards Thames estuary, the North France and Northwest Germany *(Figure 3)*. The involvement of Netherlands cities is explained by a governmental choice concerning its financial contribution to Interreg programmes, thus leading them to privilege the transnational strand against the cross-border one [5]. We may consider that by privileging far-distance cooperation, they acted as the core of a metropolised area where the border effects are side effects in territorial organisation vis-à-vis the metropolitan logic. This means that at a national level they might have generalised a strategy adopted by most metropolitan regions. The involvement of a huge number of cities in most of the Belgian territory could have been reinforced as regards the status of Brussels as the capital of the European Commission. The logics that underline the participation of Paris and London to INTERREG transnational projects is quite different: their involvement could be explained both by the institutional partners' provider status of the city and their well-developed international functions, services and connections, independently of national or proximity strategies.

Atlantic area: A rather "polycentric" organisation

In the Atlantic area, the geographical distribution of Interreg stakeholders globally seems not as concentrated and differentiated as the NorthWest Europe *(Figure 3)*. Morphologically speaking, it appears more polycentric with poles scattered all along the coastline and a decreasing density gradient towards the hinterlands.

A more detailed analysis reveals that two major mechanisms are at work: on the one hand polycentrism results from the dynamism of large and medium-size cities which take an active part in the transnational programmes. In particular one can quote the cases of Dublin and Cork in Ireland, Rennes, Nantes and Bordeaux in France, Sevilla and Santiago de Compostela in Spain, Lisbon and Porto in Portugal. On the other hand the polycentric organization seems reinforced in certain cross-borders areas which would mean a greater interest of border cities in this kind of cooperative programmes. One could highlight the very intense mobilization mainly in the Galicia-Norte area, far before the Basque cross-border area or the Andalusia-Algarve region.

The implication of the French cities is interesting to study since it allows us to mention the question of the identity of these transnational area and in particular that of the Atlantic Area. While the French cities involvement presents a quite regular distribution along the Atlantic coast, cities from Normandy and the Paris Basin are poorly represented. These regions did not join the CPMR, probably because of their strategic positioning as European well-integrated regions. They thus do not wish to take an active part in the Atlantic programme. For opposite reasons probably, Eire and Brittany seem more involved in Atlantic area than in the Northwest Europe; but their cities also participate in NWE programme: in these cases there might be a regional official strategy as regards the Atlantic and peripheral identity positioning, and a willingness of some cities to cooperate more actively with the central area.

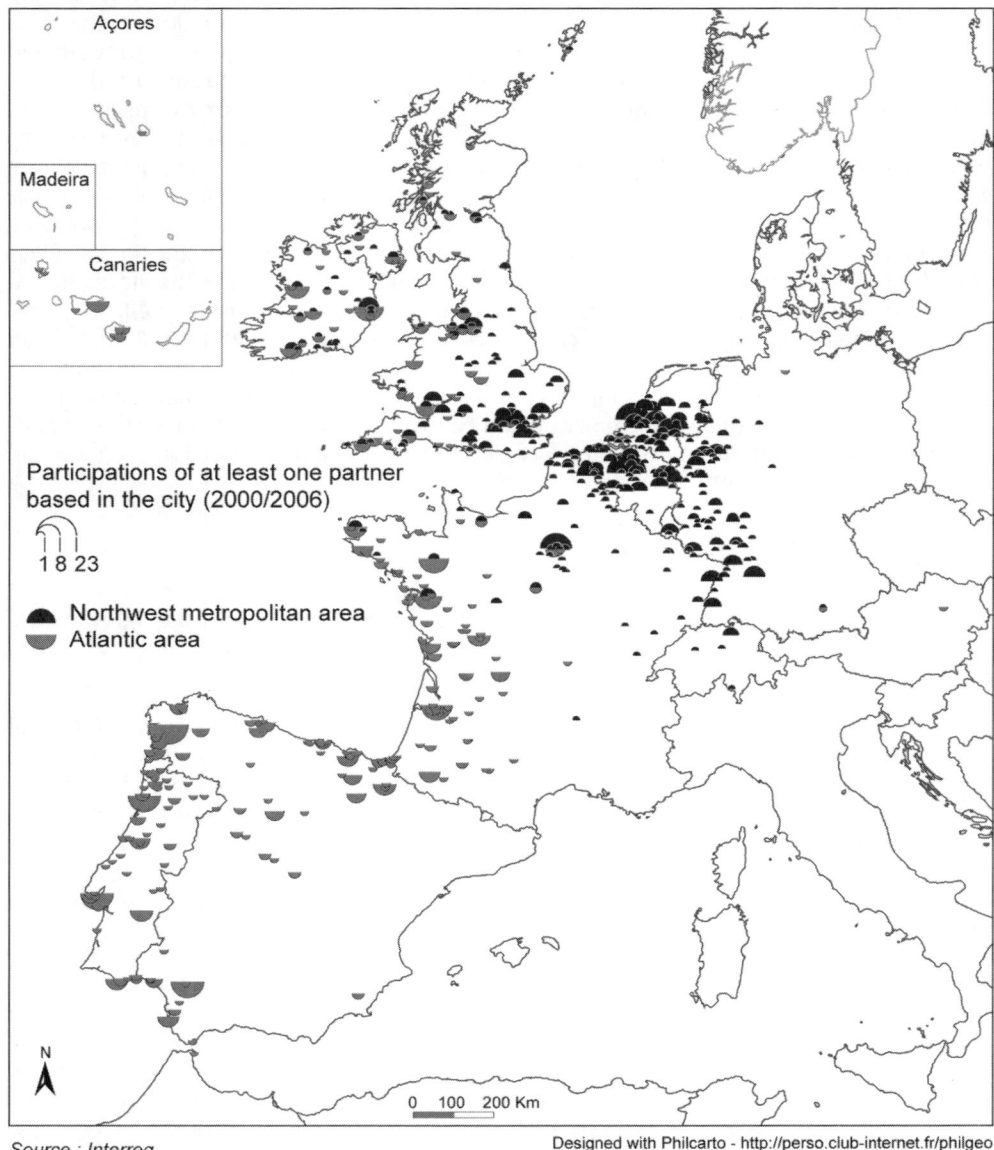

Figure 3. *The participation of North West and Atlantic Area European cities to Interreg IIIb programmes.*

THE INTEGRATION PROCESSES IN NORTH WEST EUROPE AND IN THE ATLANTIC AREA

As far as transnational cooperation aims at overcoming the barrier effect of boundaries and at furthering the relationship within large territories, the effectiveness of networking is a crucial point regarding the success of the integration aim of the programme *(Box 1)*. The location and structure of the partners' network bring information on this point following three aspects: (1) the spatial proximity, *i.e.* a preferential linkage between partners close to the borders or wherever they locate in the area; (2) the urban hierarchy, *i.e.* a preferential partnership between cities belonging to the same rank in the hierarchy or not; (3) the sectoral proximity, *i.e.* a gathering of cities having the same socioeconomic profile/sharing similar problems, or not. These three aspects display highly contrasted integration processes in both transnational spaces, North West Europe being more segmented than the Atlantic Area.

Box 1. Measuring the networking between cities

The design of city networking is not restricted, in our calculations and maps, to the relations between municipalities, but encompasses all the actors located in the city. So we consider that the relations formed between various partners of two cites may be aggregated and are meaningful of the intentional relationship between these cities.

The aggregation of partners and projects requires a methodological choice, as sometimes one partner takes part in different projects and several partners from a city can take part in the same project. So the number of participations per city takes into account any single partner, counted as many times as he is involved in different projects. The number of common projects between two cities is limited to the different projects in which at least one partner per city is involved.

Our methodology deliberately focuses on the density of partners and the strength of links. This choice is complementary to other studies based on the financial costs per partner [5].

Hierarchy and segmentation of the territory in North West Europe

The representation of the major links displays first a concentration of the network in the centre of the cooperation area *(Figure 4)*. No preferential link exists at the area fringes in Great Britain, Ireland, France and Germany. This comes indeed with no major surprise since most of the partners are located in the central zone. Dublin is here an exception, without any preferential link despite an intense participation to the programme. This can be explained by a diversification of the city partnerships *i.e.* Dublin cooperates with a great number of cities on few projects.

As far as integration is concerned, the map displays a disjunction between two kinds of partnerships: the metropolitan network and the cross-border networks.

The highest numbers of common projects are to be seen between metropolises, namely Paris, Brussels, Den Haag and London. This metropolitan network is not well balanced as two from the four cities are not connected (Paris and Den Haag). The network is actually polarised by Brussels, establishing significant links with each of the three others. The existence of such major partnerships shows that the urban hierarchy plays a role at least in terms of capital

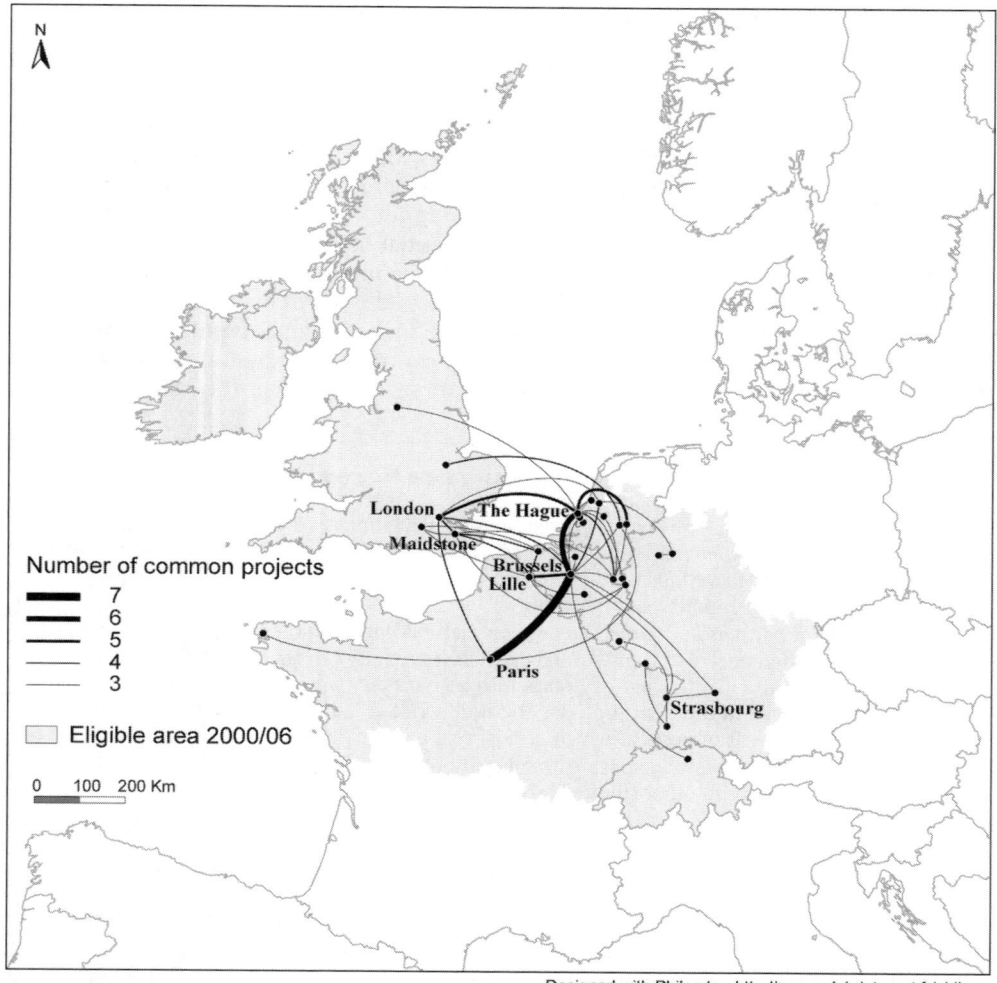

Figure 4. *Major links between cities in Interreg III B NorthWest Europe.*

city functions. Actually this observation confirms that the size of cities is less at stake than their national administrative function; for instance cooperation between central services in charge of water or the environment will occur between different public offices most often located in the capital.

Other major links can be found between border cities. Two border areas are identified, in the perimeter of the Euroregion Kent/Nord-Pas-de-Calais/Belgian regions, and between Luxembourg, Alsace and the neighbouring German Länder. In both areas cooperation between regional authorities began two decades ago, in the former to manage the impacts of the Channel Tunnel, in the latter to help the intense border work relations. The habit of working together in a cross border context is thus an asset to build larger partnerships in the transnational context. We can give the example of the project Rhinenet, "for a sustainable and participatory management of the Rhine", gathering among others partners from Saarbrücken, Stuttgart and Strasbourg, or the project WARELA, "Water retention by land use" in which partners from Luxembourg, Saarbrücken and Freiburg work together.

On this subject, the impression of a relative fragmentation of cooperation networks in NWE is reinforced when analysing the thematic priorities that cities develop. All functions as if the cooperation networks relates to specific thematic priorities *(Figure 5)*. For instance, in the priority "Water resources and prevention of flood damages" there are two major cooperation nodes, the estuaries of the Rhine and the Scheldt in the Netherlands, and the Rhine between France and Germany. The partners in the priority "Promoting territorial integration across seas" come mainly from the harbours in Belgium, the Netherlands and the South of England. Consequently, the organisation of the North West Europe INTERREG partnerships seems to proceed in part from the superposition of several sectoral networks.

As a first conclusion the city networks are not designed in a balanced and integrated way in North West Europe but rather display a segmented territory between a well-connected centre and derelict peripheries. This assertion is especially true in the case of the French NWE regions which are not part of other transnational areas, but must be nuanced for the British regions involved also in the North Sea Area and for the German ones in the CADSES.

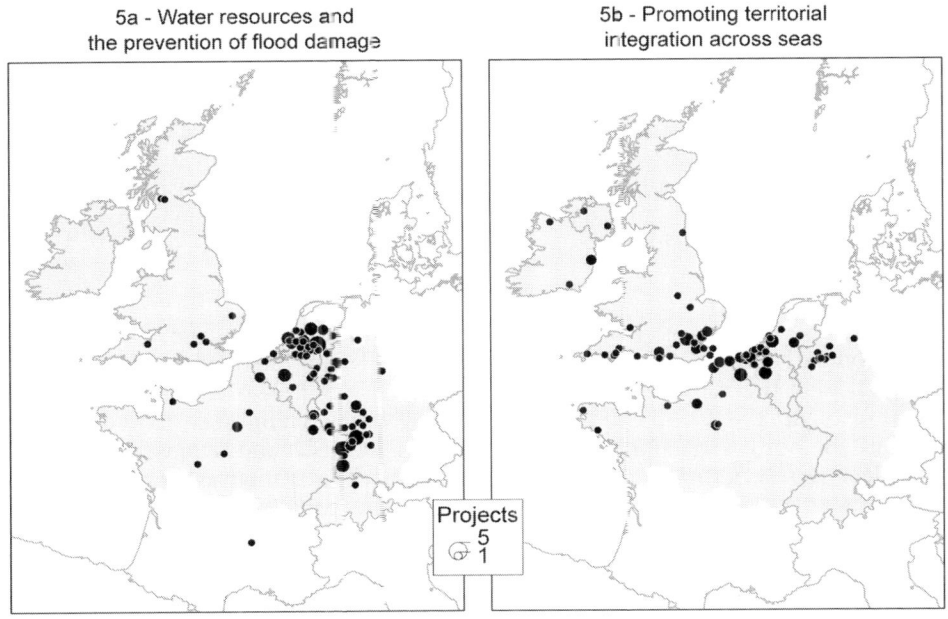

Source : Interreg

Figure 5. *The fragmentation of Northwest Europe transnational network.*

A more balanced network in the Atlantic Area

The relational pattern of cooperating partners is much more balanced in the Atlantic Area than in North West Europe. Almost any city and region of the area is linked to the others, except the Scottish ones – their situation can be explained by their involvement in two other Interreg IIIB programmes, the North Sea Programme and to a less extent the North West Europe. In this web of common links no clear logic stands out, displaying a picture of equal involvement and weak urban hierarchy. For example a big city like Manchester is poorly represented, while the higher number of participations comes to Santiago de Compostela, which is only a medium-size city *(Figure 6)*.

Moreover, Santiago de Compostela has a pivotal situation on the map of major links *i.e.* is linked to the higher number of other cities, although the city is by far smaller than other neighbouring cities like Lisbon or Bordeaux. In financial terms it is also true, as 42% of the total Spanish costs in the programme[3] are concentrated in Galicia, the region whose the capital is Santiago de Compostela. Moreover, the involvement of Galicia in transnational cooperation is not similar to the Dutch one, the latter being caused by the governmental choice of privileging the transnational cooperation (strand B of Interreg) to the detriment of the cross-border one (strand A), the former corresponding to a massive involvement in both strands[4].

How to explain this large involvement? First, as a regional capital Santiago de Compostela concentrates the main regional institutions, as well as numerous Galician lobbies. Moreover, the Galicia has adopted an active policy towards the European Union and in 1988 was one of the first Spanish regions to open a representative office in Brussels. The experience of Galician partners in managing the European projects can also be linked to the amount of Objective 1 funding allocated to the region, and to the cross-border cooperation with the Portuguese region Norte. The Galician participation contrasts with the underrepresentation of other Spanish regions like Andalusia in the Atlantic Area, which can be explained by their involvement in other Interreg IIIB areas, like the Western Mediterranean area (Medocc). Last, the Galician claims on its Atlantic and Celtic heritage finds comprehensive echoes in the Atlantic Area programme. For example the pre-existing Comité Bretagne-Galice must have been a driving force for building cooperation projects [10].

Conclusion

The territorial integration process in Europe may benefit from Interreg transnational cooperation policy on two aspects: the reinforcement of existing links and the creation of new ones. At first sight, the Atlantic Area cooperation programme is more likely to fill these conditions than the North West Europe one, considering the density and "equity" of inter-urban links independently of their rank in the urban hierarchy. The relations in North West Europe are by contrast more hindered and framed by strong pre-existing urban networks. In other

---

3. These data come from the Interreg Atlantic Area joint technical secretariat, Poitiers (situation in September 2006).
4. The border between Spain and Portugal was allocated through the Interreg strand A by far more ERDF funding than the other internal EU borders (25% of the total Community support to cross border cooperation in Europe during Interreg II came to this border).

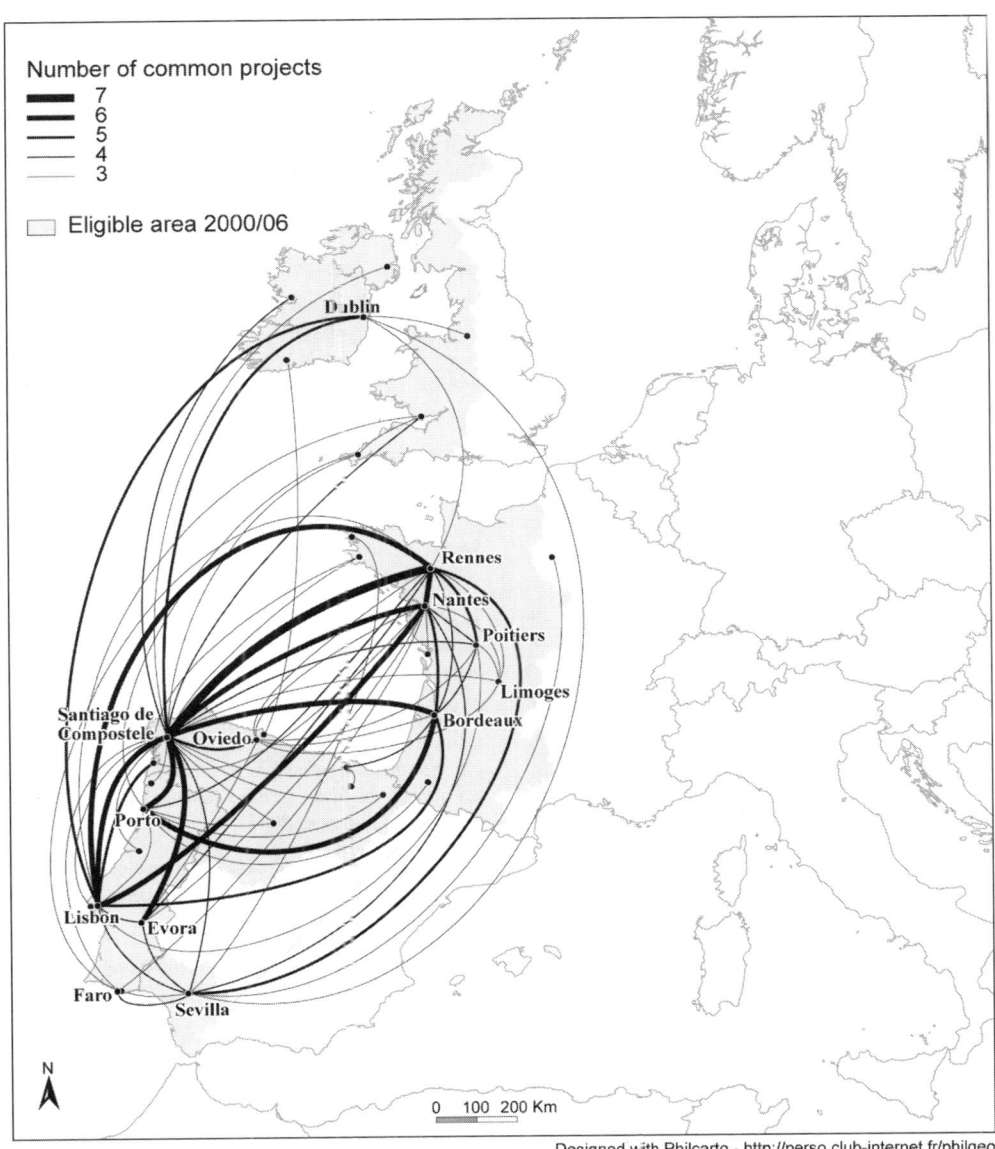

Figure 6. *Major links between cities in Interreg III B Atlantic area.*

terms, the winners in the North West cooperation are the usual winners *i.e.* the "Blue Banana" cities or the cities already used to cross border cooperation. Their international involvement existed before Interreg, while other territories stay away from the networking.

A second debate takes place on the greatest scale of cooperation. Proximity cooperation is easier to implement but is of low efficiency for the European integration. On the other side, the fragmentation of the EU territory in large cooperation areas is likely to create partitioned territories superimposed to the states, thus reproducing the centre-periphery pattern at a smaller scale. This argument is used in the struggle of Atlantic promoters for contesting the structural nature of their peripheral position. The necessity of involving stakeholders from noneligible capitals (London, Paris and Madrid) in many projects tends to put their "auto-organisation capacity" [1] into perspective.

Finally, Interreg transnational cooperation questions the differentiation of regional and urban cooperation practices. We could distinguish two embedded patterns: the cooperation between regions, which appears dominant in the Atlantic network, would be more oriented towards territorial strategies and symbolic stakes (culture, image), whereas the cooperation between cities appears more pragmatic and centred on the resolution of concrete urban planning and management problems.

References

1. Baudelle G (Ed). *La façade atlantique. Stratégies et prospective de développement*. Rennes: PUR, 1993.

2. Bundesamt für Bauwesen und Raumordnung. *Transnationale Zusammenarbeit TransCoop 05 Report*. Berichte, Band 22, 2005.

3. Carrière JP (2002). L'aménagement du territoire en Europe : vers une approche polycentrique multiscalaire. Analyse à partir du cas de l'Espace Atlantique. In : *Le développement territorial – regards croisés sur la diversification et les stratégies*. Guesnier B, Joyal A. Poitiers : ADICUEER, 2004 : 61-80.

4. Cattan N, et al. *Le système des villes européennes*. Paris : Economica, 1999.

5. Colard A. *Comportement des villes et régions francophones dans des programmes européens de coopération*. Paper submitted at the 40th colloquium of the ASRDLF, Bruxelles, 2004, September 1st-3rd, 12 p, www.ulb.ac.be/soco/asrdlf/documents/TexteFinalAlainColard_001.pdf.

6. Doucet P. Transnational planning in the wake of the ESDP: The Northwest Europe experience. In *European Spatial Planning*. Faludi A (Ed). Cambridge (MA): Lincoln Institute of Land Policy, 2002: 59-79.

7. ESPON 1.1.1, 2004. *The role, specific situation and potential of urban areas as nodes of polycentric development (2001-2006), Final Report*. http://www.espon.eu

8. Hamez G, Lesecq G. Réseaux et frontières. La coopération transnationale dans l'Europe du Nord-Ouest. In : *L'intégration européenne du territoire français : perspectives transfrontalières*. Bernard Reitel (Ed). Paris : La documentation française, 2007.

9. Nadin V, Shaw D. Transactional spatial planning in Europe: the role of Interreg IIC in the United Kingdom. *Regional studies* 1998; 32 (3): 281-9.

10. Poussard A. *L'arc Atlantique : chronique d'une coopération interrégionale*. Rennes: PUR, 1997, 241 p.

11. Zillmer S. *Alternative development paths for transnational cooperation?* Paper submitted at the Regional Studies Association conference, Leuven, 2006, June 8th-9th, 20 p.

Integrating the European space-flows and places in North West European city-region networks

Kathy Pain

The Young Foundation, Globalisation and World Cities (GaWC) Study Group, Department of Geography, Loughborough University, United Kingdom

This paper addresses a key contemporary debate about the future impact of globalisation on cities and regions in Europe. As major European cities are increasingly integrated into the global advanced service economy, what will be the likely effects on their regional hinterlands? Advanced business services are widely acknowledged as key economic activities in the European knowledge economy but to what extent can knowledge-based flows extend beyond the "global city network" to advantage "global city-regions"? These questions will be examined in the context of the recent results from the major North West Europe POLYNET study[1]. This transnational research has investigated the proposition that inter-urban flows associated with advanced business services are giving rise to a new phenomenon – the "Mega-City Region" (MCR) – a globally and regionally networked urban space. The overarching results have implications that extend far beyond North West Europe.

FROM GLOBAL CITIES TO MEGA-CITY REGIONS

Whereas the term "megacity" has been associated with mushrooming late twentieth century cities of the South, the emergent MCR is very much a twenty-first century animal. It consists of one or more towns and cities that are interconnected through processes of functional specialisation and agglomeration in the global knowledge-based economy – a space of global-local interaction. A decade ago, Manuel Castells suggested that "global cities" downplay "linkages with their hinterlands on the basis of information flows" [1]. But are global city-region relationships changing with advances in technological and institutional informationalisation? The POLYNET research has examined eight potential MCRs: South East England,

---

1. POLYNET: *Sustainable Management of European Polycentric Mega-City Regions* was funded by the European Regional Development Fund under the INTERREG IIIB North West Europe Programme. Its four empirical studies and policy analysis are reported in: Hall P, Pain K (Eds). The Polycentric Metropolis: Learning from Mega-City Regions in Europe. London: Earthscan, 2006.

Greater Dublin, the Paris Region, the Randstad, Northern Switzerland, Rhine-Main, Rhine-Ruhr and Central Belgium, to discover the answer to this question.

There has been increasing awareness in the academic literature of an intensification of global city-region functional linkages in the world-wide service economy. Advanced producer services (APS) – key sectors in knowledge production – were first identified by Saskia Sassen (1991) as distinctive global city functions. Castells (1996) recognised the importance of the "network enterprise" within the new "informational economy" in contributing to a "new spatial logic" – the "space of flows" – in a "network society", a conceptualisation of late twentieth century spatial relations that helped shape the European economic "Lisbon Agenda" [6]. APS networks have vital importance for Lisbon Strategy priorities to promote Europe's competitiveness in the global economy (European Council 2000) but do they contribute to the realisation of European Spatial Development Strategy objectives for more balanced regional economic development [2]? Research in 2001/2 on central London business clustering [15], first indicated the presence of functional interdependencies between densely clustered global APS activities in the City of London and a wide surrounding area of South East England, lending credence to Scott's assertion that global city-regions are emerging "motors of the global economy" [11]. But investigating the city-region as part of a new local-global spatial logic is not straightforward.

Since Geddes (1915) introduced the term "conurbation" to describe spreading urban development in the early twentieth century, the emphasis in urban planning has centred on demarcating the geographical extent of city-regions as functional entities. Recently, the "Functional Urban Area" (FUA) has been the basis for major European transnational analyses, notably by the GEMACA group [8] and in the ESPON Programme[2]. "Functional Urban Regions" (FURs), similarly based on population size, employment and daily commuting patterns, were used as the "building blocks" to provide initial MCR definitions in POLYNET[3]. But crucially, these analytical approaches rely on data that relates to what Castells (1996) termed the "space of places"; they do not take into account dynamic spaces of flows in globalising advanced services that are crucially relevant to European spatial policy but cannot be mapped using conventional statistical sources.

The European Spatial Development Perspective (ESDP) and North West Europe "Spatial Vision" [9] aim to promote flows from the European economic "core", or "Pentagon", to less-developed "peripheral" cities and regions, supported by Structural and Cohesion Funds. But their proposed policy tool – "polycentricity" – is based on a conceptualisation of spatial relations that originates from traditional land-use planning (spaces of places), predating contemporary theorisation [6]. Major global APS centres London and Paris, are regarded as "monocentric" cities and flows from them to other cities and regions are encouraged through the development of trans-European transport and institutional networks. But to what extent

---

2. European Spatial Planning Observation Network. Notably in ESPON 1.1.1: Nordic Centre for Spatial Development (NORDREGIO) (2004, Revised version 2005) ESPON Project 1.1.1 Potentials for Polycentric Development in Europe, Project Report, http://www.espon.lu/online/documentation/projects/thematic/1873/fr-1.1.1_revised.pdf
3. The geographical extent of the POLYNET MCR was determined by the contiguity of adjacent FURs as explained in Hall's contribution to this book and in Hall P, Pain K, Green N, 2006. "Anatomy of the Polycentric Metropolis: Eight Mega-City Regions in Overview" (Hall, Pain, 2006: 19-52).

are these and other European globally connected cities evolving into functionally multi-nuclear networked regions? POLYNET sought to develop progressive research methods to fill an analytical and policy gap by investigating MCR emergence as a morphologically situated but functionally connected urban process in the space of flows.

The key research objective was to establish how far processes of integration into inter-city APS networks are operating at a regional scale in North West Europe and to what extent this is leading to a new spatial configuration – the MCR – defined by informational flows and knowledge-based functional polycentricity? Because the subject of investigation was the functional inter-linkages conferred on cities and regions by advanced services, the starting point for in-depth study was APS firms, their networks and their implications for knowledge-based flows. Eight knowledge-intensive services were examined: banking/finance, insurance, accountancy, law, management consulting/information technology, advertising, logistics and design. Complementary quantitative and qualitative studies were conducted in tandem.

INTERURBAN LINKAGES AND POLYCENTRICITY

The quantitative method[4] was based on an "interlocking network model" developed from previous global city network analysis [12, 14]. This makes the assumption that information flows between the offices of global multi-locational APS business networks translate into knowledge-based linkages between the cities in which these offices are located. In MCR analysis, the method was used to measure the "connectivity" of towns and cities in the eight study regions within APS networks of four operational scopes – regional, national, European and global – and the inter-linkages between MCR towns and cities conferred on them by the office networks of firms.

The locations and functions of APS offices in each region were identified using web-based sources (company web-sites and business directories) and local intelligence (chambers of commerce, economic development, professional and business agencies etc.) to establish the most prominent APS network locations for each MCR. These locations are comprised of network connectivities at three geographical scales beyond the regional scale. Major cities constituting national APS centres were identified to assess network connectivity at a national scale. At the European and global scales a common set of cities was identified – 25 European cities and 25 world cities – based on global city network analysis [13]. In all, data on the office functions of 1963 service firms and 200 cities were recorded in matrices allowing the "network connectivity" of MCR towns and cities across all four scales to be computed[5] and the linkages between them modelled and mapped schematically as shown in *Figure 1 and 1bis*.

Figures 1 and 1bis reveal very different patterns of inter-urban linkage within the eight study regions. RhineRuhr and the Randstad have the largest number of significant intra-regional urban linkages bypassing their most prominent APS centres, "First Cities" Düsseldorf and Amsterdam, indicating their relative functional polycentricity for regional scope business

---

4. The quantitative method is discussed in detail in Taylor PJ, Evans DM, Pain K, 2006. "Organisation of the Polycentric Metropolis: Corporate Structures and Networks" (Hall, Pain, 2006: 53-64).
5. The algebra is explained in Taylor 2001, 2002.

Cities and networks in Europe – Networking

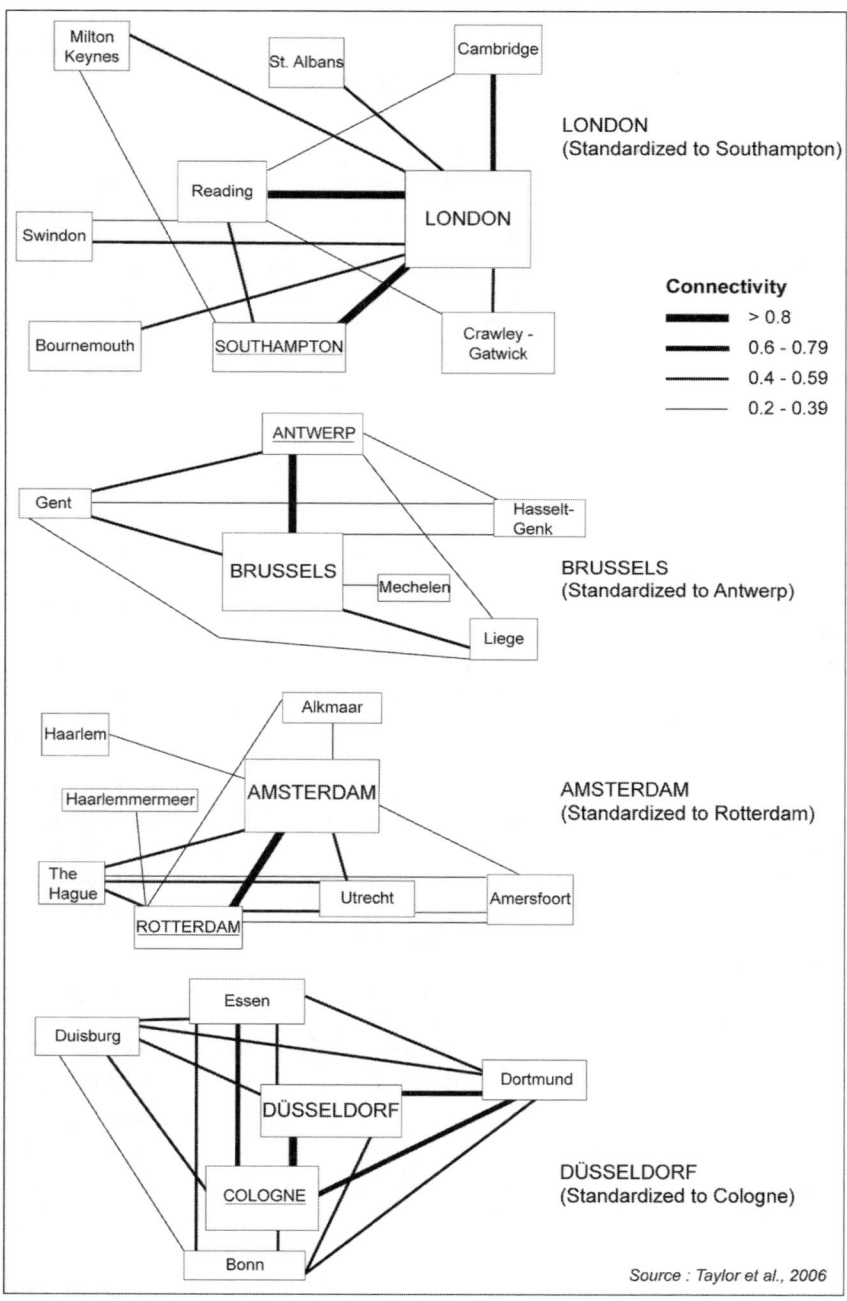

Figure 1. *"Mega-City Region intra-regional linkages"* *(office functions of service firms).*

North West European city-region networks

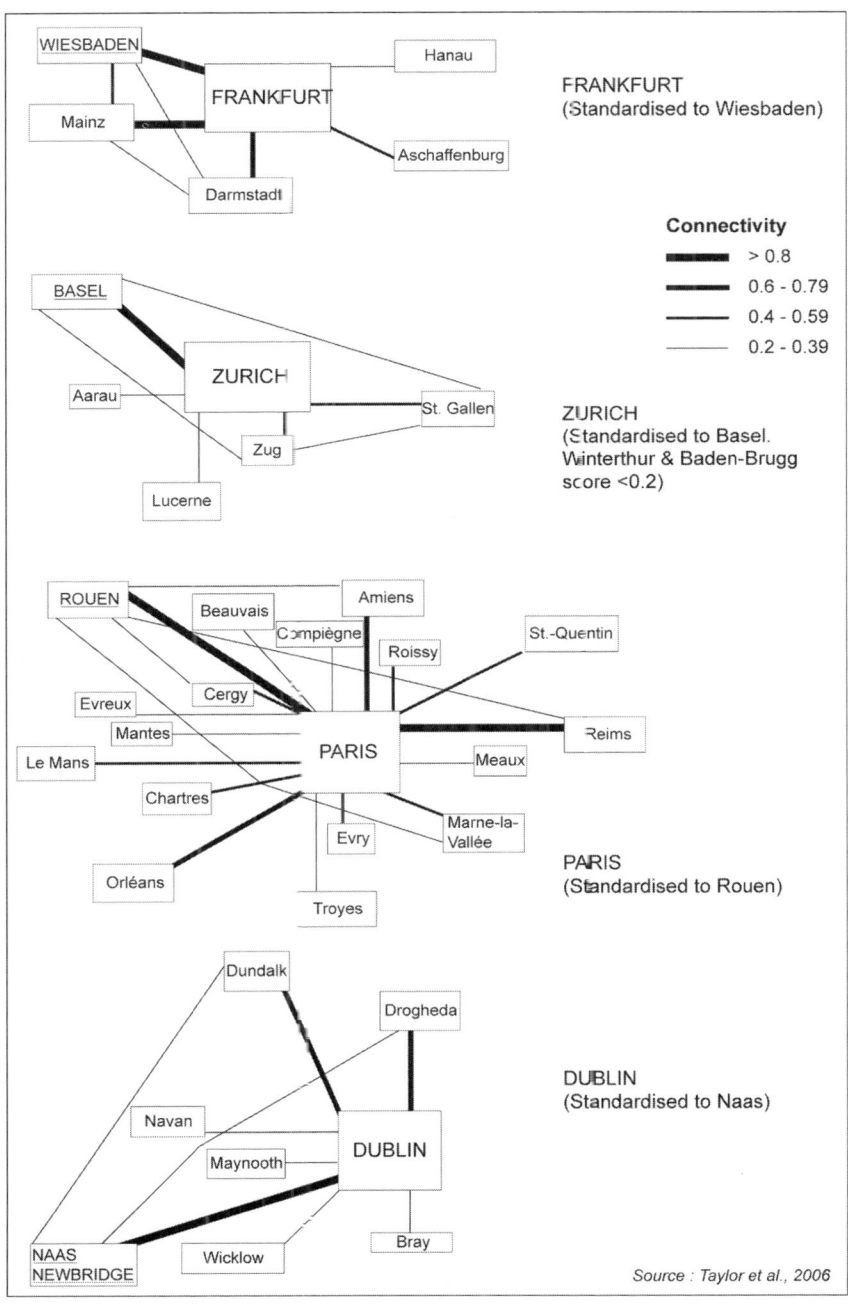

Figure 1bis. *"Mega-City Region intra-regional linkages"* (office functions of service firms).

networks. RhineRuhr appears to be the most polycentric region whereas, in contrast, Paris is a hub for strong linkages with a number of surrounding centres and therefore appears to be a relatively primate city in its region. To an extent, London belies its policy perception as a monocentric city given evidence of cross-cutting inter-urban linkages to the west of the region.

However there is a complication. In order to compare the regions in terms of their polycentricity, their intraregional linkages were calculated individually. The pair of cities with the largest link in each MCR (First Cities with the highest global connectivity in each MCR and "Second" cities) was designated the "prime inter-city link" and the value of all other linkages was computed as a proportion of this, making direct comparison of the size of inter-linkages between MCRs impossible. This is significant because global city network analysis (in Taylor 2003, table 1)shows RhineRuhr First City, Düsseldorf, for example, to have low global APS connectivity relative to other MCR First Cities whereas London and Paris rank first and second European cities (in that order) for global connectivity [13]. The value of RhineRuhr intraregional linkages is therefore likely to be lower than those of other regions yet this is not evident from *Figures 1 and 1bis*. This has important implications for effective functional polycentricity and comparisons between the MCRs with respect to this.

Detailed comparative analysis of MCR polycentricity at national, European and global scales reveals the scale dependency of functional polycentricity. In terms of global connectivity, all regions show markedly increased primacy with First Cities gaining significantly over Second Cities in connectivity. This applies even in the RhineRhur which has strong polycentricity conferred by its regional scope APS networks. Whereas Cologne has 99 per cent of Düsseldorf's regional network connectivity, it has only 58 per cent of its global connectivity, presenting a very different picture of MCR polycentricity than that shown in *Figure 1 and 1bis*. The extreme case is Greater Dublin where urban centres outside Dublin appear completely unconnected to global APS networks.

The unique value of the quantitative analysis is that it reveals for the very first time, a functional geography of city-regions that is produced by connectivity to multi-scale knowledge-based economic and urban networks. Analysis of functional polycentricity at different scales highlights the significance of network scope in constructing MCR inter-urban functional configurations. The results fill an important gap in spatial analysis however it is only by examining actual knowledge-based flows and interactions within and between offices, firms and cities that it is possible to evaluate the real contribution of organisational network connectivities to regional economic development and this calls for a different research approach.

GLOBAL-LOCAL DIMENSIONS AND INTERACTIONS

Discovering the way in which firms interact across space in practice, could only be determined by seeking out the actors who run the networks to find out to what extent their working practices result in actual information flows and knowledge transfer between cities and the intensity and value of these. A large-scale interview survey, complementary to the quantitative analysis already described, was crucial in this. A semi-structured interview methodology was chosen to allow the researchers to dig deep into the reality of MCR processes through in-depth discussion with senior business actors. A questionnaire in English, with translations into relevant languages, was designed to elicit "soft" evidence on firms within the same four network scopes used in the quantitative analysis. More than 600 in-depth face-to-face interviews with firms, trade, professional and government organisations, took place. The majority of interviewees were of chairman, vice-president, chief executive, managing director, partner or senior manager status. The interview results[6] provide a rich and detailed data-base that informs vital questions on how and where innovation occurs and knowledge is produced, how knowledge and information are exchanged, where key global command and control functions are located and the importance of different modes and places of interaction. Some key insights are summarised here.

Markets and practices

Market competition – the key driver in globalisation – was found to be a spur for MCR development. There is an increasing need for firms to compete as global and regional players, and their responses to the dynamic between these levels of interaction have locational effects. Organisational consolidation and disaggregation, knowledge specialisation and diversification, management centralisation and decentralisation, are together leading to processes of concentration and dispersion which are affecting all eight MCRs. But, importantly, these coexist as two-way flows and relate to distinct "front" and "back office", "core" and "context" business functions. Out-sourcing-in-sourcing, offshoring-onshoring, clustering-declustering, reclustering and non-clustering, are found to be complementary processes that are vital to firms' survival in increasingly competitive markets at all operational scales. Despite the high cost of concentrated "global city" central locations, these remain vital for highly complex knowledge production and exchange activities in international business, explaining the quantitative research finding on the primacy of global network connectivity in all eight MCRs. The importance of human relationships and trust, established and sustained in special city milieu for high-value business, innovation and control of risk, give the First Cities in each MCR a singular, specialised role in global service networks.

Knowledge networks

APS are "people businesses" and their reliance on relationships helps explain their specific locational logic. Frequent face-to-face contact and physical proximity are still regarded as essential despite ongoing developments in information and communication technologies (ICTs). Virtual communications are used intensively but competitiveness remains crucially dependent on "hi-tech/hi-touch" ways of working that integrate global and local spaces of flows. Central London is regarded by senior actors in global networks as the international meeting place for the European market where cross-border innovation and knowledge transfer take place. Key reasons are its openness to transnational labour supply, skills and firms and its resultant depth of infrastructure, including languages and cultural diversity. Its co-presence of financial and creative milieux (also identified in Paris), intensity and buzz, make

---

6. The transnational interview evidence is reviewed in Pain K, Hall P (2006): "Firms and Places: Inside the Mega-City Regions"; "Flows and relationships: Internal and External Linkages"; "People and Places: Interrelating the Space of Flows and the Space of Places" (Hall & Pain, 2006: 91-121).

it Europe's "global production centre". But all eight First Cities constitute MCR (and in some cases, national) hubs for global-local interaction. High value/high complexity activity is being concentrated into fewer and fewer European hubs leading to increasing concentration of global firms and functions in these special locations. This is true for all the MCRs even though their First Cities vary in size and level of global APS connectivity. Significantly, their unique role illustrates an interdependence between the "space of flows" and the "space of places", once conceptualised by Castells as two spatial logics [7]. The social, cultural and institutional structures and symbolic practices specific to First Cities, are shown to have importance in attracting scarce high-skilled, transnational people and functions required for global knowledge transfer and innovation. The most intense and high-value flows and transactions are occurring within and between these eight MCR cities, which act as "knowledge gateways" for their surrounding regions.

While the quantitative and qualitative evidence on First City global connectivity agglomeration appears to run counter to European spatial policy priorities for balanced regional development, the reality of MCR functional processes is complex. As already discussed, processes of concentration and dispersion are fluid, not fixed. Some APS functions – back office and business-to-business retail activity – can and do decentralise, facilitated by ICT. The dispersal of activity between cities at different urban and regional scales reflects a functional specialisation across space. Functions dependent on formal and tacit exchanges and requiring high levels of face-to-face interaction between many actors are densely concentrated in First Cities while other knowledge-based activities can be, and in some cases require to be, dispersed[7].

A twist in the findings is that South East England, which appears far less functionally polycentric than the RhineRuhr when considering the quantitative evidence on regional scope networks, was shown from the interview results to have the most significant knowledge-based interactions at an MCR scale – not only between the London hub and its surrounding business centres but also between them – clear evidence of effective functional polycentricity, mirroring the schematic map presented in *Figure 1 and 1bis*[8]. In practice, regional scope business networks were found to contribute least to high-value inter-urban functional linkages. London's strong connectivity to the global city network was found to allow the leverage of transnational skills and knowledge through its central APS cluster, to offer specialised services to multinational businesses outside it. Crucial in this are global network organisations with emergent MCR office networks engaging with specific sub-regional markets. But it is the development of South East England multi-sector APS clusters, also including regional and national networks, that is vitally contributing to high-value knowledge – based flows between towns and cities outside London.

Importantly for policy, this indicates that strong global connectivity agglomeration in just one regional city may be a spur to the development of a complex and geographically extensive regional knowledge economy. National policy contexts and historical development paths are shown to have a crucial impact on MCR emergence. Halbert (2006) for example suggests that in the Paris case, French national and regional policy in support of spatial polycentricity since

---

7. Functional specialisation differs from sectoral specialisation which was not found to have a clear bearing on effective functional polycentricity.
8. See Pain K, Hall P, Potts G, Walker D (2006). "South East England: Global Constellation" (Hall & Pain, 2006: 125-36).

the 1950s has been responsible for preventing the development of a deconcentration of advanced service functions at an enlarged city-region scale similar to that found outside London.

POLICY CHALLENGES AND RECOMMENDATIONS

Taken together, the research findings show that polycentricity is a much more complex concept than is currently acknowledged in European spatial policy.

First, functional polycentricity in the advanced service economy is shown to be distinct from simple morphological polycentricity. Functional specialisation cuts across urban administrative boundaries and can link cities and towns of different sizes through their complementary roles in business networks, as clearly illustrated in South East England. Whereas RhineRuhr and the Randstad are morphologically polycentric, the evidence suggests that at present their inter-urban functional linkages are relatively weak compared to other MCRs.

Second, polycentricity proves difficult to evaluate because network connectivities relate to multiple scales of analysis. Rhine-Main, for example, appears relatively primate functionally, yet it is part of a functionally polycentric national urban network in Germany. Paris appears relatively primate within its region but is part of a functionally polycentric global city network. The specificity of individual cases reflects differing historical institutional, cultural and policy contexts, calling into question the current simplistic conceptualisation of polycentricity as a regional policy tool.

Third, the need for face-to-face contact in knowledge-intensive business services has major implications for MCR development. Time-distance proximity between Secondary and First Cities is crucial to business connectivity. In the case of South East England, regionalization of high-value APS functions requires offices to also "stay close" to global skills and markets in the central London cluster. But polycentricity – morphological and functional – also generates travel between secondary centres, cross-cutting hub-and-spoke transport infrastructure. High frequency criss-cross movement is strongly car dependent in all eight MCRs for reasons of practicality, time and cost, and this has major implications for investment and management of transport infrastructure to support regional economic development alongside priorities for environmental sustainability.

Finally, what are the urgent priorities challenges and recommendations for policy and practice? The need for networking is singled out here due to its key relevance to address a governance deficit found to exist at the MCR scale of functional interaction in all cases. There is a clear need to establish a genuine noncompetitive urban politics as promoted in ESDP (1999) and Spatial Vision (2000) advice. But urban networking needs to be based on an improved understanding of specific objectives that will support both existing and potential inter-urban functional complementarities. Functional specialisation across space was found to be largely independent of territorial and administrative boundaries however institutional policies and practices that reflect jurisdictional divisions, do affect business flows. Government organisations therefore need to be better informed about barriers to business competitiveness and plan across institutional functional and territorial divisions to support agglomeration economies and flows that are vital to regional development. Management of regional infrastructure needs to be co-ordinated across its material and functional dimensions: regulation, taxation, transport, education and housing were all found important to regional knowledge economy development. Crucially, tensions identified between policy priorities for regional economic competitiveness, balanced and sustainable development need to be addressed in policy and research at a European transnational scale[9].

Conclusion

In conclusion, the research has shown North West Europe to be a highly connected functional space with complementarities between its cities that are vital to European integration in the global city network and to the development of regional knowledge economies. The MCR is an emergent scale of interaction, born of a new "spatial logic", whereby multi-scale spaces of informational flows and places are mutually constitutive through networks that involve cities. Further in-depth understanding of the complex relationships giving rise to this spatial phenomenon is essential to inform the future management of sustainable European regional development.

REFERENCES

1. Castells M. *The Information Age: Economy, Society and Culture. Vol. I: The Rise of the Network Society*. Oxford: Blackwell, 2000 (1st ed. 1996).

2. European Commission. *ESDP: European Spatial Development Perspective: Towards Balanced and Sustainable Development of the Territory of the European Union*. Brussels: European Commission, 1999.

3. European Council. *Presidency Conclusions – Lisbon European Council, 23 and 24 March*, 2000. http://ue.eu.int/ueDocs/cms_Data/docs/pressData/en/ec/00100-r1.en0.htm

4. Geddes P. *Cities In Evolution: An Introduction to the Town Planning Movement and to the Study of Civics*, London: Benn, 1968 (1st ed. 1915).

5. Halbert L. The Polycentric Region that never was: The Paris Agglomeration, Bassin Parisien and spatial Planning Strategies in France. *Built Environment* 2006; 32, 2: 184-93.

6. Halbert L, Pain K, Thierstein A. European Polycentricity and Emerging Mega-City Regions: "One Size Fits All" Policy? *Built Environment* 2006; 32, 2: 206-18.

7. Hoyler M, Pain K. London and Frankfurt as World Cities: Changing Local-Global Relations. In *Stadt und Region – Dynamik von Lebenswelten*. Mayr A, Meurer M, Vogt J (Eds). Leipzig: Deutscher Gesellschaft für Geographie (DGfG), 2002: 76-87.

8. IAURIF. *North-West European Metropolitan Regions: Geographical Boundaries and Economic Structures*. Paris: IAURIF, 1996.

9. NWMA Spatial Vision Group. *Spatial Vision for the North Western Metropolitan Area (NWMA)*. Bristol: University of the West of England, 2000.

10. Sassen S. *The Global City: New York, London, Tokyo*. Princeton: Princeton University Press, 2001 (1st ed. 1991).

11. Scott AJ (Ed). *Global City-Regions: Trends, Theory, Policy*. Oxford: Oxford University Press, 2001.

12. Taylor PJ. Specification of the world city network. *Geographical Analysis* 2001; vol. 33: 181-94.

13. Taylor PJ. European Cities in the World Network. In *The European Metropolis 1920-2000*. Dijk H. van (Ed). Rotterdam: Erasmus Universiteit, 2003. http://hdl.handle.net/1765/1021 accessed in January 2006.

---

9. The transnational research agenda developed at the end of POLYNET project is outlined in Hall & Pain, 2006: 197-211.

14. Taylor PJ, Catalano G, Walker DRF. Measurement of the world city network. *Urban Studies* 2002; vol. 39: 2367-76.

15. Taylor PJ, Beaverstock J, Cook G, Pandit N, Pain K, Greenwood H. *Financial Services Clustering and its Significance for London*. London: Corporation of London, 2003.

Why Hawaii or the Azores are an adequate representation of polycentrism?

Louis Marrou
University of La Rochelle, France

Oceanic archipelagos don't seem to be the best way to understand urban planning and networks in Europe. They are far from the core of the main continent and their urban networks are rather poor. But it seems that certain characteristics of archipelagos are rather similar to patterns of urban planning. Maritime archipelagos, such as the Azores or the Canary Islands are a good place to examine a different kind of polycentrism at work. We will consider the islands as a town, and the archipelago as an urban network in a continental situation.

Archipelago and planning

In the last decade of the 20th century French geographer Olivier Dolfus (2000) and other scientists described the new global order: the global cities which contribute to networking the world. They talk about global cities and megapoles. These global megapoles around the world (mainly Tokyo, New-York, London and maybe Paris) work as a system. O. Dolfus used the archipelago image because the Archipel Megapolitain Mondial (world megacity archipelago) is made of islands, the megacities themselves. These cities account for 80% of the scientific knowledge production and 75% of the financial flows. They surface to the top of the world as islands in the ocean. With O. Dolfus and other researchers such as Saskia Sassen, the "archipelago" appears now as a classical model in urbanism and planning.

Why is the concept of archipelago useful in thinking about polycentrism? In its classical definition, an archipelago is a group of islands. In French as in other Roman languages, archipelago is truly a polysemic term:

– the archaic name of the Aegean Sea. The Archipelago is the Aegean Sea for the Ancients;
– any sea with groups of islands;
– a set of places, or things;
– any set of things, usually similar, which can be compared to an archipelago.

In a classical French geographic definition, R. Brunet (2005) wrote that an "archipelago" is a set of islands assembled in a whole. But all groups of islands are not called archipelagos. In English, the term "islands" is used to define a group of islands rather than the term archipelago. For example, the Canaries are known more often as the Canary Islands than as the Canary archipelago. The term "group" is used the same way, like in the Vanuatu. The core notion in an archipelago is the idea of a link, a connection, which seems to be indeed the main characteristic of archipelagos. The purpose of that link could be the vicinity of islands, a community of interests, one or several shared concerns, legislation prospects or identical goals around a project.

In the different types of groups of islands, genuine archipelagos (group of islands with links) are very few in number. All the other "constellations" of islands without ties, or with very tenuous links, are what we propose to define as "conîlats".

THE REAL BIRTH OF A DEFINITION FOR ARCHIPELAGOS

If the word archipelago is old, the real birth of a definition is more recent and linked to the evolution of sea legislation. During the preliminary works of the III United Convention on the Law of the Sea (10 December 1982), different countries such as Indonesia, the Philippines, Mauritius or the Fiji Islands tried to give sense and reality to an archipelagic point of view. This implies viewing the sea as a territory: the islands, the water between the islands and the marine territories comprising them are part of a unique entity.

For the purposes of this Convention, the Part IV defines the status of the Archipelagic States (article 46). "Archipelagic state" means a state constituted wholly by one or more archipelagos and may include other islands. "Archipelago" means a group of islands, including parts of islands, interconnecting waters and other natural features which are so closely interrelated that such islands, waters and other natural features form an intrinsic geographical, economic and political entity, or which historically have been regarded as such.

WOULD IT BE POSSIBLE TO SEE THE ARCHIPELAGO AS THE PERFECT POLYCENTRIC OBJECT? THE AZORES EXAMPLE

As a geographer and planner we are used to base our work on territory. For the sake of this analysis, we will examine the Azores archipelago. The Azores is a nine-island Portuguese archipelago in the heart of the Atlantic Ocean. Santa Maria Island is 1,500 kilometres from the coast of the Iberian Peninsula. On the other side, Flores and Corvo are the two most western islands of the Azores, 3,700 kilometres from the American coast. The archipelago stretches 620 kilometres from East to West *(Figure 1)*.

The arrival of the Portuguese goes back to 1429. They came from Lisbon and the Madeira archipelago for exploration, trade, settlement and religious purposes. Thus the Azores began just an additional step during this period of "Discoveries". Here, the Portuguese found good living conditions and, within a century, they settled all nine islands. During the 16th century, part of the agricultural production was exported to the Kingdom (Lisbon) and shipped to Portuguese castles on the North African coast.

Hawaii or the Azores: adequate representation of polycentrism?

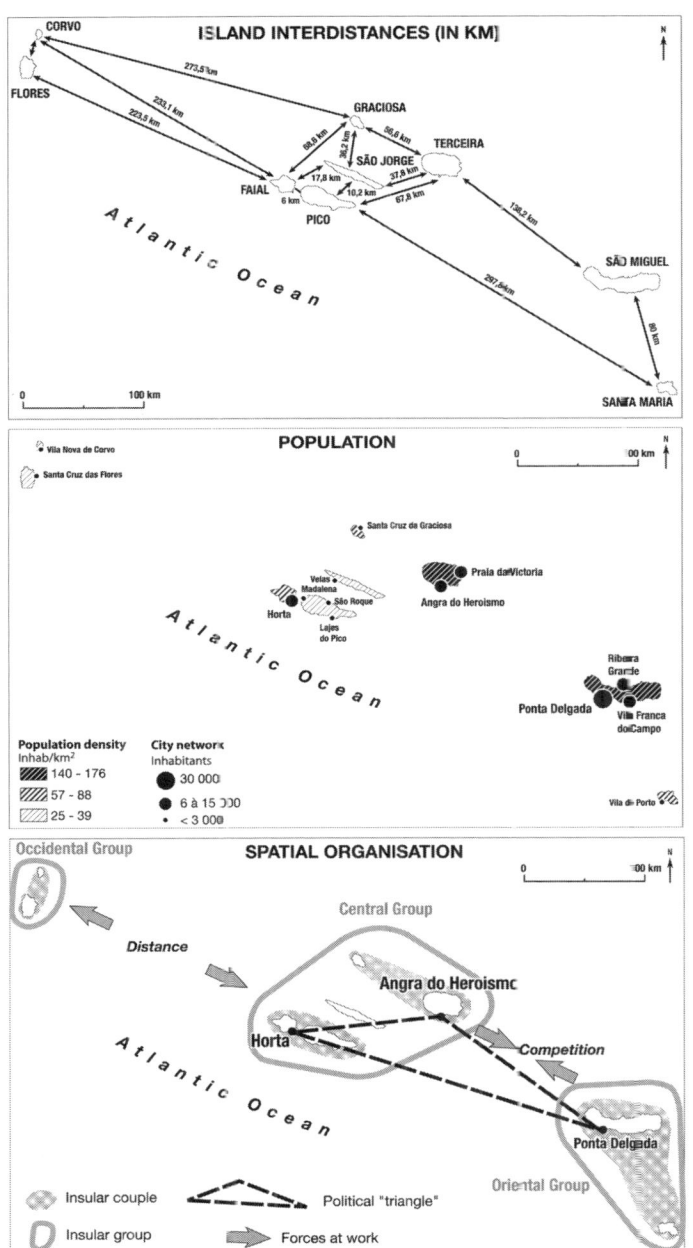

Figure 1. *The Azores*.

The success or failure of settlement on each island depends on its size, its location and the geographical conditions, for example available water resources or volcanic activity. The present demographic situation is very specific. The number of inhabitants at the beginning and at the end of the 20th century remained unchanged at about 240,000. But in the sixties, there were 100,000 more inhabitants, 340,000 total. The tradition of migration is a secular one. As early as the 16th century, people from the Azores took part in the settlement of Brazil.

São Miguel Island is a very important island: it accounts for 35% of the archipelago's surface area and 53% of the population. More than one out of two Azoreans lives in São Miguel. On the other hand, Flores and Corvo are characterised by low densities with less than 30 inhabitants per square kilometres. Flores has no more than 4,000 inhabitants.

When cities make islands!

From the early years of settlement, each island in the Azores archipelago has had specific roles. Terceira is the prime island, something like the mainland due to the presence and location of the main political, religious, judicial powers. São Miguel Island is the eternal competitor of Terceira in leading the archipelago. São Miguel has the land, the people and a large part of the power, but not the glory. Faial Island is a medium-size island but rules the second largest island in the archipelago, Pico at a distance of 6 km, which is close to it.

To summarize, one can underline that the nine Azorean islands have very different sizes. There is only one "big" island: São Miguel (768 km^2) and small islands: Santa Maria, Graciosa, Flores and Corvo. The viability of Corvo's 17 square kilometres can be seen as the fruit of Azorean solidarity. The settlement disparities between islands are even more explicit. Corvo, with 800 inhabitants, have an only and unique settlement while São Miguel presents a clear hierarchical urban network. The Azorean urban network is rather well-balanced. Ponta Delgada (28,000 inhabitants), Angra do Heroísmo (20,000 inhabitants) and Horta (6,500 inhabitants) are the main island cities (São Miguel, Terceira and Faial). Towns like Ribeira Grande and even Lagoa in São Miguel or Praia da Vitoria (Terceira) have real urban functions. The weight of each city on its island is rather small, except for Horta which concentrate significant part of the population of Faial Island.

Ponta Delgada is a small-size city among all Portuguese cities, much smaller than Funchal, the main city of the Madeira archipelago, number four after Lisbon, Porto, Coimbra. Ponta Delgada represents 21.3% of the population of São Miguel when Angra do Heroísmo gathers more than 1/4 of Terceira's population (28.6%) and Horta 43.2%. Thus the archipelagic ratio of the main cities' populations is 1 to 4, while the archipelagic ratio of the islands' total populations is 1 to 8. This fact is very revealing. The city population of Horta (6,500 inh.) is 23.2% of the city population of Ponta Delgada (28,000 inh.) when the 15,063 inhabitants of Faial are only 11.4% of the population of São Miguel (131,609 inh.). The urban network of the Azores seems to be particularly well balanced. How can we explain this situation?

Main planning characteristics of the Azores

Throughout its history, the Azores archipelago has fluctuated between complementarity and competition while trying to manage the relations between islands. Regarding the past 30 years, four major features have been identified as characteristic of the Azores' growth.

The first one corresponds to the 'Revolução dos Cravos" in April 1974: a new era begins for Portugal, its Empire and the Atlantic archipelagos. For the Azores, regionalization and the implementation of an autonomous government along with continental Portugal's power structure is still in process. It's the best way to make the archipelago a real entity (to achieve a sort of "archipelisation"). The second feature is the heavy investments and financial transfers flood in the Azores. Those funds came from the Portuguese government, the European Community, the North American communities of migrants (and indeed the Autonomous Region of the Azores). The third characteristic is that the Azores regional development has to take into account specific migration patterns. The fragmentation of the archipelago that leads to a particular distribution of influence and power is the fourth feature. This power is shared by three cities (and three islands).

In Ponta Delgada on São Miguel, one can find the headquarters of the autonomous regional government. Some ministries are housed in Angra do Heroísmo or in Horta. In Angra do Heroísmo on Terceira, the head office of the republic ministry, "Ministro da Republica", which represents the Portuguese Authority of Lisbon is localised and the Portuguese President of the Republic appoints this Minister. In Horta on Faial Island, the headquarters of the regional parliament of the autonomous region of the Azores takes place. Horta is the meeting place for the deputies of the nine islands in the archipelago.

Consequently, in the Azores there is not one capital city, but three or maybe NO capital city. This is the core of our analysis. Is an archipelago a kind of polycentric territory or a territory without a centre?

Power and archipelago

Our example is not an isolated case. The neighbouring archipelago of the Canaries is constituted of seven islands. Its history is very similar to that of the Portuguese archipelagos in the Atlantic. The Canary Islands are one of the autonomous communities of Spain. They are made up of two different provinces.

There is not one capital city for the autonomous community but two cities, which govern the territory in turn, for six months each! The cities of Las Palmas de Gran Canaria and Santa Cruz de Tenerife, on two different islands, are the two faces of the same reality. And those cases are not the only ones. The situation in the Comoros and in different island states in the Pacific Ocean demonstrates that an archipelago could be a brilliant experimentation field for observing polycentrism at work.

The keys to understanding an archipelago

One can highlight four keys to understanding what living in an archipelago means. To live in an archipelago is like learning how to live together in a fragmented territory. Living together is, first, making plans together. To define oneself in relation to something, something that is not focused on a centre, a core. To live in an archipelago involves resolving discontinuities, disregarding distances. For centuries sea was the answer and boats the solution. Now both sea and air transport ensure the accessibility of each group of islands. The combination of air and sea solutions provide a viable transport system as shown in the Canary Islands' example *(Figure 2)*.

To live in an archipelago requires playing with competition and complementarity between the elements of a whole, which leads to refusing a set pattern and choosing possibilities of fluctuating combinations. Archipelago brings forth flexibility and conciliation. This changeability applies as well to time as to space. To live in an archipelago means accepting to take time and this option isn't a good bargain.

Conclusion

Maritime archipelagos could be studied as polycentric territories because each of them seems to be:

– a well-balanced territory;
– lability seems to be a real quality of these polycentric objects. Lability could be defined as the opposite of something permanent;
– fragmentation appears as an element of recomposition. Archipelagos suggest a large number of possible answers;
– an archipelago is a meeting place and a crossroads.

Both the Azores and Canary archipelagos are characterized by excellent accessibility. European regulations in terms of transport and accessible public services have ensured a balanced treatment among all islands. In the Azores, the "archipelarity" rate, which defines the transport accessibility, is very high: 98.6%. It means that 98.6% of the population can easily reach the whole population of the archipelago.

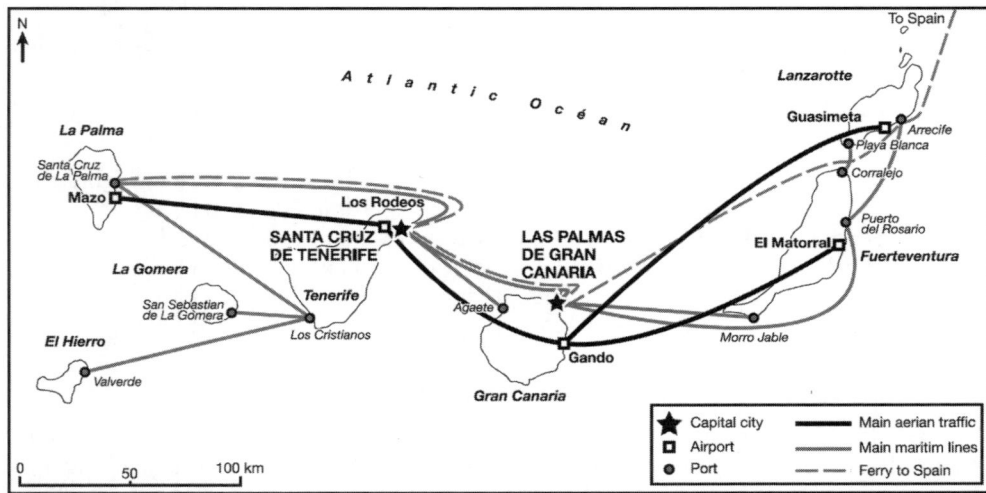

Figure 2. *Canary islands.*

Hawaii or the Azores: adequate representation of polycentrism?

In a polycentric territory like an archipelago, competition, more than complementarity between islands, poverty and migration have imposed the "archipelisation" (the formation of an archipelago), such as in the Azores for example. It means that throughout history, competition has won the process, but now, it is political forces that promote the archipelago. Polycentrism is a political choice, expensive but viable. It is based on a discerning power distribution. Many times balance in planning has been made through dependence. More than a simple object of interest in maritime geography, the archipelago proves to be an elaborate process which maps out and interprets the world around us.

References

1. Brunet R, Ferras R, Théry H. *Les mots de la géographie : dictionnaire critique*. Paris: La Documentation Française, 2005, 518 p.

2. Brunet R., Dolfus O. *Mondes Nouveaux, Tome I de la Géographie Universelle*. Paris : Éditions Belin, 2000, 480 p.

3. Depraetere C. Le phénomène insulaire à l'échelle du Globe : tailles, hiérarchies et formes des îles océanes. *L'Espace Géographique* 1991 ; n° 2 : 126-34.

4. Luis José Ángel Hernández. Temporal accessibility in archipelagos: inter-island shipping in the Canary Island. *Journal of Transport Geography*, Elsevier, 2002; n° 12 : 231-39.

5. Marrou L. *La figure de l'archipel*. La Rochelle : Université de La Rochelle, inédit scientifique d'une Habilitation à Diriger des Recherches, 2005, 362 p.

6. Mc Call G. Nissology: a debate and discourse from below. *Science and Research-Ocean* 1998; 98, 19 p. www.ocean98.org/Nisso.htm (28/11/2003).

7. Nations Unies. *Le droit de la mer. Pratique des États-archipels*. New York : Division des affaires maritimes et du droit de la mer. Bureau des affaires juridiques, 1992, 248 p.

8. Sassen S. *La ville globale*. New-York, Londres, Tokyo, Paris : Éditions Descartes, 1996, 530 p.

Part IV
Polycentrism: A view point from experiences outside Europe

Territorial development and polycentrism made in USA: Between the logic of the market and a federal organization

Cynthia Ghorra-Gobin
CNRS, Espaces, Nature et Culture, Institut d'Études Politiques de Paris, France

Adopting a comparative perspective between Europe and the United states in order to discuss the polycentrism theory, which implies a coherent spatial distribution of cities at the European scale, requires some precautions. The purpose of the comparative analysis is not to take the American mode of territorial development as a model but to reveal its hidden principles by taking into consideration the cultural representations as well as the social practices. This can be easily illustrated by the development of the railroad network which increased economic growth, urbanized the country and gave to its territory a polycentric urban form. In the 19th century, the Federal State subsidized the private railroad companies through grant lands while letting them free to decide about the layout. The configuration of the network privileged some areas to the detriment of others but the consequences of this spatial disparity have never been really discussed in the political arena.

After (1) putting in evidence the institutionalization of the polycentric form through the statute of the city in the political institutions, after (2) underlining the weight of the liberal and neo-liberal thought in the social practices through the principle of social mobility and after (3) taking into consideration the importance of the infra-metropolitan scale within the cultural representations, the analysis stresses the specificity of the American dialectic between the logic of the market and the polycentric form. In this case, polycentrism is neither really planned as such nor does it contribute to any kind of territorial cohesion.

INSTITUTIONAL POLYCENTRISM: THE STATUTE OF THE CITY IN A FEDERAL ORGANIZATION

The United States are a Federal State which started to organize its 13 colonial territories before reaching the number of 50 states. They adopted a Federal constitution in 1789 where the notion of city is completely inexistent [6]. This fact can easily be explained given the limited number of the population living in cities – as confirmed by the first census of 1790 which indicates that the urban population is less than 5% of the total population – and given the weak connotation towards the city. Urbanization is not seen as a new phase of progress for humanity. Therefore democracy is rooted in the values of the rural society and contrary to Europe it is not associated to the city. In their research, Morton and Lucia White have underlined the limited interest to the city in the writings of the American intellectuals and politicians [14]. Benjamin Franklin and Thomas Jefferson as well as intellectuals and novelists such as Ralph Waldo Emerson, Herman Melville, Nathaniel Hawthorne, Edgar Allan Poe and Henry Adams, have all underlined the inconveniences of the city for the diffusion of social values. The only exception has been Frederick C. Howe who in 1905, wrote that the city could be understood as a spatial and political organization able to diffuse the values of democracy. It follows that the vision of the city as well as of the national territory by the Federal government is extremely limited until the New Deal and later in the 60s thanks to the social mobilization of the public opinion[1].

From a judicial point of view, the city (as well as the county) is under the authority of the State. It is part of the State constitution. It is up to the State to choose its capital. Most of the States have designated a small city as the capital city in order to dissociate the spatial sphere of political power from the spatial sphere of the economic power. Hence the first three cities of the country, New York, Los Angeles and Chicago, have to follow the rules edicted by their Capital cities, Albany, Sacramento and Springfield which enjoy a nice urban environment. In the state of Wisconsin, Madison (the State capital), is much more attractive than Milwaukee which has been for a long time an industrial centre. This political choice in favour of small cities is linked to the cultural representations which value the rural country and dissociate economic dynamism and political power. The location of the federal Capital, Washington D.C. results from the choice of the President and of the Congress who were in favour of keeping their distance from the booming cities and specially Philadelphia (the most dynamic city by the end of the XVIIIth century) while being more centrally located to the west. The period of the New Deal under the leadership of president Franklin D. Roosevelt (1933-45) represents an exception which can be explained because of the Great Depression when a quarter of the active population went into unemployment. The Federal State is inspired by Keynesian ideas and decides to intervene in the economic sphere while favouring some territories. The New Deal creates programs such "grants-in-aid" which allow States to implement economic development programs. The two best examples are the Tennessee Valley Authority and the Columbian River Basin. The Federal State financed the construction of dams for the production of electricity, for improving river transportations for goods and for creating leisure areas.

The federal organization of the United States (300 million inhabitants in 2006) is defined by the Constitution and includes 50 States which are in charge of their territory. This system largely explains the lack of any sense of spatial planning or "regional planning". The federal system also presents serious problems of inter-governmental coordinations as expressed during the nine eleven terrorist attack against the World Trade Center in New York and the natural disaster in New Orleans. In New York, the mayor of the city and the chief police did

---

1. For the last two decades, the American public opinion has not been in favour for subsidizing depressed areas. This attitud is largely due to the fact that the American society is suburban and that the middle class is segregated from the inner-cities.

not know to which authority they had to ask for the closure of the airport in order to prevent a new aerial attack [6]. This federal organization explains the limited influence of the Federal State on its urban and rural territory even though it imposed the grid system.

In the 1980s, the Reagan administration largely influenced by the neo-liberal ideology worked on a program of "dereglementation" and on the retreat of central government. As a consequence of this movement, the States took initiatives in economic and territorial development on the basis of public-private partnership and the help of universities. This movement often called "new federalism" [11] helped declining industrial cities such as Pittsburgh to go through a process of economic restructuring and urban renewal. Pittsburgh succeeded in creating a new economic development based on tertiary activities. The city built new buildings in the downtown as well as new leisure and commercial centres, conventions and hotels centres.

A federal perspective linked to the ideal of flexibility in the relationship between the Federal State and the 50 States as well as the non-inscription of the city in the Federal constitution explains the limited interest of the central government for a regional planning perspective organized around city-regions. The polycentric figure of the United States is not really planned but is an outcome of the lack of spatial planning and this theoretical distinction between economic forces and political powers is embedded in the logic of the market forces.

THE INFLUENCE OF THE LIBERAL IDEOLOGY

Beyond the federal organization of the United States *per se*, the polycentric figure of the country results from its deep belief in the capacities of the individuals and their willingness to move from one place to another in order to follow the dynamic of the labour market (supply-demand). This capacity to move plays actively at two scales: between the cities on a national and regional scale or inside the same urban area.

The inter-urban system

Throughout its history, the American society has been defined as a "people on the move" ready to leave one place in order to improve their conditions of life. Domestic migrations have always characterized the American mood as well as the international migrations. The city of Los Angeles – which has been integrated to the American federation in the middle of the 19th century – has been mainly inhabited by American families and individuals coming from the East coast and later on from the Midwest, until the middle of the XXth century whereas the city of New York received flows of immigrants from Europe. Today this situation has changed since the 1970s: both cities are receiving international flows of immigrants and are responsible of domestic migrations. The belief of the American society is that "people should follow capital to new frontiers of opportunity". Capital is drawing the frontier of new economic opportunities as demonstrated by the westward movement in the 19th century. In the late 1970s President Jimmy Carter (Democratic Party) created a special task-force to advice the Federal government concerning the deindustrialization state of the economy. The economists' position was in favour of a "laisser-faire" attitude: entrepreneurs had to find by themselves new strategies and new products. People should find their own way to reach prosperity, an attitude which prevents central government to get involved in planning for economic and territorial development. This American attitude which can also be explained by the scale of the national territory – closer to the continental scale – has been reinforced with the advent of the global economy. In 1993 president Clinton clearly stated that "the era of big government is closed", a point of view which has also been the "leitmotif" of President Bush.

This lack of intervention of central government in the territorial and economic development does not mean that it does not intervene in the economy. The Federal State does not create "poles of competition" but it finances the development of research and innovation mainly in the defence sector. The close relation between Washington and some prestigious research centres linked to universities and located in the west of the country explains the economic boom of Sunbelt States. Difficult to explain the rise of the Silicon Valley without the financial help of Central government to research centres of the private university of Stanford in Palo Alto [10, 12] in Santa Clara County. Recently the State of California (after a referendum in the fall of 2004) decided to finance stem cells research. Sacramento required Californian cities willing to receive the Cell Stem Institute to write a proposal. In June 2005, the governor chose the city of San Francisco.

Sectorial programs financed by central government and by the States as well as a culture of mobility are responsible of the territorial development in the United States and its logic of polycentrism.

The infra-urban scale

In the United States, the unplanned polycentric model – which results from an institutional framework based on flexible federalism and on the liberal ideology which favours the mobility of the individuals –, could also be observed at the infra-urban and infra-metropolitan level.

The sociologist Joel Garreau was the first to clearly identify the role of Edge Cities (EC) in the dynamism of the metropolitan areas. Throughout the 19th and 20th centuries, urbanization has been mainly characterized by a process of suburbanization. People were moving out of the city in order to live in single-family houses near the nature. This residential suburbanization has been followed then by a commercial decentralization process (commercial centres and regional malls) and in the 1970s by a decentralization of the labour market. New jobs were created in the Edge Cities at the intersection of freeways. As written in the introduction of Garreau's book: *"Most of us spend our entire lives in and around these EC, yet we barely recognize them for what they are. That's because they look nothing like the old downtowns: they meet none of our preconceptions of what constitutes a city. Our new EC are tied together not by locomotives and subways, but by freeways, jetways, and jogging paths"*.

The recognition of the edge cities phenomenon meant that the urban sprawl was partly structured around polycentrism since most of the large cities got several EC. The Washington DC area encompasses 16 edge cities. Among them: Bethesda, Silver Springs, Tyson's Corner, Rosslyn/Ballston and Alexandria. The central cities of metropolitan areas have been slowly loosing jobs in favour of suburban and exurban locations (except for the financial sector).

Robert E. Lang speaks of "Edgeless cities" when he refers to exurban locations which are not characterized by a dense urban fabric.

For most American observers, EC were then recognized as being products of the marketplace even though the freeway system has been largely subsidized by the Federal State and the States [5]. However this point of view has been recently challenged by Lang who worked mainly on the Phoenix case. According to him there was a concern in the Phoenix area that office development was scattered far beyond a polycentric form: regional planners were then able to promote the growth of multiple large-scale, mixed-use business centres to capture most new office developments, leading the region to adopt various land use policies, such as density bonuses, designed to promote urban village growth. It follows then that large malls often anchored office developments. The densification process around EC happened because developers were ready to work through a zoning board. Difficult then to conclude that polycentrism at the infra-metropolitan scale is the only result of the "hidden hand" of the marketplace.

Conclusion: In the USA, polycentrism does not necessarily imply a coherent spatial pattern

In the United States, the urban system (cities and their networks) is characterized by polycentrism. These spatial characteristic results from the scale of the country, from an institutional and historical organization rooted in a flexible federalism and from a political culture favouring the liberal philosophy. The city is not mentioned in the Federal constitution and at the State level the capital city is rarely associated with the economic centres. The Federal State has never undertaken a voluntary task in favour of a homogenous spatial and economic development of its territory, except for the construction of infrastructures (dams and freeways). There is also a strong belief that it is up to individuals to look for economic opportunities and be ready to move to another place or another State if they think they can improve their conditions of life. However the Federal State seriously participates in the economic dynamism when it allocates public funds for innovative researches conducted by universities. Polycentrism is then located somewhere between the market forces and the Federal impulse through sectorial funds.

The territorial development of the United States and its polycentric characteristic (including at the infra-metropolitan level) does not result from a planned vision of the Capital city of the Federal State but relies mainly on the initiatives undertaken by its localities. In the American political culture, there is a strong and shared belief that if individuals, entrepreneurs (in the private sector as well as in the political sphere) have a clear and shared vision of what they would like to see happen they could rely on the help of the government which represents them. Cities like Los Angeles, San Diego or Phoenix (Arizona) would never be what they are given the climate conditions if local leaders and private entrepreneurs did not work together and behave as lobbyists at the Federal level in the beginning of the 20th century. The Federal State has then taken the responsibility of supplying water to urban dwellers and farmers by the construction of dams and pipes. More recently, the economist Richard Florida explains the revival of some neighbourhoods in central cities of metropolitan areas because of the emergence of a "creative class" of people that he defines as people involved in creative occupations. For Annalee Saxenian who is the scholar of the Silicon Valley, the category "creative class" includes immigrants. If creativity is being seen as a "common good" in the new economy, the probability for polycentrism to prosper is great, even if it does not imply, as in the United States, that polycentrism is necessarily associated with a coherent spatial pattern.

REFERENCES

1. Bourne LS. The North American Urban System. In *North America: A Geographical Mosaic*. Boal FW, Royle SA (Eds). Londres: Arnold, 1999: 174-92.

2. Fosler RS (Ed). *The New Economic role of American States*. NY: Oxford University press, 1988.

3. Florida R. *The Rise of the Creative Class*. New York: Basic Books, 2004 (1st ed. 2002).

4. Friedmann J, Bloch R. American Exceptionalism in regional planning, 1933-2000. *International Journal of Urban and Regional Planning* 1990; 14, 4: 576-601.

5. Ghorra-Gobin C. *Les États-Unis entre local et mondial*. Paris : Sciences Po press, 2000.

6. Ginsberg B, Lowi TJ, Weir M. *An Introduction to American Politics*. New York: Norton and Company, 2003 (1st ed. 1997).

7. Howe FC. *The City: The Hope of Democracy*. T. Fisher Unwin, 1905.

8. Kaspi A. *Les Américains*. Paris : Seuil, 1985.

9. Long L. *Migration and Residential Mobility in the United States*. New York: Russell Sage Foundation, 1988.

10. Markusen A. Defence spending: a successful industrial policy? *International Journal of Urban and Regional Research* 1986; 10: 105-22.

11. Osborne D. *Laboratories of Democracy*. Harvard Business School Press, 1988.

12. Saxenian A. *Regional Advantage: culture and competition in Silicon Valley and Route 128*. Harvard University press, 2006 (1st ed. 1994).

13. Saxenian A. *Silicon Valley's New Immigrant Entrepreneurs*. San Francisco: Public Policy Institute, 1999.

14. White MG, White L. *The Intellectuals versus the City: from Thomas Jefferson to Frank Lloyd Wright*. New York: Oxford University press, 1977.

National *versus* regional and international networking in the Arab world

Michael F. Davie

University François-Rabelais of Tours, Espaces, Nature et Culture,
University of Paris-Sorbonne, France

The question of the networking of cities and their territorial integration in nation-states or in wider regional contexts, cannot be examined similarly – and has not yet been examined as such – in both Europe and the Arab World. Geographers would expect that the spatial models they had developed were universal, and that only slight variations would affect them when they were "exported" to nonwestern contexts; they could then be explained by local cultural or historical contexts. Thus, one could surmise that the vast area stretching from the Atlantic to the Persian Gulf would show similarities with the European space. Placed so close to the European mainland, one could suppose that similar "geographical" conditions, compounded by the very presence of the Mediterranean, as well as cultural similarities and the frequency and intensity of exchanges (albeit often colonial) between the two shores, would have standardized the way most of the space was organized, used and planned in today's world. One would thus expect that the European and Arab spaces would be very similar, but just simply physically divided by the Mediterranean.

However, even a cursory observation shows that this is definitely not the case, and one is struck by the very deep differences between both sides of the Mediterranean. Politically convenient, ideologically tainted [16, 10] and easy answers have been given to explain this dissimilarity, the currently most fashionable one stressing the deep chasm between the so-called "Muslim" and "Christian" or "Western" civilizations [7]. If one follows this currently popular interpretation, religion produces cultures and thus space; the spaces of the Mediterranean's Christian northern shore cannot be in any way related to the southern, Muslim, Arab shore. While Arab space (or any other space, for that matter) cannot conceptually differ from the European case, all spaces being social constructs, one must accept that the Arab countries' recent history is radically different from Europe's. Their societies have by extension produced very real spatial differences, all materializations of social actions and of very specific political and economic investments [2], over and above whatever "natural" or "cultural" determinants may have existed or are still active.

This paper proposes an explanation as to why the spatial organization in today's Arab World is different from the models prevailing in Europe. It will stress not only that the local actors were different, but also that they had to navigate in a geopolitical jungle, dominated firstly by the colonial processes and their immediate consequences, then by the Cold War and currently in the complexity of an unipolar, globalized world. Following their formal independences, the Arab countries were forced into consolidating their national Westphallian-type identity in spaces whose borders had been neither chosen, nor were adapted to the needs of their long-term internal development; these spaces are continually changing through both local processes and the needs and constraints of a globalized economy. Western spatial legacy thus is deeply imbedded in the spatial organization of today's Arab world.

Arab space as a production of history

The differences observed on both shores of the Mediterranean can be explained by an historical approach to the production of space. Briefly, one can state that between the end of the 16th century and the end of WW1, the various territories and cities of the Arab World were very loosely administered by the Ottoman Empire, which left each space free to organize itself according to local resources and natural conditions. The Empire had neither the interest nor the means in centralizing the economy and all the various levels of the local power structures; it was just as unwilling in imposing frontiers or strict, closed regional identities. Produce and persons moved freely throughout all the territories from today's eastern Morocco to Mesopotamia, from southern Egypt and the Yemen to the Balkans. Cities and towns emerged, grew or declined, according to local or international interest; they were informally networked and even so, only by economic necessity. A hierarchical model could, of course, be applied, but one cannot discern closed, clearly-delimited spaces, which we would today call "countries"; only ethnic (Kurds, Turks, Arabs), cultural (food, music, customs, city-dwellers etc.) or religious differences (Muslims, Christians, Jews) would theoretically differentiate one space from another, while the boundaries between them were porous, ever-changing, and impossible to map. No group expressed a clear-cut sense of identity, which could be assimilated to our contemporary, Western, ideas of "Nation": all saw themselves as part of a multiethnic empire, which granted them certain rights in return for token submission to the many levels of imperial power.

On the other side of the Mediterranean however, between the middle of the 17th and the early 19th century, European space was slowly being rearranged into states, each one controlled by one exclusive power or actor, located in one particular city or region. Both cause and consequence of the birth of capitalism, these states aimed at extending absolute political or economic control over all parts of their territory. Some countries, such as Britain or France, were early in following this lead; others, such as Germany and Italy, came later. But in all cases, they aimed at guaranteeing that the capitalist mode of production was efficient on one particular space. This required forms of spatial planning, be it by the central government, the local municipal authorities, or by individual enterprise. National or nationalistic identities emerged from this spatial domination, encouraged by the power centres; each country strived to control the totality of its own internal resources, and increasingly, the external ones also, both strategically central for its own national economy.

This naturally led to the occupation, *inter alia*, of the southern shores of the Mediterranean. New warfare methods, the central role of mapping, the use of science as a tool for spatial and social control, all contributed to the ease with which the Europeans were able to take over such a vast area and progressively integrate it into their national economies. Bonaparte's Egyptian expedition, followed by the occupations of Algeria and Tunisia, were the first steps in the total control of the lands bordering the Mediterranean, which ended with the British and French occupation of the Levant during the last days of WW1.

The efficient political, economic and social control of these areas could only be attained through the export of the only model the Europeans were familiar with: clearly delimited spaces controlled by a network of power-centres in the hands of foreign or local elites. Frontiers had to be drawn and cities reorganized so as to centralize and manage the flows of goods and people to and from the European homelands, in the pure colonial tradition; simultaneously, familiar political structures (such as monarchies and republics) had to be imposed and efficiently run.

All of these very classic colonial processes, and especially the invention and imposition of frontiers, definitely restructured the previously existing "spontaneous" territories. The spaces, hitherto-organized according to local economic needs, totally porous to flows of goods, people and ideas while being largely politically autonomous, now found themselves confined in new closed structures bounded by arbitrary and hermetic limits. These new spatial entities were the answers to narrow strategic European interests, and the local populations were of course never consulted. As a result, whole populations were divided between different states; towns and cities lost their traditional spheres of influence, and nomads lost their grazing-lands. Land was confiscated, given or sold to new settlers, who could now "prove" with written deeds that the parcel was theirs, whereas, previously, oral tradition or communal property prevailed. The newly-settled European populations brought with them new agricultural and industrial techniques, as well as new languages, architecture, needs and fashions; new religions were introduced, the relations between the sexes were redefined, and history rewritten. In accordance with colonial theory and practice, the reorganization of space and society was thus total.

In both the cases of the Maghreb and the Eastern shores of the Mediterranean, the unilateral remodelling of Arab space was met with resistance. In the Eastern Mediterranean, the project of a Jewish homeland to be built in place of an Arab Palestine brought about protests, strikes, riots and armed insurrections; the antiFrench Arab Revolt of the 1920s and early 1930s shook Syria and parts of Lebanon; in Iraq, the insurrection against the British was permanent until the 1940s; the anti-Spanish and antiFrench Rif war in Morocco and the anti-Italian Libyan insurrection were long and bloody; Algerians resisted till the 1960s against the French occupation, while Egyptian protests against the British occupation were continuous. For all, the underlying reasons were as much the refusal of the colonial frontiers and the artificial separation of the Arabs, understood as being one large group sharing a common history and culture, as the refusal of being excluded from their own spaces and denied their own history by the European newcomers.

For many years, the balance of forces was undeniably on the side of the Europeans, who were thus able to imprint their own interpretation of spatial organization on these occupied lands. However, on the northern side of the Mediterranean, just after the Second World War and during the 1950s, the economic and political situation had radically changed. The European states, exhausted by WW2, decided to re-centre their universe and give birth to a new spatial entity, which would forgo the previous national and nationalistic bases, and, to a large extent, the classical colonial model. The founding fathers of this new territorial composition decided to progressively erase the frontiers between their own states, to network their cities and spaces, to encourage complementary interactions and economies of scale, making their space even more efficient. The overseas colonial spaces, now formally independent, would however remain strategic and useful appendages for the economic survival of Europe.

THE POST-COLONIAL PERIOD: TOP-DOWN *VERSUS* OPEN-ENDED NETWORKING PROCESSES

The decision by European powers to disengage from their overseas possessions implied an end to the physical control of these spaces. With the notable exception of Palestine, the Arab countries from the Maghreb to the Machrek became independent, but their inherited colonial frontiers were never questioned, as they constituted the very foundations of each country's claimed identity and the legitimacy of the struggles for national liberation. Each independent country occupied the exact footprint of the colonial territory, *de facto* continuing the colonial spatial processes. Furthermore, the new countries remained very closely related to their former colonial powers through economic and cultural links, and their internal spatial organization, a reflection of this order, continued over time. The strict intangibility of the frontiers, confirmed by the United Nations, was vehemently defended, for opposing reasons, by both the states themselves and by the major superpowers during the Cold war.

Another contributing factor that can explain the fossilization of the previous colonial situation was the unchallenged personal powers of the countries' rulers. Those allied to the West guaranteed the previous colonial links and advantages, while those close the Socialist block simply changed economic partners for the same resources: oil, minerals, communication facilities, strategic bases. In return, their personal power went unquestioned, and was maintained in the face of growing local opposition. In both cases, the external powers often intervened militarily in favour of their local allies.

In this geopolitical game, the Arab leaders territorialized their national space in such a way as to forbid the emergence of any local counter-powers or forms of internal resistance. Continuing the colonial period's logics, the capitals were the only economic and cultural centres of the states. As in the past, these spaces concentrated the countries' riches and strategic value: they were assets that had to be controlled and defended, and political power had to be concentrated in the capital at the top of all possible hierarchies. The strategic necessity of consolidating each country's independence and national identity thus left no room for any sort of regional specificity. As the economy was centralized and totally controlled in the capital by the new nations' elites, who often maintained very close links with the ex-colonial powers, any forms of partnerships were excluded between internal spaces that did not consolidate the centre's. As these central spaces were also very often marked by ethnic, cultural, religious, historical or linguistic particularities, the ruling powers saw any signs of inter-regional cooperation as proof of secessionist tendencies and did everything to interdict local autonomy. In a nutshell, the centre decided for the rest of the country, continually confirming that the national spaces and cities were all hierarchically subordinated to the capital, that networking was dangerous and against the national interest. The frontiers were often made impenetrable, hermetically sealed to all, including the nomads, ensuring that pre-colonial historical, ethnic, cultural or religious territories could never emerge once again across internal or external frontiers.

This put an end to any thought about the possibility of networking cities located in different countries, yet spatially very close. In the Levant, Beirut, Damascus and Amman, for example, could never be complementary. Tunis could not be networked with the cities of Eastern Algeria, although culturally and historically very close. The cities along the coast between Lattakia in Syria and Tyre in Lebanon (or even further south, to Gaza, in Palestine) could never be part of any coastal Eastern-Mediterranean networking project. Even the possibility of efficiently networking cities inside a same country could pose problems: the cities of the Nile delta, those of the Moroccan and Algerian steppes or of the wider Sahara can put forward as examples. Uniform national curricula and state-controlled radios and TVs did the rest to homogenize the various national spaces.

Sequitur, networking particular regions or cities in the Arab world with their counterparts on the other side of the Mediterranean was equally impossible. For purely economic reasons, such networking could lead to more efficient capitalism by reducing the "frictions" of space and time. In theory, a totally open free market would have been necessary to achieve these goals; it would have implied the end of state control of the economy and free movement of capital, and thus the end of the centralized power structures. This option was anathema to the national movements during the period between the 1960s and the end of the last millennium. Thus, while the north of the Mediterranean was slowly being reshaped to the needs of modern capitalism, the south was evolving into stodgy, fossilized, ineptly managed spaces. In turn, the West easily controlled these anachronistic spaces, politically, economically and militarily.

Thus, Europe, an association of states with clear worldwide ambitions, saw the Arab world as just its immediate periphery, its interface with Africa or Central Asia. Instead of physically occupying each and every Arab state according to now-obsolescent colonial doctrines, Europe (and more generally, the "West") simply subordinated these spaces in accordance with its own vital strategic interests. By controlling the discovery, transport and distribution of oil and related products, it *de facto* required the control, surveillance and submission of the regimes on the spaces that produced this resource. By monopolizing research and development of high technology, or by mass-producing consumer goods, it controlled the internal markets of the so-called "lesser-developed" countries. Europe maintained unpalatable regimes in place, draining the financial resources of the countries, while effectively capturing long-term markets. In effect, it just continued the previous colonial policies, but on a much larger and a more efficient scale.

Internally, the lack of credible or efficient local elites, compounded with the lack of capital, and, later on, the end of the Cold War and the effects of the globalization of the economy, contributed to brake any local tendencies towards pooling resources and spaces within the Arab world or with the northern shores of the Mediterranean.

It was certainly not in the interests of Europe to encourage the emergence of a next-door, well-networked Arab space. Many examples can be put forward to illustrate networking possibilities at this scale, though never put into effect: Tunis with Southern Italy; the Moroccan

Atlantic and Mediterranean coasts with those of Spain and Portugal, along the "Atlantic Arc"; the Algerian coastal regions with those in Italy, Spain or France; Libya's coastal regions with Italy or Greece; the Levant with Cyprus, Greece or Turkey. Similarly, even major Arab cities, networked as possible emerging polycentric satellites linked to Europe, could not be envisaged. Surprisingly, even Beirut, Algiers, Tunis or Tripoli are very weakly linked to coastal cities of the North and the few formal bilateral cultural, economic or political cooperations signed with European cities or autonomous regions do not constitute efficient, integrated networks, the engines of sustainable development or of strategic shared identities.

Researchers and professionals working on the question of spatial planning in the different Arab countries have interiorized all of these internal and external factors. No serious official project has been put forward proposing regional transfrontier links, or to effectively network cities while bypassing the capital, or even just networking the main cities with others. Engineers, planners, urbanists and financiers have refused to address the question of the change of scale, which would effectively have put an end to the postulate of the Nation-State, of centralized government, or of the sacredness of frontiers. The dominant model is still that of the total superiority of the capital and of the total subordination of the other national spaces. Very little attention has been given to encouraging culture, to the very necessary cosmopolitanism of cities, to the common foundation of the Arabs' identity, which can all be expressed in spatial terms. Each and every country has been fascinated mainly by the improvement of the internal transport infrastructure polarized by the capital, with centralized one-way links with the West; they also opted for copying and imposing out-dated European architectural and urban models.

Briefly then, the North of the Mediterranean was developing into a vast integrated space, in which cultural or political differences were tolerated as long as they did not disrupt the functioning of the economy. In the south, however, the colonial spaces and links were forcefully maintained, albeit in independent states. While on one side space was being continuously and consciously remodelled, on the other, it was maintained in unquestioned obsolescent models, with the capital city forcibly occupying the top of the urban hierarchy. This physical, economic, cultural and symbolic domination by the West questions the very possibility of independent networking in the Arab countries, and even that of mutually respectful networking between the North and the South.

One would quite naturally expect, then, that today's Arab world is everywhere composed of closed-in, dominated, and introverted spaces. This is certainly not the case, and Arab space is not everywhere identical, and surprisingly, new forms of networking are visible or are emerging.

COUNTER-EXAMPLES IN TODAY'S ARAB WORLD

Dubai, a networked point

Perhaps the most original locus, in terms of networking, is the Gulf emirate of Dubai. It is far better networked with the Western and Asian world and economy than with its immediate Gulf environment, or more generally with the Arab World. It can be seen as a sort of enclave in which everything is organized to satisfy the needs of the globalized economy. Dubai is an international airline hub between Europe and the Far East; it organizes internationally recognized fairs and competitions, and has massively invested in high-quality international tourism. Its markets and duty-free shops have made it the regional emporium for goods from around the World; its communications and educational facilities are recognized by all. As an international financial centre, it has polarized the economic activity of the Gulf, the Eastern Mediterranean and parts of the Indian sub-continent. The city's architecture stuns, and its residential projects (the now-famous "Palm" islands) are geared for an international upper-class clientele [13]. Its population is so mixed and cosmopolitan that the question of national identity is largely irrelevant.

Dubai has emerged over the last twenty years as a World City existing only by its position and role as a porous interface between European, US and Asian economies and financial markets. It produces little, except added value through transactions and commerce. It thus offers the quintessence of the *modus operandi* of modern capitalism, and by necessity, it is networked to the rest of the World through Cyberspace, without any intermediate, national, "physical" space. Here space and territory are reduced to a point, with other loci such as Abu-Dhabi, Qatar, or Sharjah being other relays for the globalized economy, and with Kuwait and Oman acting as military bases to defend them.

Palestine and Israel as contradicting counter-models

Palestine constitutes an extreme counter-example, with the total destruction of all pre-existing networks and of all current endeavours to network, at all scales. Whole cities have been isolated from their immediate environment by military encirclement, settlement-building and physical obstacles. On the one hand, the annexation of Eastern Jerusalem to Israel in 1967 has redirected that part of city's networks from the West Bank and Jordan to Israel proper. Even at the intraurban scale, networking has been redefined over the last quarter-century: the Old city of Jerusalem is now divided into Jewish and Arab quarters, which studiously ignore each other; their respective suburbs are now linked by separate road networks.

Further up on the scale, simple physical communication between towns, villages or cities have been progressively rendered extremely difficult by several "security fences" or for military reasons. Contacts between major towns such as Nablus, Ramallah, Bethlehem and Hebron or those between lesser-sized ones such as Jenin, Kalkilya and Jericho are now reduced to a mere trickle. Finally, all the occupied territories are totally isolated from the surrounding Arab countries, or from the Mediterranean and thus from the nodal points of current networks.

On the other hand, networking between the Jewish areas is being developed, through the physical fusion of expanding colonies, by the building of a network of interconnecting roads. These settlements are totally integrated into the Israeli economy, itself well intermeshed with the West's. This is the case of Tel Aviv and other cities of the Coastal plain, which constitute "the hard core of Israel's post-industrial, globally oriented economy" [9]. At another scale, Israel itself can be seen as an important outpost of the modern liberal economy, itself highly networked, in the Middle East. Its links are overwhelmingly centred on the USA and Europe (and increasingly with China and Japan), while being inexistent with Arab World. Israel's culture and politics, its architecture and life-styles are clearly Western, as are its continuous references to its contemporary history. Israel's cities, its town-planning models, its scholarly research on spatial thematics, all reflect the deep links – the networking – with European or American spaces and models.

Thus two very different types of networking affect the same physical space: Israel's centralized and efficient state-dominated network as part of the globalized economy and a proto-Palestinian disintegrated and "dis-networked" territory.

Iraq and the end of all efficient networking

Iraq is another counter-example, with the apparent end of the previous national logics and their replacement by a different model. The re-networking of the post-Saddam Iraqi national spaces has failed, and the civil war has led to a break-up of the country along ethnic or religious lines.

An example can be given by the now semi-autonomous northern Kurdish area which is struggling to network its space with southern Turkey's or western Iran's while at the same time losing its links with central Iraq. However, these links are either just simple commercial exchanges or the consolidation of shared ethnic origins on both sides of the border.

Everywhere else, the fragmentation of Iraq's national space also affects the intraurban scale, with a breakdown of urban networks, and a progressive isolation of quarters along religious or ethnic lines. In the process, forms of ethnic cleansing are under way, effectively destroying whatever local urban networking may have existed, and creating new, spatially smaller ones, in effect semi-autonomous ghettoized quarters.

The only trace of networking would be though the Iraqi and Kurdish diasporas, mainly settled in Turkish, Jordanian, Syrian and European cities. However, it is feeble and insufficient to maximize the efficiency of the stagnating local economy, and is certainly of no interest for the decision-centres of the globalized economy. But as with the Palestinians, these diasporas are the strategic link with the more efficient networks located abroad.

The difficult post-war re-networking of Beirut

Finally, Beirut, with its reconstruction project, which rested on the assumption that the previous networks forged between the 1940s and 1975 were still operational [4, 6, 15], gives another example of the extreme splintering of Mediterranean territories. The premise was based on the assumption that if networking was severed or suspended (*e.g.* by wars), it could be reconstituted *in situ*, and kick-started to function again once the temporary local problems were solved. Networking was associated to forms of hysteresis, "normality" bouncing back once the war was over. Networking (and thus space) was thus understood as being distinct from the historical, cultural, political and economic environments that once produced it; it was seen as a fact, tool that existed *per se*, which required no effort to fuel.

The premise for Beirut was that the post-civil war city would maintain its position as the centre of the financial and transport network of the Middle East, a strategic and irreplaceable link between the Eastern Mediterranean, the Arabian Peninsula and Europe. The reconstruction of the city's centre (or rather the building of a new centre) was also aimed at rebuilding Beirut's pre-eminency as the Lebanon's only city of any importance, confirming its real and symbolic position in national space [12]. For a series of complex reasons, the vision of networking the city and its advantages with the rest of world's economy was far better managed by Dubai's, which has effectively positioned itself as the place to be, rather than Beirut.

Today's networking of Beirut is now a subtle mix of those networks that survived the war, those that were constituted during the war years, and new ones developed during the reconstruction period. These are being continuously recomposed in time, the July-August 2006 war being the latest example. At the same time, other spaces in the city show signs of effective and vigorous networking with specific loci or sectors, in both Europe and the rest of the world.

Conclusion

The histories of these two spaces, Europe and the Arab World, are so different that their spaces cannot be compared. The inexistence of spatial planning on inter-regional scales, the interference of the political sphere in all things technical, and the constant intervention by the various superpowers, all explain the paucity of efficient national and international networking of many spaces and cities.

Whatever official networking that can be observed can only be understood as being opportunistic, provisional, and spatially weak. However, in ever-increasing cases, cities in the Arab World no longer function exclusively through official, state-controlled channels. The informal sector, the diasporas, the various migrant populations, the underground economy, the NGOs and the religious groups [3], all contribute to networking national spaces with the outside world. They require neither planned space, nor officially sanctioned links. Though invisible, these forms of networking compensate the weaknesses of many state economies, while paradoxically enriching the central power structure in return for its noninterference. The State, in effect, acts as a predator by siphoning off parts of the profits created by the networks and thus consolidates the personal powers of the local strongmen. The central powers of many Arab states thus are reduced to dispensers of "protection" to ephemeral, informal groups that very efficiently compensate the states' economic and social inefficiency. These networks have replaced the top-down hierarchical networking state system by a form of spontaneous, unorganized, spatially indifferent and continuously remodelled type of networking, stressing both the micro-local and global scales [17] rather than the national one. It would seem that while the Arab states have all of the Jacobin trappings, they can now only survive if informal, unregulated and invisible networking is allowed to thrive.

The apparent danger of this model is that these very informal networks can also act, in certain conditions, as efficient alternative powers, destroying the very foundations of the claimed legitimacy of the Arab states or of their leaders, albeit the "protectors" of this very informality. Perhaps the clearest expression of these parallel networks is the undeniable cosmopolitanism of many of today's Arab cities, criss-crossed by multiple cultural flows and influences, by diverse languages and fashions, by the presence of large foreign populations, by the widespread use of the Internet, by the adoption of opinions that differ with official political orthodoxy [8] or with imposed social norms. The spaces produced by these ephemeral and opportunistic combinations are expressions of Bauman's "liquid modernity" [1] that characterises much of today's postmodern world and its globalized economy, and by extension, particular spaces of many Arab cities [14]. They express personal choices rather than institutional ones, which can on occasion reconstitute "tribes" [11]; they can change overnight according to the whims of the economic actors; they are difficult to locate and to map, but they efficiently integrate people in the globalising world. Their very reason for existing requires a total indifference to state-building national ideologies and to state planning. They offer an effective counter-model to nationalistic discourses, and survive in a love-hate atmosphere with the State and its apparatus. This can be clearly observed in Beirut, and in Iraqi, Palestinian and Maghrebi cities.

Finally then, it is perhaps at this level that networking between the North and the South of the Mediterranean is the most efficient. It would be through informal, spontaneous, opportunistic "menu-hopping" postmodern networking, that multilayered societies on both shores meet and link, and not only through the familiar paradigm of formal, state-run institutions.

REFERENCES

1. Bauman Z. *Liquid modernity*. Cambridge & Malden MA: Polity Press & Blackwell, 2000, 228 p.

2. Braudel F. *La Méditerranée et le monde méditerranéen à l'époque de Philippe II*. Paris : Librairie Armand Colin, 1979.

3. Corm G. *La question religieuse au XXIe siècle. Géopolitique et crise de la postmodernité*. Paris : La Découverte, 2006, 215 p.

4. Davie MF. Beirut's city centre as an expression of global, national and local identities and confrontations. *Working Papers in Local Governance and Democracy*, 1999; 99, 2: 29-38.

5. Dear M (Ed). *Spaces of Postmodernity. Readings in Human Geography*. Oxford: Blackwell's, 2001, 512 p.

6. Gavin A, Maluf R. *Beirut Reborn. The Restoration and Development of the Central District*. London: Academy Editions, 1996, 148 p.

7. Huntington SP. *The Clash of Civilizations and the Remaking of World Order*. New York: Simon & Schuster, 1997, 367 p.

8. Insel A. La postdémocratie. Entre gouvernance et caudillisme. *Revue du MAUSS* 2005; 26, 2005/2: 121-36.

9. Kipnis BA. Tel Aviv, Israel – a world city in evolution: urban developement at a deadend of the global economy.

Research Bulletin 2002; 57, http://www.lboro.ac.uk/gawc/rb/rb57.html.

10. Kobayashi A. Geography, spatiality, and racialization: the contribution of Edward Said. *The Arab World Geographer* 2004; 7, 1-2: 79-90.

11. Maffesoli M. *Le temps des tribus. Le déclin de l'individualisme dans les sociétés postmodernes*. Paris : La Table Ronde, 2000 (3rd ed), 330 p.

12. Makdisi S. Laying claim to Beirut: urban narrative and spatial identity in the age of Solidere. *Critical-inquiry* 1997; 23, 3: 660-705.

13. Pacione M. City profile. Dubai. *Cities* 2005; 22, 3: 255-65.

14. Quataert D. Historical and Postmodern Cities of the Middle East. *Journal of Urban History* 2003; 29, 3: 347-53.

15. Rowe PG, Sarkis H (Ed). *Projecting Beirut. Episodes in the Construction and Reconstruction of a Modern City*. Munich, London, New York: Prestel-Verlag, 1998, 303 p.

16. Said EW. *Orientalism*. New York: Vintage Books, 1979, 369 p.

17. Yacobi H, Shechter R. Rethinking cities in the Middle East: political economy, planning, and the lived space. *The Journal of Architecture* 2005; 10, 5: 499-515.

East Asia: An example of regional integration via networks and flows

Patrice Cosaert
University of La Rochelle, France

The first aim of this article is to provide researchers and players in the field involved in the organisation and development of the European territorial area with a particular viewpoint, by way of comparison with the processes of regional integration via networks and flows at present occurring in East Asia; this will enable confrontation of the European view with the largely spontaneous trends that can at present be observed on the Pacific coasts of the Asian continent[1].

PERSISTENCE OF A MERIDIAN GROWTH AXIS IN EAST ASIA[2]

From the straits of Singapore to the Korean straits, there is an axis, or corridor, of growth that focuses all the economic dynamics of East Asia. There is no longer any doubt as to the material reality of this axis, which is structured by several major circulation "nodes" (Singapore, Hong-Kong, Tokyo-Yokohama): the flows it involves structure the whole of eastern Asia. Today this axis has seen its functions and activities multiplied, and the nodes paired by the extensions of Singapore towards Bangkok, Tokyo-Yokohama towards Seoul-Pusan, and Hong Kong on the one hand towards Taipei-Kaohsiung, and on the other towards Shanghai. This extension of their outreach has reinforced their role as forces of integration. Maritime trade, which has been modernised by container transport, has been used by the countries in this region to develop their export strategies; it also links them one to the other, as inter-regional exchange develops. The expansion of air transport has not altered circulatory flows, since the main airports are positioned along the same axis. Information "highways", which use means connected with this axis, also contribute to reinforcing it. And the even more immaterial monetary flows also run with it *(Figure 1)*.

---

1. The author refers widely to the work conducted by the NORAO group (Nouvelles Organisations Régionales en Asie Orientale), which comprises some forty researchers, and of which he is also a member; these researchers are from different disciplines (geography, history, political science, economy, urbanism,, ethnology, sociology, etc.) and all are involved in issues of spatial analysis and territorial reconfiguration. This work led to the publication in 2004 (by Les Indes Savantes) of two large volumes of 388 and 496 pages respectively: "Identités territoriales en Asie orientale", coordinated by Philippe Pelletier, and "Intégrations régionales en Asie orientale", coordinated by Christian Taillard.
2. This introduction has been written with the collaboration of Philippe Pelletier and Christian Taillard.

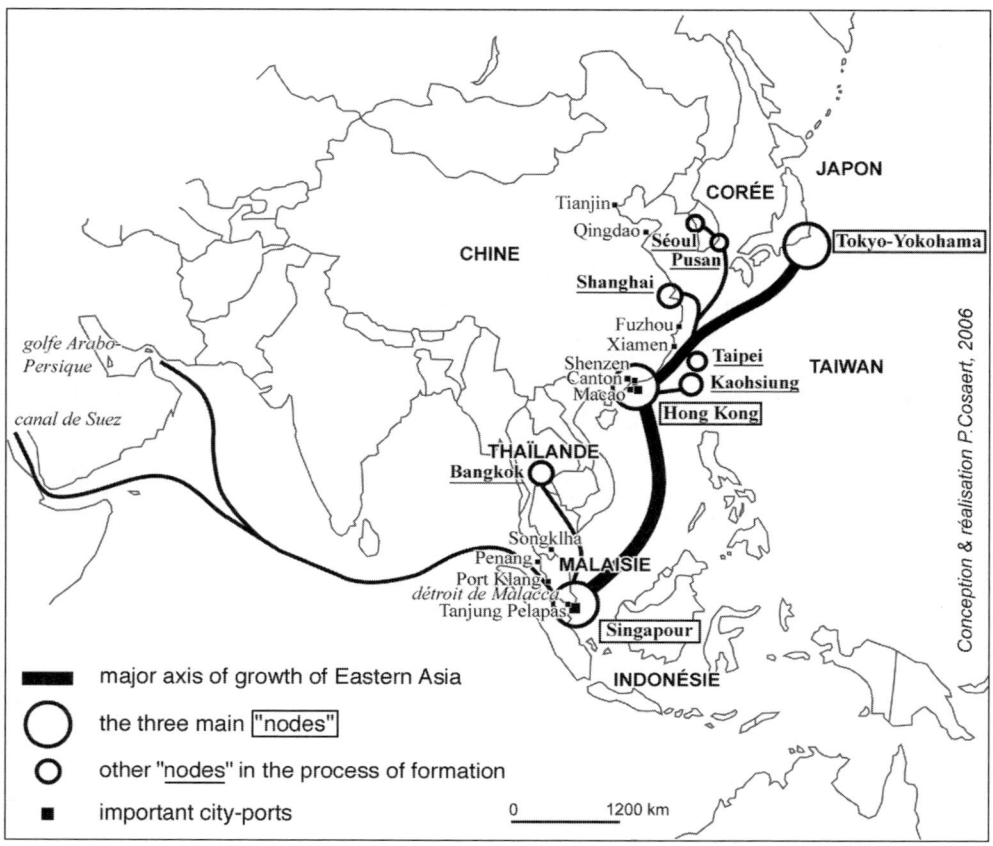

Figure 1. *Axes of growth in Eastern Asia.*

Until the 15th century, the maritime route linked China, and also Japan to some extent, to the eastern coasts of India. With the different Western colonisations, the limits were pushed westwards to the western coasts of Europe, and eastwards to the western coast of the USA. Thus the straits of Japan on the one side and the straits of Malacca on the other became the essential ports of entry to this maritime route in eastern Asia.

This axis of growth therefore follows the former trade route used by Western trader-navigators at the time when they settled in a durable manner in the region in the 19th century. For a period it also coincided with the Cold War "front" after the Second World War and the shift of China to the communist world. Today it is part of the trans-global container transport route, under the control of Asian shipowners.

The general configuration of the present network was established as early as 1855 by the British: it was then that Hong Kong, as a third node at the centre of the axis, was added to the two existing entries focusing Tokyo-Yokohama in the east, bridgehead of the Japanese archipelago, and Singapore to the west at the end of the Malacca straits (replacing the previous trading-posts on the western coasts of Malaysia). This third node is strategically positioned at the entrance to the Formosa (Taiwan) straits, linking the South and East China Seas, also dividing North-East from South-East Asia. From this time on, despite the fact that it was characterised by the arrival of nation-states, it was the reticular organisation of the maritime route, rather than former national constructions, that imposed these two city-states produced by the British maritime empire at the commands of two of the three major nodes on the meridian axis.

Today, the geography of the meridian axis is still dominated by the different straits, even if certain poles are tending to develop into a hierarchy around the three main nodes. It is worth noting that no other important platform has emerged, beyond the colonial trading posts, whether on the Vietnamese or Chinese coasts. Ports such as Haiphong and Saigon on the one hand, and Tianjin, Qingdao and Shanghai on the other, have been restricted to transshipment functions at national level, unable thus far to gain international relay status. This particular configuration is partly explained by the fact that China and Vietnam were closed, as a result of the Communist revolution in the early fifties which lasted through the Cold War period; it is also explained by the meridian structure of the coastal spaces, whereby differentiated economic units are found in succession from north to centre to south in each one. It is however the reproduction of this tripartite meridian model on the scale of East Asia as a whole that appears to be the determining factor. Indeed, the maritime axis has remained structured over time around its three main nodes, even if each one of these is tending towards greater complexity today.

The modernity of the metropolises in the Asian "maritime corridor" has always been founded on services: an emporium model for Malacca, or later a warehouse model in Singapore and Hong Kong. Today, the "service integrator" model has taken over, with a particularly evolved form in Hong Kong. The main new logistic platforms have indeed had to assume several functions and combine different professions, from identification of sources of supply to information management, and, of course, the management of maritime trade, increasingly complex as time passes. Thus the East Asian maritime corridor comprises several large ports or port areas, at once complementary and rival, the future of which depends on their ability to combine high quality infrastructures with sophisticated services:

– The Pearl River complex, where Hong Kong orchestrates the different synergies, in particular with the ports in the Shenzhen zone.

– Singapore further south, a powerful transshipment platform at the western entrance to the Pacific.

– Kaohsiung in Taiwan, the great rival of Hong Kong and Singapore, but with the handicap of its poor relationship with China.

– And finally Shanghai, which remains a transshipment port rather than a genuine dispatch platform.

There are three regional examples of integration via networks and flows that are worth examining in more detail: Hong Kong and the Pearl River delta, Singapore and the Malacca Straits, and the Formosa (Taiwan) Straits which form and increasingly active interface between Taiwan and mainland China.

THE TRANS-BORDER REORGANISATION OF HONG KONG

Hong Kong was a British colonial creation located, as has been seen, on a major circulation node in the Asian maritime corridor. It successively assumed the roles of a ware-house port, of an industrial agglomeration working for the world market, and finally a centre providing high level services. In the face of the problem of the confinement of its territory, Hong Kong put its stakes on the internationalisation of its economy, while at the same time, paradoxically, delocalising its production units to areas in the immediate neighbourhood, in the Chinese province of Guangdong. Thus there is a spatial pattern that relates at once to that found in the large metropolises worldwide, and at the same time to a trans-border spatial organisation pattern. Its retrocession to China in 1997 has not fundamentally altered the situation, since there is still a watertight border between the special administrative region of Hong Kong and Guangdong province, and hence considerable disparities, whether in income and qualification scales, or in regulatory and taxation issues. The Hong Kong delocalisations, which first benefited the special economic zone of Shenzen (created in 1979), later shifted and spread throughout the Pearl River delta, in particular towards Canton (Guangzhou), and then along a western axis from Canton to Zhuhai (the Macao special economic zone), towards the North of Guangdong province and towards neighbouring provinces (Fukian, Guanxi, Hainan). Guangdong province has thus become a sort of "workshop" province for Hong Kong, which for its part has gradually lost most of its employment in industry; the transport infrastructures in the Pearl River delta have been reorganised accordingly (creation of new specialised ports, airports in Shenzen, Canton and Macao, motorways, and a bridge linking Hong Kong to Macao, from island to island across the delta). The urbanisation and industrialisation of rural areas has completely changed Guangdong province, which now attracts very numerous migrants from other Chinese provinces. The integration of Hong Kong and Guangdong province has been facilitated by the existence of family ties, and a shared culture epitomised by the use of Cantonese on either side of the border, as well as by the main television channels. This de facto integration does not however mean the loss of identity for Guangdong province, which enjoys a considerable degree of autonomy in the social and economic fields with respect to Beijing, and it even possesses its own financial institutions, and considerable freedom in managing its production infrastructures. The integration of Hong Kong and Guangdong province also creates a very large conurbation (comprising Hong Kong, Shenzen, Canton, Zhuhai and Macao), which, in due proportion, recalls the Randstad in Holland, although the heart of it is not green but the blue of the Pearl River delta!

THE SPATIAL ORGANISATIONS OF THE MALACCA STRAITS[3]

The Malacca Straits constitute one of the main maritime passages between Europe (via the Suez Canal) or the Persian Gulf and the ports of North-East Asia (China, Japan and Korea). It is also an inland sea surrounded by a densely inhabited world, between two coastlines, that of the island of Sumatra (Indonesia), and that of the Malaysian peninsula.

---

3. This paragraph was written with the collaboration of Nathalie Fau.

The meridian flows overall, mostly transoceanic, first of all form an integrated and hierarchised space on the scale of the straits, dominated by the port of Singapore (top world ranking). This port platform is situated at the centre of a complex set of regional maritime and air interconnections which endow it with a vast international hinterland. The ports on the straits, which are only one branch of the network, are reduced to a relatively subsidiary role, for instance Singapore re-exports 90% of container exports from Penang and Belawan.

The surrounding countries vary in the view they take of this supremacy. For the eastern coast of Sumatra and southern Thailand, the port of Singapore is an advantage, enabling them to overcome their peripheral location. The volume and the value of exports from the ports of Palawan and Songkhala are insufficient to warrant stopover by large shipping firms. Since exports represent much larger volumes than imports, freight involves paying extra taxation on empty containers. The proximity of Singapore thus enables daily connections with world trade circuits, without incurring the related costs. In contrast, for the Malaysian government, this dependency is politically unacceptable, and all its policies for modernisation of the port infrastructures of Port Klang and Penang are aimed at attracting part of the maritime exchanges away from the city-state of Singapore. Port Klang and Tanjung Pelapas, by housing important European maritime trade companies, have indeed already taken over part of Singapore's container traffic [8].

The meridian configuration of the straits, extending 300 kilometres, also generates a spatial organisation into sub-units that have functioned for a long time in two distinct networks at either end. Far from disappearing today, this north-south divide in the straits is strengthening. The limits of the trans-border cooperation zone, that has been known since 1990 under the generic term of the "growth triangle", in fact correspond to the borders of the former sultanates and the economic regions created around the Straits Settlements in the 19th century:

– The southern triangle, known under the denomination of SIJORI, is a trans-border cooperation zone comprising Singapore, Johor state in Malaysia, and the islands of the Riau archipelago in Indonesia. Its borders correspond to those of the former sultanate of Johor-Riau. When Singapore was created in 1819, the Riau islands became a major contact zone between the new British trading post and the archipelago as a whole. They were at once a storage zone for raw materials from the Dutch Indies before re-export through the port of Singapore, and a redistribution pole for manufactured goods imported from Singapore.

At the start, the purpose of the SIJORI zone, initiated in 1989 by Goh Chok, then deputy prime minister of Singapore, was to find a solution to the shortage of labour and ground space in Singapore by relocating part of its production activity to neighbouring areas. The development of SIJORI however took place without any very strict regulation. Since they saw themselves as secondary players, the governments were consistently reluctant towards any form of institutionalisation, thus leaving any initiative to the private sector. Despite an agreement concluded between Singapore and Johor state, the federal government in Kuala Lumpur broke off the agreement by which Malaysia found itself in the position of a secondary power under the domination of Singapore.

The SIJORI zone, which is an unprecedented economic achievement in the region, is seen by governing bodies in South-East Asia as an example of development policy that merits attention. Despite its success, the expression of "growth triangle" applied to the SIJORI zone is in fact insufficient to describe the functioning of the trans-border cooperation zone: relationships within it are more bilateral than trilateral [5]. Practically speaking, the investment flows from Singapore and Johor have split the Indonesian province of Riau into two distinct areas of influence. Economically, Singapore has absorbed the insular part of the province (Riau kepulauan), while the Johor Corporation, an Indonesian state firm founded in 1970, assists and supports investment projects in the "mainland"part of Riau province (Riau daratan, part of the island of Sumatra). The Indonesian government has condemned massive purchases of land in Riau province by Malaysians, and the imperialist mentality of investors seeking cheap land and labour but refusing to develop downstream processing activities in the province. This trans-border cooperation zone has thus gradually become a force opposing the central power in Indonesia. As for the third side of the triangle linking Malaysia to Singapore, proximity, the quality of transport infrastructures and massive investment have integrated the south of Johor state into the Singapore economic space. The inauguration in January 1998 of a second bridge between Tuas (Singapore) and Gelang Patah (Johor) has further strengthened this integration, making Johor state a back-yard of the city-state: it provides its water, food commodities, and labour, as well as green and leisure areas, and cheap shopping for the population of Singapore, which suffers from the confinement of its territory.

– The northern triangle comprises four small states of northern Malaysia (Perlis, Perak, Kedah and Penang), Southern Thailand, and two provinces in north Sumatra (Aceh and North Sumatra). This region corresponds to the zone of influence of the former sultanate of Aceh, and to an economic region that formed around Penang following the establishment of the British trading post in 1786. The northern triangle in a sense establishes the influence of Kuala Lumpur. Prime Minister Mahathir Mohamad decided its creation in August 1991, and from the outset gave it national priority status. The north-west coast of the peninsula was to play a role, with regard to southern Thailand and the eastern Sumatra coast, similar to that played by Singapore with regard to Johor and Riau. Unlike the southern triangle, the partners of this northern triangle signed a trilateral inter-governmental agreement as early as June 1993. The creation of the northern triangle cannot be dissociated from plans for restoring balanced growth within the different national territories involved. The peripheral areas in Thailand and Indonesia saw this project as a development opportunity, and a bid for autonomy. On the Malaysian side, the formation of the northern triangle was part of the development programme for the states in the northern part of the Malaysian peninsula (Perlis, Kedah and Perak), Penang becoming a regional growth pole[5].

The northern triangle rests on the exploitation of complementary spatial and economic factors. If southern Thailand and northern Sumatra appear in many ways to be underindustrialised in comparison with the Malaysian area, the availability of space and labour is on the other hand a major advantage. The northern part of the Malaysian peninsula, for its part, is experiencing a situation that bears similarities with that of Singapore twenty to thirty years ago. Thus the northern triangle has formed around the pole constituted by Penang, which is establishing preferential relationships with its two neighbours. However, since the economic structures of the regions belonging to Thailand and Sumatra are similar in nature, no bilateral cooperation has developed between them. As Fau remarks, the development of these relationships that extend beyond national boundaries but continue to give precedence to the geographical continuum shows that globalisation, far from ignoring the local scale, is generating new forms of proximity between the two shores of the straits.

THE STRAITS OF FORMOSA: TASK SHARING AND COMPETITION AMONG PORTS ARE SHAPING THE INLAND SEA OF CHINA

The straits of Formosa (Taiwan) are an important maritime route in Eastern Asia, since they are the shortest passage from North-East Asia to Hong Kong, Singapore and the Malacca straits, and the obvious gateway towards India and Europe. The main feature of these straits, however, is that for the last half century they have separated two political entities that resulted in 1949 from the Chinese civil war: the People's Republic of China, and the Republic of China in Taiwan. The island of Taiwan covers only 36 000 km^2 (equivalent to the surface area of Belgium), although there are 23 million inhabitants It has succeeded in exemplary manner in overcoming underdevelopment in a single generation, to become an economic and financial power that carries weight in Asia and in the world. It is a full democracy, and enjoys de facto independence, but its relations with Beijing (which considers it to be a renegade province) have no legal framework. Thus relationships are tense, or even conflictual. Even so, commercial and financial exchanges between the two, while indirect, are nonetheless considerable today.

Most navigation companies use the straits, in particular the regular shipping lines. Some concentrate on the mainland ports, this obviously being the case for the Chinese national company COSCO. However most serve one or several Taiwanese ports on their way from Hong Kong to Japan or South Korea (Kaohsiung of course, but also Keelung and Taichung). Taiwan, by its remarkable economic growth has indeed become a major receiving and dispatching platform for maritime traffic to and from the whole world, so that the straits of Formosa can no longer be viewed as a mere north-south passage for goods in transit. The situation is however in no way comparable to that of Singapore, or even that of Hong Kong, despite the scale of container transport through Kaohsiung, since, for the moment, the Taiwanese ports are not centres of redistribution of goods, or dispatch ports economically integrated into their region. To achieve this, direct maritime links need to function without restriction between Taiwan and the mainland. At first sight, any transversal traffic of this sort would appear negligible. From 1949 direct maritime (and air) links between Taiwan and mainland China were banned. It was only in 1997 that they were unobtrusively re-established between the two main ports in Fujian province, Xiamen and Fuzhou, and the main port in Taiwan, Kaohsiung. However they can only involve goods in transit, and to date volumes have been small. In fact, it is well known that exchanges between Taiwan and the People's Republic of China have developed markedly, but they transit through Hong Kong (and secondarily through Macao), and it is this port that enjoys the status of a regional hub (until, possibly, it is replaced in this by Shanghai).

In addition to a vast market that is already opening up to some of their products, in mainland China Taiwanese enterprise can find cheap labour, raw materials, and the space which they lack, as well as less stringent regulations for pollution and environmental protection. In addition, their counterparts speak the same language. The authorities in the People's Republic, whether at central, provincial or local level, of course value the arrival of their "countrymen", who bring with them capital and know-how, create employment and facilitate access to the international market for their products.

The two Chinese entities now seem clearly complementary from the economic standpoint. For an increasing number of Taiwanese firms, investing in mainland China has become essential: not only do these investments constitute an increasingly significant source of profit, but above all they appear inevitable. China is in itself a fast-growing market, but, over and above that, it is an ideal production platform towards third party markets. It remains that the exchanges across the straits, although indirect, are already considerable, and it would be sufficient for the political obstacle to be raised for the traffic to develop exponentially. Can the political situation change in the near future? It is easy to see that, at this stage in regional economic integration, the answer to this question will determine whether or not the Formosa straits become a genuine Chinese inland sea, within which flows would be as readily transversal as meridian, and in which Kaohsiung could become a major distribution port serving the ports of Fujian province. François Gipouloux (2004) notes, on the basis of projections established by the Taiwan Transport Institute, that if direct links were to be allowed, the ports of Fujian province would transship 40 to 50% of their freight in Taiwan. He remarks elsewhere that although several large companies already stop off in Xiamen, and although the container traffic in this port is developing fast, this should not markedly reduce the chances of Kaohsiung in the short or medium term, because the logistics and port services are at present incomparably better in Taiwan than on the mainland.

Should there be an agreement between the two Chinese entities, if not formal and legalised, at least de facto, considerable development of the traffic across the straits can be expected. The straits area, stretching from Hong-Kong to Shanghai, would become the centre of the Chinese world, a sort of trapeze-shaped inland sea, the wide base running from Hong Kong to Shanghai, and the smaller base from Kaohsiung to Keelung. This scenario appears all the more credible if one considers that the different demographic components of the trapeze thus formed are fairly well balanced, and that the existing disproportion in economic and financial terms is constantly reducing [4].

Conclusion

To conclude, everything tends to confirm the importance of the coastal axis in the structuring of the development patterns of Eastern Asia, which has become a region (in the wide sense) in its own right, rather than merely a destination for capital and tourists, or a place from which goods and labour are exported. Diversified flows continue to consolidate it, capital and skills meet, as well as increasing numbers of workers and tourists, also mobilising the new information and communication technologies. These growing and convergent flows produce, de facto, economic integration which is a condition for regionalization (in the local meaning of the term) in this part of the world. For political reasons, however, this integration takes on different forms:

– Very marked integration, with specialisation of each player, in the case of the Pearl River delta, which comprises the special administrative regions (SARs) of Hong Kong and Macao, part of Guangdong province, and the special economic zones (SEZs) of Shenzhen and Zhuhai, administrative entities which ultimately all belong to the People's republic of China, despite their particularities and diverse status which give them a large degree of autonomy with respect to the central authority;

– Trans-border-type spatial organisation into fairly loose sub-units in the case of the straits of Malacca, which are shared by four sovereign states. It should however be noted that it is the smallest of the four, Singapore, that derives most benefit from this organisation, since it is the only one to possess a global-scale metropolis;
– *De facto* economic integration between the two shores of the straits of Formosa (Taiwan and Fujian province in mainland China) on account of obvious complementary economic features that come to bear on the local players, despite a fundamental political disagreement between the two governments.

In all three instances, however, it should be noted that the delocalisation of numerous activities towards neighbouring areas (rather than on the other side of the world as is the case for many of the world's large metropolises) accentuates further the internationalisation of the economies of Hong Kong, Singapore and Taiwan, which continue to dominate the local scene.

REFERENCES

1. Antheaume B, Bonnemaison J, Bruneau M, Taillard C. Asie *du Sud-Est, Océanie, Géographie Universelle*. Belin-Reclus, 1995.

2. Boillot JJ, Michelon N. *Chine, Hong Kong, Taiwan, une nouvelle géographie économique de l'Asie*. La Documentation française, 2001 (coll. Les Études).

3. Chancel C, Pielberg EC. *La façade asiatique du Pacifique*. PUF, 2004.

4. Cosaert P. Le détroit de Formose : mer intérieure chinoise ou voie maritime internationale entre l'Asie du Nord-Est et l'Asie du Sud-Est ? In : *Intégrations régionales en Asie orientale*. Taillard C (Ed). Les Indes savantes, 2004 : 263-78.

5. Fau N. Enjeux et organisations spatiales du détroit de Malacca. In : *Intégrations régionales en Asie orientale*. Taillard C (Ed). 2004 : 295-314.

6. Foucher M (Ed). *Asies nouvelles*. Belin, 2002.

7. Gentelle P, Pelletier P. *Chine, Japon, Corée, Géographie Universelle*. Belin-Reclus, 1994.

8. Gipouloux F. Les nouvelles fonctions portuaires du corridor maritime de l'Asie orientale. In *Intégrations régionales en Asie orientale*. Taillard C (Ed). 2004 : 63-78.

9. Jan M, Chaliand G, Rageau JP. *Atlas de l'Asie orientale*. Le Seuil, 1997 : 223 p.

10. Ohmae K. *De l'État-Nation aux États-Régions, comprendre la logique planétaire pour conquérir les marchés régionaux*. Dunod, 1996.

11. Pelletier P (Ed). *Identités territoriales en Asie orientale*. Les Indes Savantes, 2004.

12. Sanjuan T. *À l'ombre de Hong Kong, le delta de la rivière des Perles*. Paris, L'Harmattan, 1997.

13. Taillard C (Ed). *Intégrations régionales en Asie orientale*. Les Indes Savantes, 2004.

Acknowledgements

I would like to thank Hélène Martin-Brelot for her assistance in the final reading and editing procedures. I also thank Liliane Lizzi for her cartographic expertise to finalizing the maps and figures.

N. Cattan

Achevé d'imprimer par Corlet, Imprimeur, S.A.
14110 Condé-sur-Noireau
N° d'Imprimeur : 104537 - Dépôt légal : juin 2007
Imprimé en France